CHRISTIAN MENN BRÜCKEN BRIDGES

Diese Brücke ist Kultur, sie ist ein Kunstwerk. Nicht nur ihr Aussehen, auch wie sie zustande gekommen ist. Nicht erst die fertige Brücke verbindet Menschen. Schon die Planung und der Bau sind ein Gemeinschaftswerk, bei dem alle menschlichen und technischen Elemente zusammenspielen.

«A bridge cannot be built by one man alone. It is the work of many hands.» («Eine Brücke baut nicht nur ein einzelner Mensch. Daran sind viele beteiligt.») Das sind die Worte von Christian Menn. Die heutige Feier gilt auch ihm, dem grossen Brückenkünstler der Schweiz. Christian Menn hat schweizerische Ingenieurskunst – und wenn ich sage Kunst, meine ich Kunst – in alle Welt gebracht.

Christian Menn steht mit seinen Werken in der Tradition so bedeutender Brückenbauer wie Guillaume-Henri Dufour, Othmar Ammann, Richard Coray und Robert Maillart. Die Salginatobelbrücke und die Sunnibergbrücke machen das Prättigau zu einem Mekka des Brückenbaus. Es sind Brücken zur Welt.

Ausschnitt aus der Rede von Bundesrat Moritz Leuenberger
zur Eröffnung der Umfahrung Klosters am 9. Dezember 2005

This bridge is culture. It is a work of art not just in appearance, but also in how it came about. What brings people together is not just the finished bridge, for its planning and construction were also collective undertakings entailing the interaction of all the various human and technical elements.

"A bridge cannot be built by one man alone. It is the work of many hands." The words are those of Christian Menn. And today we celebrate not just this bridge, but Switzerland's great bridge builder too, a man who has spread Switzerland's art of engineering – and I use the word "art" deliberately – throughout the world.

Christian Menn stands in a long line of bridge builders of note, among them such towering figures as Guillaume-Henri Dufour, Othmar Ammann, Richard Coray, and Robert Maillart. The Salginatobel Bridge and Sunniberg Bridge have made the Prättigau Valley a Mecca for bridge enthusiasts, becoming bridges to the world.

Excerpt from a speech by Federal Councilor Moritz Leuenberger
at the opening of the Sunniberg Bridge on December 9, 2005

CASPAR SCHÄRER · CHRISTIAN MENN HRSG. | EDS.   FOTOGRAFIEN | PHOTOGRAPHS RALPH FEINER

CHRISTIAN MENN   BRÜCKEN BRIDGES

SCHEIDEGGER & SPIESS

INHALT
CONTENT

11 Vorwort
Preface

15 Christian Menn: Meine Philosophie des Brückenbaus
Christian Menn: My philosophy of bridge design

25 Caspar Schärer: Interview mit Christian Menn
Interview with Christian Menn

29 David P. Billington: Der Einfluss von Robert Maillart und Othmar Ammann auf Christian Menn
The influence of Robert Maillart and Othmar Ammann on Christian Menn

Projekte des Ingenieurbüros 1957–1971
Projects by the Engineering Firm 1957–1971

36 01 Crestawaldbrücke, Sufers
01 Crestawald Bridge at Sufers

48 02/03 Averserrheinbrücken Cröt und Letziwald, Avers
02/03 Cröt Bridge and Letziwald Bridge over the Avers Rhine at Avers

64 04 Grünebrücke, Splügen
04 Grüne Bridge at Splügen

72 05 Rheinbrücke, Bad Ragaz
05 Bridge over the Rhine, Bad Ragaz

82 06 Rheinbrücke, Tamins
06 Bridge over the Rhine at Tamins

94 07 Nanin- und Cascellabrücke, Mesocco
07 Nanin and Cascella Bridges at Mesocco

108 08 Salvaneibrücke, Mesocco
08 Salvanei Bridge at Mesocco

118 09 Viamalabrücke, Zillis
09 Viamala Bridge at Zillis

128 10 Isolabrücke, Mesocco
10 Isola Bridge at Mesocco

136 11 Pregordabrücke, Mesocco/Soazza
11 Pregorda Bridge at Mesocco/Soazza

146 12 Valserrheinbrücke, Uors/Surcasti
12 Valserrhein Bridge between Uors and Surcasti

154 13 SBB-Überführung, Buchs
13 Swiss Federal Railways overpass at Buchs

162 14 Viadukt Mühle Rickenbach, Wil
14 Mühle Rickenbach Viaduct at Wil

170	15 Limmatbrücke, Würenlos	316	28 Visionen. Brücken mit Spannweiten von 3000 Metern
	15 Bridge over the Limmat at Würenlos		28 Visions. Bridges with spans of 3000 meters
178	16 Felsenaubrücke, Bern		
	16 Felsenau Bridge at Berne		

Politik, Geschichte und Kultur
Politics, History, Culture

Essay
Essay

193 Luzi Bärtsch: Brückenbau aus der Sicht des Politikers
     Bridge building from the politician's perspective
197 Werner Oechslin: Harmonie und Eleganz aus Kalkül und Ökonomie
     An ideal balance of harmony and elegance
201 Joseph Schwartz: Zur Architektur im Brückenbau
     On architecture in bridge building

322 Iso Camartin: Brückengeschichten
     Bridge stories

Anhang
Appendix

Entwürfe und Beratungen nach 1971
Designs and Consultancy Projects after 1971

334 Biografie Christian Menn
     Biography Christian Menn
336 Werkverzeichnis
     List of works
340 Projektbeteiligte
     Project participants
342 Epilog
     Epilogue
345 Dank
     Acknowledgments
349 Bildnachweise
     Credits
     Impressum
     Imprint

208 17 Ganterbrücke, Ried-Brig
     17 Ganter Bridge at Ried-Brig
226 18 Viadotto della Biaschina, Giornico
     18 Biaschina Viaduct at Giornico
240 19 Pont de Chandoline, Sion
     19 Chandoline Bridge at Sion
246 20 Leonard P. Zakim Bunker Hill Memorial Bridge, Boston
     20 Leonard P. Zakim Bunker Hill Memorial Bridge in Boston
264 21 Sunnibergbrücke, Klosters
     21 Sunniberg Bridge, Klosters
280 22/23 Al Showah Island Bridges, Abu Dhabi
     22/23 Al Showah Island Bridges in Abu Dhabi
290 24 Brücke über den Grimselsee, Guttannen
     24 Bridge over Lake Grimsel at Guttannen
296 25 Hoover Dam bypass bridge
     25 Hoover Dam bypass bridge
302 26 Peace Bridge, Buffalo
     26 Peace Bridge, Buffalo
310 27 Reussbrücke, Wassen
     27 Reuss Bridge, Wassen

VORWORT
PREFACE

CHRISTIAN MENN

Vor 2000 Jahren war der Pontifex – wörtlich übersetzt der «Brücken-Macher» – ein Priester mit geheimnisvollen Verbindungen zu den Göttern, aber auch ein genialer Baumeister, der im Römischen Reich Aquädukte über Schluchten und Täler baute. Die mit grossen Steinquadern errichteten Bauwerke bestanden aus Bogenreihen und wiesen oft ein sehr kleines Gefälle auf; es kam kaum zu Wasserverlusten. Eine der grössten und schönsten Brücken dieser Art ist der ungefähr 50 n. Chr. erbaute Pont du Gard in Südfrankreich.

Zur selben Zeit entwickelte sich auch der eigentliche Brückenbau für Verkehrswege; anfänglich vor allem für zentrale, für alles mögliche genutzte Verbindungen in bedeutenden Städten an Flüssen. Einfache Holzstege bewährten sich auf Dauer aber nicht. Sie fielen oft extremen Naturereignissen zum Opfer oder wurden in Kriegen zerstört; so leider auch die schönsten und kunstvollsten Brücken des Ostschweizer Ingenieurs Hans Ulrich Grubenmann, der im 18. Jahrhundert Holzkonstruktionen mit enormen Spannweiten baute. Die meisten einfachen Holzstege wurden mit der Zeit durch beeindruckende, wunderschöne Steinbrücken wie etwa die Karlsbrücke in Prag ersetzt. Auch Leonardo da Vinci war vom Brückenbau fasziniert: Berühmt geworden ist sein Entwurf für eine gewaltige Brücke über das Goldene Horn in Istanbul. Und für viel Aufsehen sorgte in Paris der von Louis XV. veranlasste und von Jean-Rodolphe Perronet von 1768 bis 1772 ausgeführte Bau des Pont de Neuilly. Der König liess Aussichtsplattformen erstellen, damit die Bauarbeiten gebührend bewundert und gewürdigt werden konnten – für sich und sein Gefolge auf der einen Seite der Brücke und für die Öffentlichkeit am anderen Seineufer.

EISEN UND BETON
Um die Jahrhundertwende vom 18. zum 19. Jahrhundert wurde im Rahmen der politischen, technischen und industriellen Umwälzungen neben vielen anderen Neuerungen das Schmiedeeisen für die Herstellung von Walzträgern, Schienen und Drähten entwickelt. In Amerika und in Europa entstanden weit verzweigte Eisenbahnnetze, die einen gewaltigen Aufschwung im Eisenbrückenbau zur Folge hatten. Berühmte Eisenbrücken des 19. Jahrhunderts sind etwa die Eads Bridge über den Mississippi in St. Louis, Gustave Eiffels Garabit-Brücke in Frankreich, die vielen grossartigen Bogen-, Gitter- und Fachwerkbrücken in Deutschland und schliesslich

In ancient Rome, the highest priests held the title of pontifex, which means builder of bridges. By providing a link between gods and men, these pontifices were indeed builders of spiritual bridges between heaven and earth. Ancient Rome also had able builders of bridges in the earthly realm, who distinguished themselves by the aqueducts they built across steep canyons and broad valleys. These structures, usually made up of a series of semicircular stone arches, were built to very slight grades yet allowed only minimal loss of water. One of the largest and most beautiful such structures, the Pont du Gard, built around A.D. 50 in southern France, provides compelling evidence of the immense talent and skill of Roman builders.

Simple timber structures spanning rivers that cut through cities were the earliest bridges for human transportation. The wooden bridges of Hans Ulrich Grubenmann stand out as some of the most beautiful and elaborate of the 18th century. Practically all the timber bridges of antiquity, as well as Grubenmann's, no longer exist.

Timber was gradually replaced by stone, a material that could withstand the test of time. Many early stone bridges, such as the Charles Bridge in Prague, were impressive works of great beauty. The Pont de Neuilly, commissioned by Louis XV and built by Jean-Rodolphe Perronet, created a sensation when it was opened in 1772. The king required that the bridge be provided with observation platforms, on one side of the bridge for himself and his entourage, and on the other side for commoners, so that the elegant features of the structure could be admired.

IRON AND CONCRETE
The turn of the 19th century, a time of great upheavals in politics, technology, and industry, produced two innovations of crucial importance to bridges: the steam engine and wrought iron. The steam engine led to the construction of vast railway networks in America and Europe, which created an unprecedented demand for bridges. The industrial production of beams, rails, and wires, made possible by wrought iron and its successor steel, provided a means to satisfy this demand by enabling bridges to be built faster, cheaper, and for much longer spans than could be built in timber or stone.

Among the most famous iron and steel bridges of the 1800s are the Eads Bridge over the Mississippi at St. Louis, Eiffel's Garabit

die Firth-of-Forth-Brücke in Schottland. Alle diese Brücken wurden damals bewundert und waren anerkannt als Meisterwerke der Technik.

Neben den besonders für Spannweiten im Bereich von 50 bis 100 Metern geeigneten Eisenbrücken wurden im 19. Jahrhundert nach wie vor viele Natursteinviadukte mit Spannweiten um die 30 Meter und Bogenbrücken mit Spannweiten um die 50 Meter gebaut. In der Schweiz erreichten die Natursteinbrücken am Übergang vom 19. zum 20. Jahrhundert den Höhepunkt beim Bau der Rhätischen Bahn.

Für Spannweiten über 100 Meter wurde im 19. Jahrhundert das uralte Tragsystem der Hängebrücken zur Erhöhung der Tragkraft und der Stabilität mit Tragkabeln aus dem neuen Material Eisen weiterentwickelt. Bei den ersten Brücken bestand das «Tragkabel» aus normalen Ketten; später, bei der 176 Meter weit gespannten Menai-Brücke in North Wales verwendete Thomas Telford Ketten von sogenannten Augenstäben, bis dann 1823 Henri Dufour, damals noch Kantonsingenieur in Genf, die wegweisenden Drahtkabel entwickelte. Der 1834 vom französischen Ingenieur Joseph Chaley erbaute Grand Pont Suspendu in Fribourg wies bereits Parallel-Drahtkabel auf. Diese Hängebrücke über die Saane hielt mit einer Spannweite von 273 Metern ein paar Jahre lang den Weltrekord. Die berühmteste Hängebrücke des 19. Jahrhunderts war dann aber ab 1883 mit einer Spannweite von 486 Metern Johann August Roeblings Brooklyn Bridge in New York, damals ein technisches Weltwunder.

Mit dem Eisenbeton tauchte gegen Ende des 19. Jahrhunderts ein neuer Baustoff auf, der rasch eine gewaltige Verbreitung fand und bald aus dem Bauwesen gar nicht mehr wegzudenken war. Im Gegensatz zu den stabförmigen Baustoffen Holz und Eisen ist Eisenbeton ein leicht formbarer, flächiger Baustoff, der sich besonders gut für Platten, Scheiben und Schalen eignet. Er zeichnet sich gegenüber Holz und Eisen auch durch einfachste Verbindungen und eine multifunktionale Tragwirkung aus (Tragfähigkeit gleichzeitig als Balken, Platte und Scheibe). Von den grossen Pionieren des Eisenbetons nutzten François Hennebique und Robert Maillart diese Eigenschaften konsequent aus, während Emil Mörsch eher stabförmig traditionell damit konstruierte.

In der ersten Hälfte des 20. Jahrhunderts wurden vor allem an der amerikanischen Ostküste für den rasch wachsenden Motorfahrzeugverkehr immer noch viele grossartige Eisenbrücken erstellt. Der Bau der Hängebrücken wurde vom schweizerisch-amerikanischen Ingenieur Othmar Hermann Ammann mit der 1931 eröffneten George Washington Bridge über den Hudson River in New York revolutioniert. Nie zuvor und auch nie danach wurde die aktuelle Rekord-Spannweite um das Doppelte – damals 500 Meter – übertroffen. Und es ist Ammann zu verdanken, dass ein paar Jahre später die Golden Gate Bridge in San Francisco nach seinem neuen Konzept ausgeführt wurde, und nicht nach den ursprünglich vorgesehenen Plänen.

In der unsicheren Zeit zwischen den beiden Weltkriegen entstanden in Europa nur wenige Brücken. Immerhin zählen die im Hinblick auf den Lehrgerüstaufwand effizient konzipierten und elegant gestalteten Brücken Maillarts und einige imposante Eisenbe-

Viaduct in France, and the Firth of Forth Bridge in Scotland, all of which are recognized as masterworks of engineering.

Although iron and steel bridges were particularly economical in the 1800s for spans between 50 and 100 m, stone continued to be used for multiple arch viaducts with individual spans of about 30 m, and for single arch spans of about 50 m. The pinnacle of stone bridge design was reached at the turn of the 20th century with the bridges of the Rhaetian Railway in the Swiss Alps.

In the 1800s, spans longer than 100 m were generally built as suspension bridges. The strength and stability of this ancient structural system were greatly increased by cables made of iron and steel. Initially, main cables were built using common iron chains. This was followed by chains of forged eyebar links, which were used on the 176 m span of Thomas Telford's Menai Straits Bridge. Eyebar chains were later replaced by parallel wire cables, developed in 1823 by Henri Dufour. Parallel wire suspension cables were used in the Grand Pont Suspendu in the Swiss city of Fribourg, built in 1834 by the French engineer Jean Chaley. Its span of 273 m was for several years the world's longest. The most famous suspension bridge of the 19th century is John Roebling's Brooklyn Bridge over the East River in New York, completed in 1883. This bridge, which has a main span of 486 m, is to this day universally regarded as a marvel of engineering.

In 1867, reinforced concrete was patented by the French gardener Joseph Monier. Although his first use of this new material was to build flower pots, he soon applied it to larger scale construction. Reinforced concrete was quickly adopted throughout the world for every type of structure and soon became ubiquitous. Contrary to wood and iron, which are generally limited to linear structural members, reinforced concrete can easily be formed into surfaces of any given shape, including slabs, panels, and shells. It also differs from wood and iron by the ease with which monolithic connections can be made, and by enabling components to assume multiple structural functions. Among the notable early designers of reinforced concrete structures, the German Emil Mörsch created works composed primarily of linear elements, whereas the Frenchman François Hennebique and the Swiss Robert Maillart created structures of much greater variety and significance by consistently exploiting the unique properties of this new material.

In the first half of the 20th century, many great steel bridges were built as components of rapidly expanding highway networks, in particular on the east coast of the US. Othmar Ammann revolutionized the design of suspension bridges with the George Washington Bridge, which exceeded the previous record span by a factor of two, a feat that has never been duplicated. Ammann's intervention on the design of the Golden Gate Bridge ensured that this magnificent structure was not built according to the original, questionable concept.

Due to political and economic instability, few bridges were built in Europe between the two world wars. Nevertheless, the elegant and efficient bridges of Maillart, as well as a number of imposing reinforced concrete arch bridges built in Germany, Sweden, and France stand out as particularly noteworthy works from this period.

ton-Bogenbrücken in Deutschland, Schweden und Frankreich heute noch zu den bemerkenswertesten technischen Bauwerken überhaupt.

GEGEN DEKORATION

Ende der 1930er Jahre erfand der geniale französische Ingenieur Eugène Freyssinet den Spannbeton. Dabei wird dem Eisenbeton mit gespannten Drähten, Litzen oder Stangen ein Spannungszustand überlagert, der den äusseren Einwirkungen (teilweise) entgegenwirkt. Der entscheidende Vorteil des Spannbetons besteht jedoch darin, dass hochwertiger Stahl verwendet und voll ausgenützt werden kann. Dem Eisenbeton-Brückenbau wurden mit der Vorspannung neue Spannweitenbereiche eröffnet, und bei kleinen und mittleren Spannweiten wurden fast nur noch aufgestelzte Trägerbrücken gebaut.

Die erste grössere, 287 Meter lange Spannbetonbrücke in der Schweiz wurde von 1955 bis 1958 von Hans Eichenberger über die Thur bei Andelfingen gebaut. Die Einweihung der Brücke mit der dazu erschienenen Festschrift war ein denkwürdiges Ereignis. Im Beitrag *Die Weinlandbrücke als Kunstwerk* schrieb der Kantonsbaumeister Heinrich Peter: «Mit der für die Weinlandbrücke gefundenen Form wird ein denkbar geringer Teil der reizvollen Thurlandschaft verdeckt.» In diesem Satz wurde der Brückenbau als technische Spitzenleistung in Frage gestellt. Ein paar Jahrzehnte später standen Brücken in der Öffentlichkeit nach 2000 Jahren der Bewunderung meistens nur noch für notwendige Zweckbauten und wenig erfreuliche Umweltbelastungen. Das führte dazu, dass Bauherren und Brückeningenieure bei der Konzeptentwicklung und Gestaltung Architekten und Landschaftsplaner engagierten. Der Brückenbau wurde damit bunter, aber bestimmt nicht wirtschaftlicher; und absurde, masslos übertreuerte Brücken wurden mit der Floskel «Ästhetik ist Geschmackssache» schöngeredet.

Der Bruch nach über zwei Jahrtausenden kontinuierlicher Entwicklung des Brückenbaus ist nachvollziehbar, nahmen doch neue Technologien wie Informatik, Biologie, Medizin und Weltraumforschung in kürzester Zeit einen gewaltigen Aufschwung. Gegen seine schwindende Bedeutung wollte sich der Brückenbau in letzter Zeit mit Ornamentik und aufdringlicher Originalität behaupten, was sich aber oft kontraproduktiv auswirkte. Im vorliegenden Buch, das sich nicht nur an Ingenieure und Architekten, sondern auch an Behörden und die Öffentlichkeit richtet, steht deshalb die Förderung des Verständnisses für echten Brückenbau im Vordergrund. Mit Blick auf interessierte Laien wird deshalb bei den Beschreibungen in der Regel nicht die korrekte wissenschaftliche, sondern eine vereinfachte, verständliche Sprache angewendet. Kräfte, Gleichgewicht, Balance und Tragwerkseffizienz sind natürliche Phänomene, die – visualisiert und anschaulich dargestellt – Wirtschaftlichkeit und natürliche Ästhetik reflektieren. Optimale Tragwerkseffizienz beziehungsweise optimale Balance von Wirtschaftlichkeit und natürlicher Ästhetik bedürfen keiner Ornamentik, Dekoration und fragwürdiger, teurer Originalität. Brückenbau ist und bleibt eine Ingenieursaufgabe; die Mitarbeit eines Architekten kann wertvoll sein, wenn eine produktive Zusammenarbeit entsteht.

AGAINST DECORATION

In 1928, the brilliant French engineer Eugène Freyssinet patented prestressed concrete. His concept was to reinforce concrete using high-strength steel that was put into tension before the structure was loaded. This creates a permanent state of compression in the concrete that reduces or eliminates tension due to external load. More importantly, however, prestressed concrete provides a means to utilize the full capacity of high strength steel. Prestressing enabled concrete structures to be built for spans that were previously thought possible only for steel. The highway construction boom of the 1960s gave a major impetus to prestressed concrete bridges. For short and medium spans, prestressed concrete girders supported on piers soon replaced practically all other structural systems.

Switzerland's first major prestressed concrete bridge was the 287 m long Weinland Bridge over the Thur at Andelfingen, designed by Hans Eichenberger and completed in 1958. The official opening of the bridge was commemorated by a book describing all aspects of design and construction. In his contribution to this volume, the architect attached to the project, Heinrich Peter, wrote, "The form selected for the Weinland Bridge makes only a minimal intrusion into the charming landscape of the Thur valley." With this comment, bridges were for the first time regarded not as achievements to be celebrated, but rather as environmental impacts to be minimized. Since then, this perspective has become increasingly popular, eroding the widespread admiration for bridges that had prevailed for over two thousand years. As a result, bridge engineers and owners now routinely retain architects to lead the conceptual design of bridges. The works thus produced show greater variety of shaping than their predecessors but are generally more expensive. In extreme cases, grossly extravagant bridges are now justified as beautiful according to the formula that aesthetics are a matter of taste.

This transformation in the way bridges are regarded, following two thousand years of technological development, is understandable to some extent since the public interest has been seized by rapid new developments in areas such as electronics, biology, and medicine. Recent developments in bridge design, on the other hand, which focused on ornamentation and flashy originality, have failed to generate genuine interest. This book was written to foster an understanding of the true nature of bridges. It is intended to be read not only by engineers and architects but also by the general public. The description of every bridge included in the book is therefore preceded by a simple introduction suitable for laymen.

The book is based on the following principles: Forces, equilibrium, balance, and structural efficiency are natural phenomena which can be given visual expression. They can thus reflect economy and natural aesthetics. Structural efficiency, which can be regarded as an optimal balance of economy and natural aesthetics, never requires ornamentation or extravagant originality. Bridge design is and will remain the task of engineers. The contribution of architects can however be of value to engineers who are able and willing to communicate with architects.

MEINE PHILOSOPHIE DES BRÜCKENBAUS
MY PHILOSOPHY OF BRIDGE DESIGN

CHRISTIAN MENN

VORGESCHICHTE EINES BRÜCKENBAUS

In der Regel beschliesst die öffentliche Hand, konkret das entsprechend zuständige Baudepartement, den Bau einer neuen Verkehrsverbindung und lässt eine Studie mit Linienführung und Kosten erarbeiten. Die Studie wird als Baueingabe publiziert, damit sich alle interessierten Körperschaften, Verbände und Personen zum Bauvorhaben äussern können. Wenn alle Einsprachen bereinigt sind und die Finanzierung gesichert ist, kann der Baubeschluss gefasst werden und das Bauamt erteilt die Aufträge zur weiteren Projektierung. Zunächst wird die genaue Linienführung der neuen Verbindung festgelegt. Wenn sie eine aussergewöhnliche Brücke enthält, wird für das erforderliche Bauwerk ein Wettbewerb ausgeschrieben und die Wettbewerbsjury wählt unter den eingereichten Beiträgen den besten Vorschlag zur Weiterbearbeitung aus.

WETTBEWERBE

Wettbewerbe sollten keine Lotterie sein. Deshalb müssen die Jurymitglieder unbedingt über eine hohe fachliche Kompetenz verfügen.

Wettbewerbe sind notwendig, da die neuen Ideen den Fortschritt fördern. Es gibt unzählige Arten von Brückenwettbewerben. Fast alle stellen hohe Anforderungen an den Umfang der funktionellen Nachweise, denn die Machbarkeit der vorgeschlagenen Lösung muss auch in dieser frühen Phase einwandfrei nachgewiesen werden. Die Ausgangslage des Wettbewerbs sollte nicht zu eng gefasst sein; so sollte die Linienführung des Verkehrsweges in einem räumlichen Korridor frei wählbar sein. Bei speziellen Bedingungen muss darauf hingewiesen werden, ob sie verlangt oder erwünscht sind, und entsprechend ist die vorgeschlagene Lösung zu beurteilen. Und schliesslich sollte auf einer egalitären Kostenbasis der ästhetische Wert der Projekte bezüglich Konzept und Gestaltung im weiträumigen und lokalen Umfeld ermittelt werden.

NORMEN

Normen sind keine Gesetze und dürfen den Fortschritt nicht behindern. Abweichungen von den Normen sind deshalb zulässig; bei Mängeln infolge dieser Abweichungen muss aber der Konstrukteur die volle Verantwortung für zusätzliche Bauzeit und Kosten übernehmen.

Die Tragwerksnormen regeln hauptsächlich die drei Bereiche Einwirkungen, Baustoffe und Anforderungen an das Tragwerksver-

THE ANTECEDENTS OF A BRIDGE DESIGN

In most cases, a bridge design begins with a decision by the public agency responsible for transportation to provide a link between two points, which will entail the construction of a highway, railway, or other facility. The agency's staff will then undertake a study of route location and preliminary costs. The competed study is then published as part of a formal application for permission to build. All concerned political bodies, organizations, and individuals then have an opportunity to express their opinions on the overall plan. When all objections have been successfully dealt with and financing has been secured, a formal decision to build can be concluded, and on this basis the transportation agency can award assignments for further stages of design. The alignment of the proposed link will first be finalized. When the alignment contains one or more complex bridges, design competitions will be held, and the competition jury will select for a given bridge the best proposal for final design.

COMPETITIONS

Competitions must not be lotteries. Jury members must therefore have a high level of competence in their respective disciplines.

Competitions are absolutely necessary, since they foster progress through new ideas. There are many types of bridge design competition. Almost all, however, place high emphasis on verifying the technical aspects of the project entries, since the recommended solution must be buildable without impediment. The terms of reference must not be too restrictive. Instead of providing entrants with a rigid definition of the alignment, for example, it should be possible for entrants to select the alignment themselves within a specified corridor. Special requirements must be clearly defined as compulsory or merely recommended, and the entries must be judged accordingly. The aesthetic value of entries must be determined in consideration of both the local and wider surroundings and on an equitable cost basis.

STANDARDS

Standards are not laws and must not impede progress. Deviating from standards should therefore be allowed. Responsibility for any delays or additional costs of construction resulting from deviation from a standard, however, must be borne entirely by the designer.

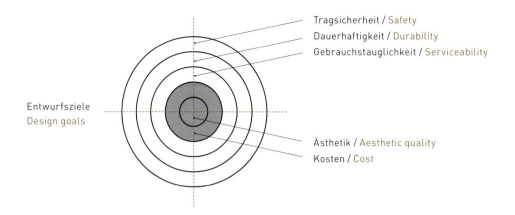

Fig. 1
Allgemeingültige Zielsetzung im Brückenbau
Generally applicable goals of bridge design

halten. Diese drei Bereiche sind durch Berechnung und Konstruktion miteinander verknüpft. Einwirkungen und Anforderungen werden in Normenkommissionen festgelegt und sind bis zu einem gewissen Grad subjektiv. Die Genauigkeit und Ausführlichkeit der Berechnungen sollten deshalb in einem vernünftigen Verhältnis zu den von den Kommissionen mit nicht zu unterschätzenden Unsicherheiten festgelegten Vorschriften stehen. Es ist viel wichtiger, nicht oder ungenügend normierte Einwirkungen im Sinn der Normen zu beachten und Mängel in der konstruktiven Durchbildung zu vermeiden als jenseits eines vernünftigen Verhältnisses zwischen Genauigkeit der Berechnung einerseits und Zuverlässigkeit der normierten Einwirkungen andererseits eine sinnlose Geschäftigkeit zu entfalten.

ZIELSETZUNGEN IM BRÜCKENBAU
Brückeningenieure sind verpflichtet, im Rahmen der Normen schön, ökonomisch und ökologisch/baustoffsparend zu bauen.

Brücken sind anspruchsvolle Zweckbauten der Verkehrsinfrastruktur für Fussgänger, Motorfahrzeuge, Eisenbahnen und Schiffe. Sie müssen verkehrstechnische, funktionelle, ökonomische, ökologische und baukulturelle Anforderungen erfüllen.

Die verkehrstechnischen Anforderungen betreffen die räumliche Linienführung und die Querschnittsausbildung für die betreffende Nutzung.

Die allgemeinen, funktionellen Zielsetzungen umfassen die normierten, technischen, imperativen Ziele: Tragsicherheit (Sicherheit vor Kollaps des Tragwerks oder einzelner Komponenten); Dauerhaftigkeit (unterhaltsfreie Nutzungsdauer des Tragwerks während etwa 75 Jahren); Gebrauchstauglichkeit (Beschränkung von Verformungen und Schwingungen etc.); die subjektiven, kreativen, nicht normierbaren Anforderungen: eine angemessene Wirtschaftlichkeit unter Berücksichtigung von Baukosten, Unterhalt und Abbruch; eine hohe ästhetische Qualität bezüglich Umfeld und Bauwerksgestaltung.

Es bestehen weitere bauwerkspezifische Zielsetzungen wie minimale Bauzeit, Vermeidung von Verkehrsbehinderungen etc.

Die technischen Zielsetzungen sind miteinander kompatibel und ohne kreative Anforderungen mit technischen Massnahmen erfüllbar. Wirtschaftlichkeit und Ästhetik sind in der Regel nicht

Structural design standards relate to the following three areas: actions on structures, materials, and requirements relating to structural behaviour. These three areas are mutually related through calculations and detailing. Design standards are written by committees and are thus to some degree subjective. The precision and refinement of calculations should thus be kept in proportion to the degree of variability, which should not be underestimated in provisions that have been written by these committees.

Given that there is no real basis for taking design standards as completely authori-tative, it is far more important to pay attention to actions that are not covered or insufficiently treated by standards and to prevent faults in structural details than to busy oneself unnecessarily in performing exhaustive calculations of extreme refinement.

Although structural design standards have become increasingly extensive in recent decades, many fundamental improvements have yet to be implemented. Significant improvement, for example, is possible with respect to structural safety. As a given bridge proceeds from design to construction and operation, knowledge is gained each step along the way. This knowledge can often justify a reduction in the safety factors used in the safety checks. At all stages in the life of a given bridge, the computed margin of safety would need to exceed the corresponding minimum limit computed on the basis of factors of safety that corresponded to the level of knowledge at that stage. If not, measures would need to be taken to guarantee the required margin of safety. Two different standards, one for design and the other for operation, would then be superfluous.

THE GOALS OF BRIDGE DESIGN
Bridge engineers have the duty to design bridges that satisfy all applicable standards and are beautiful, economical, and environmentally sustainable.

Bridges are functional objects that play an essential role in transportation systems, carrying pedestrians, highway traffic, railways, and even ships. They must satisfy challenging and complex requirements relating to transportation, structural function, economy, the environment, and culture.

The goals originating from transportation engineering relate to the three-dimensional highway alignment and the cross-section necessary to perform its required function. The goals related to

zueinander kompatibel; optimale Balance, Harmonie und Gleichgewicht lassen sich nur mit Kreativität beim konzeptionellen Entwurf erreichen.

Die Erfüllung der normierten Zielsetzungen – Tragsicherheit, Dauerhaftigkeit und Gebrauchstauglichkeit – ist lernbar. Das Rüstzeug wird an den Universitäten oder Hochschulen vermittelt und ein junger, gewissenhafter Ingenieur ist in der Lage, aus einem Vorprojekt selbstständig das Detailprojekt zu erarbeiten. Er braucht dazu weder Erfahrung noch Kreativität oder Fantasie, aber er kennt die Berechnungsverfahren und Normen unter Umständen besser als sein erfahrener Vorgesetzter.

Die Erfüllung der nicht normierbaren Zielsetzungen – Kosten und Ästhetik – erfordert einerseits Erfahrung in der Bautechnik und in der Kostenermittlung und andererseits Kreativität und Fantasie bei der Wahl des Tragsystems und dessen Ausgestaltung im Hinblick auf landschaftliches Umfeld, kulturelle Bedeutung, Exposition, Anwohner und Nutzer.

TRAGSICHERHEIT

Die Tragsicherheit ist mit dem Kollaps infolge Gleichgewichtsverlusts, dynamischer Instabilität oder anderer Ursachen – z. B. Feuer – klar definiert. Die Normen enthalten die zu beachtenden Vorschriften, die eine ausreichende Tragsicherheit gewährleisten.

DAUERHAFTIGKEIT

Die erforderliche Dauerhaftigkeit ist mit der bauteilspezifischen, unterhaltsfreien Nutzungsdauer festgelegt. Diese ist für Abdichtungs- und Belagssysteme, Leitungen, Lager und Fugenkonstruktionen, externe Kabel und deren Verankerungen sowie die eigentliche Tragkonstruktion nicht gleich. Wichtig für die Gewährleistung der unterhaltsfreien Nutzungsdauer sind vor allem die Baustoffqualität, die konstruktive Durchbildung und die Sorgfalt bei der Herstellung. Ein Minimum an Kontrolle und lokalem Unterhalt gehört ebenfalls zu den unentbehrlichen Massnahmen für ausreichende Dauerhaftigkeit.

GEBRAUCHSTAUGLICHKEIT

Die Gebrauchstauglichkeit erfordert bezüglich Nutzerkomfort und visuellem Bauwerkszustand die Gewährleistung folgender Kriterien: Beschränkung der Tragwerksverformungen, Tragwerksschwingungen und Rissbreiten sowie eine wirksame Entwässerung der Fahrbahn und ausreichenden Schutz der Tragwerksteile gegen Regenwasser und vor allem gegen chloridhaltiges Wasser.

WIRTSCHAFTLICHKEIT

Die Kosten einer Brücke sind in erster Linie abhängig vom Konzept und vom Bauvorgang. Berechnung und Bemessung haben auch einen Einfluss; aber man sollte nicht versuchen, die Kosten durch eine möglichst knappe Bemessung zu reduzieren. Die Kosten umfassen nicht nur die Erstellungskosten, sondern auch Unterhalt, Abbruch und Entsorgung. Da die Lebensdauer einer Brücke aus vielen Gründen – beispielsweise Änderung der Verkehrsführung oder

structural function consist of the following compulsory technical requirements defined by standards: Structural safety, which is understood to mean safety against the collapse of the entire structure or of individual components. Durability, which is usually understood to mean a service life free of major maintenance of about 75 years, and serviceability, which includes limits on deformations and vibration.

The subjective, creative requirements, which cannot be governed by standards, are: A suitable degree of economy, which encompasses the cost of construction, maintenance, and demolition at the end of service life, and a high standard of aesthetic quality, which includes both the form of the bridge and the way the bridge relates to its environment.

Additional goals, such as minimizing the duration of construction or impact on existing traffic during construction, may be of relevance in specific cases.

The technical requirements are mutually compatible and can be achieved using only technical means without drawing on the designer's creative faculties. Economy and aesthetic quality are normally incompatible, and an optimal balance between these two goals can only be achieved with creativity during conceptual design.

Satisfying the goals that have been specified in standards – safety, durability, and serviceability – can be learned. The required skills are taught at universities, and a young, knowledgeable engineer is generally able, on his own, to complete a final design based on a good design concept. For this, he requires neither experience nor creativity or imagination. His knowledge of methods of calculation and design standards will in some cases be even better than that of his more experienced supervisors.

Satisfying the goals that cannot be defined by standards – economy and aesthetic quality – is focused on the choice of structural system and its visible form. This task, which must consider the bridge's environment, cultural meaning, visual exposure, nearby residents, and users, requires experience in the technical aspects of design, construction, and estimation of costs, as well as creativity and imagination.

SAFETY

Safety is a now clearly defined in terms of preventing a collapse due to loss of equilibrium, dynamic instability, or other less common factors such as fire. Design standards contain relevant provisions that, when satisfied, will guarantee an acceptable level of safety. In cases where specific actions on structures or aspects of structural capacity are not precisely determined in design standards, they must be defined in a project-specific safety plan.

DURABILITY

The required level of durability is associated with a service life free of major maintenance. Required service life of components such as wearing surfaces, deck waterproofing, barriers, bearings, expansion joints, as well as external tendons and their anchors, will generally differ from the required service life of the structural system proper. The most important factors that affect service life are the

Denkmalschutz – nicht vorhergesagt werden kann, sollten die Gesamtkosten für einen Zyklus von 75 Jahren ermittelt werden, der etwa der unterhaltsfreien Nutzungsdauer des Tragwerks entspricht. Nach 75 Jahren muss ohnehin mit einer anders gearteten Verkehrsstruktur gerechnet werden, die unter Umständen wesentliche Verstärkungen, Verbreiterungen oder andere Massnahmen erfordert, die zum Zeitpunkt der Bauwerkserstellung noch nicht abzuschätzen waren.

ÄSTHETIK

Die ästhetische Qualität zählt zu den wichtigsten Bestandteilen der Baukultur. Sie ist aber nicht direkt quantifizierbar. Man kann höchstens aufgrund eines Kostenvergleichs für verschiedene Projektvarianten den finanziellen Wert unterschiedlicher ästhetischer Qualität abschätzen. Brückenästhetik besteht einerseits aus der Beziehung zwischen Bauwerk und Umfeld und andererseits aus der Gestaltung der Brücke selbst.

ÄSTHETIK IM BRÜCKENBAU

Brückenästhetik besteht in der Visualisierung eines effizienten Tragwerks, das sich optimal in sein Umfeld einfügt und sorgfältig elegant gestaltet ist.

Im Grunde gibt es zwei Arten von Ästhetik. Einerseits die kreative, «man made» Ästhetik (Bild 2), die nicht unbedingt identisch ist mit Kunst, und andererseits die natürliche Ästhetik (Bild 3), die ohne menschliches Zutun in der Natur, aber auch in der Physik und Geometrie enthalten ist.

Ästhetik ist ein abstrakter Begriff, der zum besseren Verständnis mit konkreten Eigenschaften eines Objekts wie etwa Form, Farbe, Glanz, Struktur oder Originalität in Verbindung gebracht wird. Der Entwurf genuiner Brücken beruht im Wesentlichen auf naturwissenschaftlichen Grundlagen. Er reflektiert deshalb vor allem eine natürliche Ästhetik, die sich am treffendsten mit dem überragenden Begriff des Gleichgewichts verbinden lässt: im physikalischen Sinn mit Gleichgewicht zwischen Einwirkung und Tragfähigkeit und im metaphorischen Sinn mit Gleichgewicht als Ausgewogenheit und Harmonie zwischen dem Bauwerk und seinem Kontext sowie zwischen den verschiedenen Bauwerksteilen und -komponenten.

Das Gleichgewicht zwischen Brücke und Kontext – die optimale Einfügung der Brücke in ein historisches und landschaftliches quality of materials, structural details, and the quality of construction. Minimum inspection and local maintenance are also essential measures that contribute to durability.

SERVICEABILITY

Serviceability relates primarily to user comfort and an acceptable visual condition of the structure. Providing an acceptable level of serviceability requires satisfying limits on structural deformations, vibrations, and crack widths. In addition, it is necessary to provide effective bridge deck drainage, adequate protection of structural components against rainwater, and in particular water containing chlorides.

ECONOMY

The costs of a given bridge depend primarily on the structural concept and method of construction. Calculations and dimensioning of components also have an impact on cost, but one should not attempt to reduce costs by dimensioning as close as possible to the bare minimum. Overall cost includes not only the construction cost, but also the cost of maintenance, demolition, and disposal. Due to factors such as changes to the transportation system, changes to functional requirements, and historical preservation, it is usually not possible to determine the life of a given bridge in advance. For this reason, overall costs should be determined for a design life of about 75 years, which should generally coincide with the expected service life before major maintenance is required. After 75 years, it is likely that major changes to transportation requirements must be considered. These will often require significant strengthening, widening, or other measures that cannot be foreseen at the time the bridge is designed.

AESTHETIC QUALITY

Aesthetic quality is the most important component of the cultural essence of a given bridge. It cannot be quantified directly. It may be possible, however, to compare the cost of several alternative designs and relate this to a cost of aesthetic quality. Bridge aesthetics encompass both the visible form of a given bridge considered on its own, and the relation between the bridge and its visible environment.

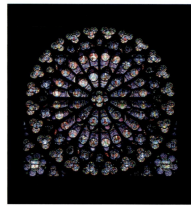 

Fig. 2
Kreative Ästhetik
Man-made aesthetics

Fig. 3
Natürliche Ästhetik
Natural aesthetics

Gefüge – wird durch zeitliche und räumliche Aspekte sowie die mehr oder weniger starke Betonung der Zeichenhaftigkeit des Erscheinungsbildes hergestellt. Die zeitlichen Aspekte umfassen Geschichte und Tradition des lokalen Brückenbaus und das aktu-elle Niveau der lokalen Baukultur und Brückenbautechnik. Die räumlichen Aspekte bestehen aus Charakter und Massstab der weiträumigen, natürlichen oder städtebaulichen Landschaft, der Exposition der Brücke und deren Bedeutung als mögliches Wahrzeichen. Das Einfügen der Brücke in ihr unmittelbares, lokales Umfeld erfordert die optimale Berücksichtigung von Topografie und Geologie, Baugrundeigenschaften, örtlicher Bausubstanz, vorhandener Verkehrssituation, Lichtraumprofilen, Gewässercharakteristik, Gewässerverlauf und einiges mehr.

Für die Ästhetik des Tragwerks selbst ist die wichtigste Voraussetzung für Ausgewogenheit und Harmonie eine klar organisierte, aus dem Konstruktionskonzept abgeleitete, räumliche Struktur, die nicht zweidimensional (auf einem Blatt Papier) zu entwickeln ist. Grundsätzlich sollte ein schlankes, transparentes, elegantes Tragwerk angestrebt werden, das sich durch technische Effizienz auszeichnet. Daneben sind folgende Aspekte zu beachten: Ganzheitlichkeit des Tragsystems (das Zusammenwirken möglichst vieler Tragwerksteile), Einheitlichkeit der Tragwerksstruktur (ein durchgehendes Stab- oder Flächentragwerk sowie formal ähnliche Querschnittsformen), Visualisierung des Kraftflusses durch sorgfältige, der Beanspruchung entsprechende Variation der Querschnittsabmessungen und Betonung der räumlichen Tragwerksstabilität.

Die Ornamentik sollte sich auf ein Minimum beschränken. Gewünscht werden jedoch oft Profilierungen bei relativ grossen Flächen und konstruktiv sorgfältig aufgebaute Regelflächen mit Stäben oder Kabeln. Bei Kabeln ist unbedingt zu beachten, dass den Blick verwirrende Überschneidungen vermieden werden.

Insgesamt sollte die Ästhetik einer Brücke an einem Modell oder mit einer Computervisualisierung überprüft werden. Modelle sind dreidimensional: Die räumliche Wirkung kommt damit gut zur Geltung; andererseits sind Modelle meistens zu klein und werden oft aus einer Perspektive betrachtet und fotografiert, die kein Betrachter in Realität einnehmen kann. Besonders wenn im Modell die Brücke und ihr ganzes Umfeld weiss gestrichen sind (was bei Architekturmodellen üblich ist), gehen Kontraste verloren, und Fotografien sind dann kaum mehr brauchbar.

Computervisualisierungen und Fotomontagen mit der geplanten Brücke in der realen Landschaft sind in der Regel wesentlich aufschlussreicher als Modelle. Der einzige Nachteil besteht darin, dass die Dreidimensionalität nicht befriedigend zur Geltung kommt.

Im Tätigkeitsbereich der Ingenieure und Architekten zwischen den Polen Naturwissenschaft (die keine subjektive Kreativität zulässt) und Kunst (die vor allem auf Kreativität beruht) steht die Architektur näher bei der Kunst und das Ingenieurwesen näher bei der Naturwissenschaft. Architekten bevorzugen deshalb eher die kreative, dekorative Ästhetik und Ingenieure eher die natürliche, konstruktive. Das kann zu Missverständnissen zwischen Architek-

BRIDGE AESTHETICS

Bridge aesthetics consist of the visual expression of an efficient structure that is integrated optimally into its surroundings and that has been given an elegant shape.

Aesthetic quality is the most important component of the cultural essence of a given bridge. It cannot be quantified directly. It may be possible, however, to compare the cost of several alternative designs and relate this to a cost of aesthetic quality. Bridge aesthetics encompass both the visible form of a given bridge considered on its own, and the relation between the bridge and its visible environment.

Aesthetic quality springs from two distinct origins. On the one hand, there is beauty that originates from human creativity, which will be referred to as man-made aesthetics (Fig. 2). *Man-made aesthetics* are not necessarily the same as art. On the other hand, there is beauty that originates without human intervention from sources such as nature, physics, and geometry (Fig. 3). This will be referred to as *natural aesthetics.*

Aesthetics are an abstract concept. To understand it better, it is often considered in terms of properties such as form, colour, splendor, structure, or originality. The design of genuine bridges is based primarily on scientific foundations. For this reason, bridges reflect primarily natural aesthetics, which are most closely related to the overarching concept of equilibrium in both the physical sense (equilibrium of structural demand and capacity) and in a metaphorical sense (balance and harmony between the bridge and its environment as well as among the various structural components).

The equilibrium of bridge and environment, i.e. the optimal adaptation of a bridge into its environment, is given visual expression primarily by means of temporal and spatial qualities as well as, in some instances, symbolic qualities. Temporal qualities include the relation of the bridge to its historical context, the local bridge building tradition, and the current state of the art in bridge technology and culture. Spatial aspects are defined by how the bridge relates to the character and scale of the broader landscape, both natural and man-made, the visual prominence of the bridge, and, in some instances, how these aspects give special meaning to the bridge as an icon. Adapting a given bridge into its immediate local environment requires consideration of diverse factors such as topography, geology, relevant geotechnical properties, nearby works of construction, existing transportation conditions, drainage characteristics, etc.

The most important basis for achieving balance and harmony in works of structural engineering is a clearly organized three-dimensional visible form that originates directly from the structural concept. This form is essentially three-dimensional and thus must not be developed using two-dimensional means, i.e., on a sheet of paper. The goal should be a slender, transparent, elegant structure that projects technical efficiency. In this regard, the following factors are particularly important: (1) The unity of the structural system (as many components as possible working together), (2) the unity of the visible form (a continuous arrangement of members or

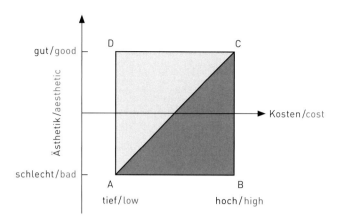

Fig. 4
Verhältnis Kosten/Ästhetik
Ratio of cost to aesthetic quality

Positionierung der Brücken in einem schematisch-fiktiven Kosten-Ästhetik-Diagramm
Schematic diagram relating cost and aesthetic quality

ten und Ingenieuren führen. Mit den immer umfangreicheren Normen, Richtlinien, technischen Vorschriften, Nachweisen und Kontrollen hat sich das Ingenieurwesen in jüngster Zeit zunehmend in Richtung Naturwissenschaft verschoben, während die Architektur sich mit dem Streben nach Originalität und Kreativität selbst bei der Lösung aktueller bauphysikalischer Probleme mehr der Kunst angenähert hat. Dieses Phänomen schadet dem gegenseitigen Verständnis der beiden Berufe, die früher enger zusammengehörten. Viele Ingenieure sind heute durchaus bereit, den Architekten die konzeptionelle Gestaltung der Brücken zu überlassen, und die Architekten erwarten von den Ingenieuren, dass sie mit den heute zur Verfügung stehenden Mitteln auch noch so skurril gestaltete Tragwerke «gesund»-rechnen können.

Es wäre viel fruchtbarer, wenn Ingenieure und Architekten wieder aufeinander zugingen, wenn bei den Ingenieuren das Verständnis für die Architektur und bei den Architekten das Verständnis für die Konstruktion gefördert würde. Grundsätzlich sollte der Ingenieur mit seiner Übersicht über die konstruktiven Möglichkeiten mit dem Architekten als Berater das Konzept entwickeln; bei fortschreitendem Entwurf kann der Architekt die Verfeinerung des rohen Konzepts leitend übernehmen und der Ingenieur sollte dabei beratend mitwirken.

BALANCE VON KOSTEN UND ÄSTHETIK
Ein gutes Brückenkonzept soll im Rahmen der imperativen, normierten Anforderungen ein überzeugendes Kosten-Ästhetik-Gleichgewicht aufweisen.

Bei der Balance der Entwurfsziele – Kosten und Ästhetik – spielt die konstruktive Kreativität – von der Wahl des Tragsystems über die Gestaltung des Tragwerks bis zur Verfeinerung der Details – die dominierende Rolle. Ein wichtiger Aspekt bei der Beurteilung eines Konzepts ist der zusätzlich für die ästhetische Qualität erforderliche Kostenaufwand gegenüber der einfachsten, wirtschaftlichsten Lösung. Folgende Grenzwerte sollten nicht überschritten werden: Bei Grossbrücken ca. 5 Prozent, bei mittleren Brücken (Länge weniger als 500 Meter, mittlere Spannweite etwa 100 Meter) ca. 15 Prozent und bei kleinen Brücken (Länge unter 100 Meter, mittlere Spannweite etwa 50 Meter) ca. 25 Prozent. Bei Fussgängerbrücken sind je nach erwünschtem Brückenerlebnis auch grössere zusätzliche Kosten vertretbar. Begründen lassen sich die von der

surfaces, as well as visually similar shapes for cross-sections), (3) the visual expression of the flow of forces by means of a carefully shaped variation of cross-section dimensions corresponding to these forces, and (4) Giving visual emphasis to the three dimensional stability of the structure.

Ornamentation should be kept to a minimum. It may, however, be desirable to give texture to large surfaces and provide special treatment to the surfaces formed by large numbers of members or cables. Particular attention should be paid to the arrangement of cables intersections. Arrangements that appear haphazard should always be avoided.

The overall aesthetic impact of bridges should be validated by means of models or digital imagery. Models are true three-dimensional objects. They therefore give a faithful representation of spatial relations. They are usually too small, however, and are often viewed and photographed from perspectives that are not realistic. When a model and its surroundings are painted white (which is common for architectural models), contrast is lost and photographs are generally not usable. Computer-generated imagery, in which bridges are incorporated into their real landscape, is generally richer in information than models. Its only disadvantage is that true three-dimensionality is sometimes not faithfully reproduced.

The activities of engineers and architects can be regarded as a spectrum that ranges between pure science at one end and pure art at the other. Science permits no subjective creativity, whereas art deals primarily with creativity. The practice of architecture can be regarded as closer to art, while engineering can be regarded as closer to science. As a result, architects tend to prefer a more creative, decorative perspective on aesthetics, whereas engineers prefer a natural perspective more closely related to structural function. This can lead to misunderstandings between architects and engineers. With the proliferation in recent years of standards, guidelines, technical requirements, checks, and inspections, engineering has shifted its orientation increasingly towards science, whereas architecture has moved closer to art, even to the extent of trying to apply creativity and originality to the solution of technical problems. This phenomenon hinders the mutual understanding of the two professions, which actually belonged together in the past. Today, many engineers see nothing wrong with letting architects take over the con-

Brückengrösse abhängigen Abstufungen damit, dass die Kosten der Haupttragelemente, die wenig Einfluss auf die Ästhetik haben, mit zunehmender Brückengrösse stark ansteigen und Grossbrücken allein schon mit ihren Abmessungen eindrücklich wirken.

In einem Kosten-Ästhetik-Koordinatensystem lassen sich alle Brücken schematisch in ein von den Punkten A, B, C und D aufgespanntes Rechteck einordnen.

A wirtschaftlich, aber ästhetisch schlecht
B teuer und ästhetisch schlecht
C teuer, aber ästhetisch gut
D wirtschaftlich und ästhetisch gut

A, C und D sind je nach Exposition und Grösse der Brücke akzeptabel, das heisst, dass Positionen über der Diagonalen A – C möglich, darunter jedoch abzulehnen sind.

DIE ENTWICKLUNG DES BRÜCKENKONZEPTS

Ein Brückenkonzept soll den aktuellen und lokalen Stand des konstruktiven Ingenieurbaus reflektieren. Es soll effizient, einfach und klar sein. Die verwendeten Baustoffe sollen dem System entsprechen und ökonomisch, funktionell und synergetisch verwendet werden. Das Konzept ist erst dann gut, wenn man nichts mehr hinzufügen muss und nichts mehr wegnehmen kann.

Wenn man davon ausgeht, dass Brücken bei ihrer Nähe zur Naturwissenschaft eine natürliche, im Gleichgewicht stehende Ästhetik aufweisen sollen, besteht kein Grund, den Entwurf mit künstlerischen Elementen anzureichern; schon gar nicht, wenn diese zur Hauptsache aus einem seltsamen Tragsystem, tragwerksfremden Dekorationen, teuren Baustoffen oder Millimeter-Toleranzen bestehen und damit in den Bereich unter die oben erwähnte Diagonale A – C rutschen. Innovation und Originalität sind nur dann echte, wertvolle Qualitätsmerkmale, wenn sie nachhaltig sind, also etwa in ähnlicher Form kopiert und verbreitet werden können. Andernfalls handelt es sich dabei nur um teure Originalitätssucht, PR-Aktivitäten und eitle Selbstdarstellung.

Eine pragmatische Entwurfsentwicklung besteht im Prinzip aus vier Schritten: Im ersten Schritt muss ein Tragsystem gewählt werden, das sich einwandfrei in den näheren und weiteren Kontext einfügen lässt und aufgrund erster Abschätzungen ein hohes Potenzial bezüglich Wirtschaftlichkeit und Ästhetik aufweist. Im zweiten Schritt muss untersucht werden, ob die Zusatzkosten im Vergleich zur Minimallösung unter dem zulässigen Grenzwert liegen, da sonst das Konzept verworfen werden sollte. Im dritten Schritt erfolgt mit der Ermittlung der optimalen Strukturabmessungen die Weiterbearbeitung des Tragsystems zum Tragwerk. Im vierten Schritt werden schliesslich die Querschnittsabmessungen dem Kräftefluss entsprechend variiert – soweit es die Kosten zulassen – und die konstruktiven Details sorgfältig verfeinert.

Die Visualisierung und Beurteilung der mit Gleichgewicht – also mit Ausgewogenheit und Harmonie – in Beziehung stehenden natürlichen Brückenästhetik ist nicht einfach Geschmackssache. Wenn einmal das generelle Tragsystem mit Rücksicht auf das Brü-

ceptual design of bridges, and architects expect that engineers will be happy to take ludicrous concepts that bear absolutely no relation to structural function and "make them work".

It would be much more fruitful for engineers and architects to come back to together, by promoting a mutual understanding of each other's profession. Fundamentally, the engineer who understands the possibilities and implications arising from the choice of a structural system should develop the design concept with the architect, acting as his advisor. As the design progresses, architect, can take the lead on refining the raw concept, with the engineer now playing the role of his advisor.

THE BALANCE OF COST AND AESTHETIC QUALITY

Good bridge concepts must, in addition to satisfying requirements prescribed in design standards, exhibit a convincing balance of cost and aesthetic quality.

Creativity in design – as applied to tasks including the choice of structural system, the definition of the structural form, and the refinement of details – plays the most important role in achieving a suitable balance between cost and aesthetic quality. Although the simplest, most economical solution need not necessarily be chosen, the increase in cost of a given concept relative to the most economical solution should not exceed the following limits: For large bridges: about 5 %; for medium bridges (total length less than 500 m, average span about 100 m): 15 %; for small bridges (total length less than 100 m, average span about 50 m): 25 %.

For pedestrian bridges, depending on the desired experience for users, even higher increases can be allowed. Defining these increases as a function of the size of the bridge can be justified since the cost of the primary structural components, which have relatively little impact on aesthetic quality, increases rapidly with increasing size, and large bridges can be impressive merely by virtue of their size.

The relationship between cost and aesthetic quality can be represented graphically by the rectangle shown in Figure 4. The meaning of the vertices of this rectangle is defined as follows:

Point A: Economical bridges with low aesthetic quality
Point B: Expensive bridges with low aesthetic quality
Point C: Expensive bridges with high aesthetic quality
Point D: Economical bridges with high aesthetic quality

Depending on the exposure and size of the bridge, A, C, and D can all be acceptable. So points above the A – C diagonal represent possible combinations of economy and aesthetic quality, whereas concepts with points below this line should not be chosen.

THE DEVELOPMENT OF A BRIDGE CONCEPT

Bridge concepts should reflect the current and local state of the art of engineering design. They should be efficient, simple, and clear. The materials used should be suitable for the structural system and should be used economically, functionally, and synergetically. More is not better. The concept is good when nothing more needs to be added and nothing can be taken away.

ckenumfeld festgelegt ist, muss das entsprechende effizienteste Tragwerk ermittelt werden. Grobe Mängel der Tragwerksoptimierung lassen sich ohne Weiteres mit Modellen und Computerbildern feststellen. Man kann sofort unterscheiden zwischen leichter Eleganz und klobiger Plumpheit, zwischen funktional geeigneten und ungeeigneten Baustoffen, zwischen effizienten und ineffizienten Tragsystemen, zwischen erforderlichen und überflüssigen Elementen des Tragwerks, zwischen Konstruktion und Dekoration und zwischen konzeptionellen Ansätzen, die sich wohl im Hochbau, aber nicht im Brückenbau eignen. Entwerfer sollten vermeiden, auf weit hergeholte Vergleiche (das oder jenes sieht aus wie...) hinzuweisen. Brücken sollten, abgesehen von kleinen, nostalgischen Stegen, (auch mit ihrem Aussehen) natürliche, mathematisch-physikalische Schönheit im Rahmen des aktuellen Stands der Dinge widerspiegeln. Der Brückenbau ist nicht eine Kunst im engen, wörtlichen Sinn. Ästhetisch missratene Brücken als Folge visueller Unverträglichkeit mit ihrem Umfeld, schlechter Gestaltung, eines ungeeigneten Tragsystems oder nicht zweckmässiger Baustoffe sollten nicht mit Begriffen wie «moderne Kunst im Brückenbau» schöngeredet werden.

Bei genaueren Untersuchungen ist ein sorgfältig geschultes Formgefühl ausserordentlich nützlich. Gutes Formgefühl, das auf einem soliden Verständnis von Statik und Konstruktion beruht, korreliert (fast immer) mit optimaler Tragwerkseffizienz. Echter Brückenbau folgt nicht architektonischen Trends und Modeströmungen.

Based on the premise that bridges, by virtue of their closeness to science, should project a visual impression that originates from equilibrium, there is no reason to augment a design with artistic elements, especially if these consist of ludicrous structural systems, decoration unrelated to structural function, expensive materials, or construction tolerances of a millimeter or less. These concepts will always lie below the A – C diagonal in Figure 4. Innovation and originality can only be genuine and valuable hallmarks of quality when they are worthy of being repeated and emulated on other bridges. Otherwise, they are merely expensive instances of originality for its own sake, exercises in public relations, and expressions of the designer's vanity.

A pragmatic design process consists primarily of the following four steps: A structural system is selected. The system must be integrated perfectly into the bridge's surroundings and possess a high potential for economy and aesthetic quality. The additional costs of the concept relative to the minimal cost solution must be estimated. If these costs exceed the applicable limit, then the concept must be abandoned and another chosen. The structural system is developed into a structure by means of optimizing structural dimensions. Provided it can be done cost-effectively, the cross-section dimensions can be varied according to the flow of forces. The structural details can also be refined.

The visual expression and assessment of natural aesthetic quality, which is related to balance and harmony, is not a simple matter of taste. Once the overall structural system has been determined relative to its surroundings, the associated and most efficient structure must be determined. Major problems regarding structural optimization can be readily discovered using models and digital imagery. It is certainly possible to distinguish between light elegance and heavy crudeness, between materials that are well suited to their function and those that are not, between efficient and inefficient systems, between design and decoration, and between conceptual approaches that are well suited to the design of buildings but not of bridges. Designers should also avoid far-fetched references to other bridges. Apart from small, nostalgic works, bridges should reflect natural beauty in harmony with the principles of physics and mathematics, consistent with the state of the art of engineering design. Bridge design is not an art in the strict literal sense. Poorly advised bridges that exhibit visual incompatibility with their surroundings, bad shaping, inappropriate structural systems, or impractical materials should not be praised as "the modern art of bridge design".

For more exact studies, a carefully schooled sense of form is extremely useful, since choices that arise from a good sense of form, founded on a sound understanding of statics and design, almost always correspond with structures of optimal efficiency. True bridge design does not follow architectural trends and fashions.

IM GLEICHGEWICHT
PERFECT POISE

CHRISTIAN MENN IM GESPRÄCH MIT CASPAR SCHÄRER / CHRISTIAN MENN IN CONVERSATION WITH CASPAR SCHÄRER

Erinnern Sie sich an Ihre erste Brücke?

Ja natürlich, das war die Crestawaldbrücke. Sie wurde im Juli 1959 betoniert, als meine älteste Tochter Claudia geboren wurde. Ich hatte natürlich schon ein bisschen Angst; das Absenken des Lehrgerüstes hatte bei mir einen gewissen Stress ausgelöst. Und im Nachhinein muss ich ehrlich sagen, dass ich bei der Crestawaldbrücke etwas mehr Wert auf die erwünschte Form als auf die beste Konstruktion legte. Ich wollte unbedingt den Bogen als Sichel formen. Der Zweigelenkbogen ist aber vom grundsätzlich Konstruktiven bei einer Brücke wie dieser nicht richtig, er könnte eigentlich eingespannt sein. Aber ich fand, dass die Sichel schöner aussieht.

Sie haben also die Ästhetik über die konstruktive Vernunft gestellt?

Ja, das kann man vielleicht so sagen. Der Bogen ist etwas breiter, als er sollte und damit am Rand stärker Regen, Schnee und der salzhaltigen Schwarzräumung ausgesetzt, doch es ist nach wie vor eine hübsche Brücke.

Welche Ihrer Brücken haben Sie besonders gern?

Die Brücke in Boston – die letzte, die ich bisher gebaut habe. Eigentlich hätte die Brücke in Abu Dhabi die letzte sein sollen; die Bauarbeiten hatten bereits angefangen, dann kam diese amerikanische Firma und hat uns einfach rausgeschmissen. Jetzt wird da etwas Himmeltrauriges hingebaut. Man muss sich doch ein bisschen bemühen! Eine Brücke ist nicht einfach nichts. Ich möchte mit diesem Buch einen Anstoss geben, dass man sich mehr Mühe gibt in der Gestaltung – und bereit ist, je nach Standort und Bedeutung der Brücke auch etwas dafür zu bezahlen.

Es scheint nur sehr wenige Brückenkonstrukteure zu geben, die auf die Gestaltung achten.

Ich habe den Eindruck, dass früher mehr Wert auf die Gestaltung gelegt wurde. Und ich meine damit nicht das 20. Jahrhundert, sondern viel früher. An den Brücken der Römer und des Mittelalters erkennt man ein Gespür für die Gestaltung.

In früheren Zeiten dauerte der Bau viel länger und da konnten sich die Baumeister wahrscheinlich mehr dazu überlegen – während es heute rasch gehen muss. Heute ist es nochmals ganz anders. Ungefähr in den 1970er Jahren fand ein starker Wandel statt, als

Do you remember your first bridge?

Yes, of course, that was the Crestawald Bridge. The concrete was cast in July 1959, when my eldest daughter Claudia was born. Naturally I was a little scared; the subsidence of the falsework worried me. And with hindsight I have to admit that for the Crestawald Bridge, I attached rather more importance to the desired form than to the best possible construction. I wanted the arch to be crescent-shaped at all costs. But from an engineering point of view, a two-hinged arch is not the right choice for a bridge like this one; it could just as well have been a simple span. But the crescent was more attractive to my mind.

So you gave aesthetics priority over engineering rationale?

Yes, you could perhaps say that. The arch is somewhat broader than it should be and hence more exposed to rain, snow, and the salty grit used to keep the road clear in winter; but it's a beautiful bridge nonetheless.

Which of your bridges are you especially fond of?

The bridge in Boston—the last one I built. The bridge in Abu Dhabi was supposed to be the last one, actually, and we had already begun building it when along came this American contractor and threw us out. And what they're erecting is so pitiful! You have to at least try! A bridge is not nothing. I would like this book to give people a nudge, to inspire them to take more care over the design—and to be willing to pay for it, too, depending on the bridge's location and how important it is.

It seems there are not many bridge builders around who pay heed to design these days.

I too have the impression that design used to count for more. And I'm not even talking about the twentieth century, but rather long before that. You can see a feeling for form even in Roman and medieval bridges.

Building a bridge used to take much longer than it does now, so those who built them presumably had more time to think things over, whereas these days everything has to be done as fast as possible.

Today it's different again. A major change took place in the seventies or thereabouts, when architects got into the business of

die Architekten als Brückengestalter auf den Plan traten. Die Brücken wurden bunter und lebendiger, aber sie wurden auf keinen Fall wirtschaftlicher. Ich habe mir von Anfang an Gedanken über die Ästhetik von Brücken gemacht und seither immer und immer wieder. Daraus schälte sich ein Begriff heraus, der für mich zu einer erhabenen Grösse wurde: das «Gleichgewicht» als ein physikalischer, aber eben auch als ein bildlicher Begriff. Im «Gleichgewicht» enthalten sind «Balance», «Harmonie» und «Ausgewogenheit». Hinzu kommt die «Einheitlichkeit», die ebenfalls sehr wichtig ist.

Hat sich Ihr Verhältnis zur Ästhetik im Laufe der Zeit gewandelt?

Meine Überlegungen zur Gestaltung sind gewachsen und ich hatte diesen unbändigen Willen, mich laufend weiterzuentwickeln. Wenn ich aus heutiger Perspektive an meinen ersten Vortrag zurückdenke, den ich vor langer Zeit in den USA hielt, erscheint mir das damals Gesagte nur noch läppisch. Ich habe mich bemüht, mich zu verbessern, auch wenn ich nicht immer ans Ziel gelangt bin.

Sie haben sich vor allem durch das Bauen von Brücken weiterentwickelt.

Vor allem mit den Bogenbrücken habe ich mich intensiv auseinandergesetzt. Aber ich habe leider viel zu spät herausgefunden, wie sie besser funktionieren könnten. Mein Projekt für eine Brücke beim Hoover Dam (vgl. Seiten 296 ff.) sah einen 300 Meter weit gespannten Dreigelenkbogen vor, der in einem neuartigen Bauvorgang mit Hilfe von Fachwerktürmen hätte hergestellt werden sollen. Es wäre eine moderne und elegante Brücke geworden. Die Brücke in Tamins (vgl. Seiten 82 ff.) ist im Vergleich dazu eine konventionelle Brücke. Wenn ich die Idee mit den Fachwerktürmen schon früher gehabt hätte, wäre alles viel einfacher gewesen und wir hätten eine neue Form von Bogenbrücken gesehen. Ich habe damals richtiggehend etwas verpasst, und das reut mich heute natürlich. Wahrscheinlich war ich zu bequem und zu stark auf die Wirtschaftlichkeit fokussiert. Wir Ingenieure waren selber an diesem Wettrennen beteiligt und haben untereinander diskutiert, welche Brücke nun pro Quadratmeter wieviel kosten würde.

Dennoch waren die 1960er und 1970er Jahre eine interessante Zeit für Brückenbauer. Überall wurden Brücken gebaut und Ihr Wissen und Können war gefragt.

Das Nationalstrassennetz mit seinen ursprünglich 1800 Kilometern Autobahn war der Auslöser für die meisten Brücken. Der Kanton Graubünden erkannte die Gelegenheit und nutzte die Nationalstrasse, um endlich eine wintersichere Verbindung ins Misox zu bauen. Wenn man früher im Winter ins Misox fahren wollte, musste man einen gewaltigen Umweg auf sich nehmen und sieben Kantone durchqueren. Und so setzte der Kanton Graubünden durch, dass der San-Bernardino-Tunnel als erster Alpentunnel des Nationalstrassennetzes gebaut wurde.

designing bridges. That made them more colorful and more exciting, but definitely not more economical. I gave a lot of thought to the aesthetics of bridges right from the start—and have done so ever since, over and over again. This gave rise to a concept that for me became the hallmark of the sublime. I'm talking about the concept of "poise" as both a physical property and a visual quality. "Poise" implies "balance", "harmony", and "equilibrium"; to which we could add "integrity", which is also very important.

Has your relationship to aesthetics changed over the years?

My thoughts on design have grown and I always had this fierce determination to keep developing my whole life long. Thinking back to my first lecture from where I am today, it seems to me that what I said all those years ago in America was actually pretty wishy-washy. I've made an effort to improve, even if I haven't always hit the mark.

You've developed mainly by building bridges.

The main focus of my engagement has been on arched bridges. Unfortunately though, I didn't discover how they could work better until it was too late. My project for a bridge at the Hoover Dam (cf. pp. 296 ff.) envisaged a three-hinged arch with a 300-meter span, which thanks to a new building method using truss towers could in fact have been built. It would have been a modern and elegant bridge. The bridge in Tamins (cf. pp. 82 ff.) is conventional by comparison. If only I had come up with the idea of truss towers a bit earlier! It would all have been so much easier and we could have had a new form of arched bridge. I missed something groundbreaking back then, and naturally regret it now. Probably I was too complacent and too fixated on the economic aspects. We engineers were ourselves complicit in this race and took to discussing which bridge cost how much per square meter even among ourselves.

Yet the sixties and seventies were an interesting time for bridge builders. Bridges were going up everywhere and your knowhow and skills were in demand.

Most of my bridges were needed for the national highway network, which was to be 1800 km long originally. The Canton of Graubünden spotted the opportunity presented by this nationwide undertaking and seized it to finally provide a winter-safe road link to the Misox Valley. Prior to that date, anyone who had wanted to drive there in the winter had needed to make a huge detour through seven different cantons. So it was thanks to the Canton of Graubünden that the San Bernardino Tunnel was built—the national highway network's first Alpine tunnel.

But there were also one or two bridges to cross on the road from Thusis to Roveredo, both before and after the tunnel…

Yes, indeed, over a dozen of them in fact.

Vor und nach diesem Tunnel gab es dann auf dem Weg von Thusis bis Roveredo die eine oder andere Brücke, die sie gebaut haben...

Ja, das waren gut und gern ein Dutzend Brücken.

Konnten Sie noch Einfluss nehmen auf die Lage der Brücken oder war das alles schon fixiert?

Die Linienführung war vom Kantonsingenieur vorgegeben. Ich hätte vielleicht da und dort schon diskutieren können, aber man hat das damals nicht gemacht. Alles musste schnell gehen. Aus heutiger Sicht muss ich sagen: Wir hätten uns mehr Zeit nehmen sollen. Wir hatten die einmalige Chance, eine Strasse über einen Pass zu bauen, und hätten alles ganz sorgfältig planen und bauen sollen. So wie bei der berühmten Sustenpassstrasse auf der Berner Seite oder bei der Albulabahn. Bei diesen beiden Projekten wurden grosse Infrastrukturbauten mustergültig in die Landschaft eingebettet.

Wann kommt im Verlauf eines Brückenprojektes die Ästhetik ins Spiel?

Sie kommt ganz am Anfang. Denn am Anfang steht nicht die Brücke, sondern die Umgebung. Es gibt einen räumlichen und einen zeitlichen Einfluss; das Räumliche ist der Massstab und der Charakter der Landschaft und der Topografie; das Zeitliche ist die Geschichte und die Tradition. Im Grunde genommen sind das ganz einfache Dinge, und doch werden sie immer wieder vergessen. Da vergreift sich einer im Massstab, dort übergeht ein anderer einfach die Brückenbautradition einer Stadt. Erst wenn man das Umfeld einer Brücke betrachtet und untersucht, kann man bestimmen, welche Struktur dazu passt.

Eine Bogen-, eine Balken-, eine Kabel- oder eine Hängebrücke...

Richtig. Die Brücke hat erst eine ganz rohe Form, die ich dann verfeinern muss. Soll ich jetzt den Träger oder den Bogen dicker oder feiner ausformulieren; wie verhält sich die Fahrbahnplatte; wie wird die Brücke gebaut? All das sollte in einem Gleichgewicht sein. Die Gestaltung einer Brücke erfordert einerseits viel Wissen, andererseits braucht man ein gewisses Gefühl dafür. Ich habe allerdings auch eine Brücke mit einigen gestalterischen Mängeln gebaut.

Welche Brücke war das?

Der Pont de Chandoline in Sion (vgl. Seiten 240 ff.). Die beiden Pfeiler in der Rhone mussten extrem tief fundiert werden und wurden deshalb rund ausgeführt. Darauf kommt der Träger mit der Fahrbahnplatte zu liegen, und darüber erheben sich schliesslich die zwei Pylone mit den Seilen. Die Pylone sind rechteckig, die Pfeiler unten im Fluss sind rund. Das sieht einfach nicht gut aus! Und dann sind die Pylone oben breiter als unten. Noch so ein Fehler!

Wer hat das denn entschieden?

Ich war das selber. Ich habe nicht intensiv genug an dieser Brücke gearbeitet; ich hätte ein richtiges Modell bauen sollen, dann hätte ich die Probleme wahrscheinlich erkannt. Diese Fehler tun mir weh und ich fahre nicht gerne dort vorbei. Zum Glück war das vor der

Did you have any say in the location of the bridges, or had that already been decided?

The route had been fixed by the cantonal engineer. I could perhaps have discussed this or that part of it with him, but that's not what actually happened. It all had to be done quickly. Looking back, I have to say that we should have given ourselves more time. We had this once-in-a-lifetime chance to build a road over a pass and should have taken a lot more care over both the planning and building of it; just as they did on the Berne side of the famous Susten Pass or on the Albula Railway. In both those cases, major infrastructural developments were embedded in the landscape in an exemplary way.

How do aesthetics come into play in the course of a bridge project?

They're there right from the start. Because what you start with is not the bridge but its surroundings. There is a space factor and a time factor: The space factor is the scale and character of the landscape plus the topography; the time factor is history and tradition. These are actually very basic things, yet time and time again they're forgotten. This one gets the scale wrong, that one disregards a city's own bridge building tradition... Only by studying a bridge in its larger context can you decide which structure is the right one for it.

Whether it should be an arch or a beam bridge, a cable-stayed or a suspension bridge...

Exactly. The form looks pretty crude at first and it is my job to refine it. Should the girder or the arch be thicker or finer? How will the road deck on top of it behave? How is the bridge to be built? All of these things have to be perfectly balanced. Designing a bridge calls for a lot of engineering know-how; but you have to have a feel for it as well. Having said that, I did once build a bridge with certain design defects.

Which bridge was that?

The Pont de Chandoline in Sion (cf. pp. 240 ff.). The two piers in the Rhône had to be sunken extremely deep into the riverbed, which is why we made them round. Resting on them is the box girder with the road deck and mounted on that are the two pylons with cable stays. The pylons, however, are rectangular, whereas the piers in the river are round. It just doesn't look good! And then the pylons are wider at the top than at the bottom. Another mistake!

Who decided that?

I did! I simply didn't work hard enough on that bridge; I should have built a proper model and then would probably have spotted the problems right away. The mistakes still pain me which is why I try to avoid driving anywhere near it. Fortunately it came before the one in Boston. There could be no repeat of that on a huge bridge running right through the middle of a big city. This time I would get it right. And the result really was better.

Brücke in Boston. Bei dieser grossen Brücke mitten in der Innenstadt durfte das nicht noch einmal passieren. Dieses Mal wollte ich es richtig machen. Und das Resultat war viel besser.

Blicken wir kurz noch etwas weiter zurück. Sie sind Sohn eines Bauingenieurs. War Ihr Weg also schon früh vorgezeichnet?

Mein Vater war bei einem Bauunternehmen und an vielen Brücken beteiligt; er hat sogar in Persien Brücken gebaut. Aber auf mich hatte das keinen Einfluss. Am Gymnasium habe ich mir noch keine grossen Gedanken über einen künftigen Beruf gemacht. Medizin hätte mich interessiert, doch ich konnte mir nicht vorstellen, jemanden zu operieren. Mathematik wäre eine andere Option gewesen – ich war recht gut in Mathematik –, aber es hat mich nicht sonderlich gereizt, jahrelang an einer Primzahl herumzustudieren.

Später an der ETH waren Sie ein Schüler von Pierre Lardy. Was hat er Ihnen mit auf den Weg gegeben?

Pierre Lardy war kein typischer, fantasievoller Bauingenieur, aber ein ganz besonderer Mensch. Zuerst war er am Konservatorium, dann studierte er Chemie, später Mathematik und wurde erst dann Bauingenieur. Er lud mich oft in die Kronenhalle ein: Wir haben uns dort ausführlich über Brückenquerschnitte unterhalten. Könnte man nicht noch diesen oder jenen Querschnitt ausprobieren? Solche Fragen halt, neue Ideen. Wir haben immer versucht, einander neue Ideen zu vermitteln. Lardy hat mich wirklich ernst genommen. Auch wenn viele dieser Diskussionen im Sand verliefen, haben sie mir enorm geholfen. Manchmal, wenn ich zurückdenke, habe ich das Gefühl, dass ich dieses Glück gar nicht verdient habe. Ich habe mir in meiner Laufbahn einige Mal gewünscht, dass ich dieses oder jenes Problem mit Lardy hätte besprechen können.

Wie erging es Ihnen später, als Sie bei Pier Luigi Nervi in Paris gearbeitet haben?

Ich durfte an dem Projekt für den Hauptsitz der UNESCO mitarbeiten. Es gab da ein verzwicktes Problem, an dem ich lange gerechnet und überlegt habe. Diese Deckenschale war gerade mal 8 Zentimeter dick, aber an einer bestimmten Stelle brauchte ich mindestens 14 Zentimeter. Ich war ganz verzweifelt und wandte mich an den Bürochef. Er wollte jedoch nur wissen, ob man die Verdickung sehen würde. Als ich das verneinte, sagte er, dass ich sogar auf 30 Zentimeter Dicke gehen solle. Da war ich also schon erschüttert, wie locker die das nahmen. Nervi hat leider keine Brücken gebaut; es hätte mich interessiert, wie er vorgegangen wäre.

Was würden Sie als erfahrener Konstrukteur einem jungen Ingenieur in Ausbildung mit auf den Weg geben?

Ich würde dazu raten, sich im Studium nicht zu lange aufzuhalten, die Ausbildung aber ordentlich abzuschliessen und dann so bald wie möglich raus in die Welt zu gehen. Zu meiner Zeit gab es für jeden Ingenieur die Möglichkeit, zu Othmar Ammann nach New York zu gehen. Ich hatte das ursprünglich auch vor, aber es kam dann nicht dazu.

Let's go back a bit further. You are the son of a civil engineer. Was it inevitable that you would follow in your father's footsteps?

My father worked for a building contractor and was involved in several bridge projects; he built bridges even in Persia. But that had no influence on me. I didn't give much thought to my future career while still at high school. Medicine would have interested me, but I couldn't imagine cutting someone open. Mathematics would also have been an option – I was pretty good at math – but the prospect of spending years studying prime numbers didn't really appeal.

Later, at the ETH, you were a student of Pierre Lardy. What did you get out of that?

Pierre Lardy was not your typical civil engineer brimming with ideas; but he was a very special person. First he was at the conservatory, then he switched to chemistry, then mathematics, and only then civil engineering. He often invited me to the Kronenhalle restaurant where we talked at length about bridge cross sections. Couldn't this or that cross section be tried out too? Questions like that. New ideas. We were constantly bouncing ideas off each other. Lardy took me very seriously. And even if many of our discussions ran aground sooner or later, they helped me enormously. Sometimes, when I think back, I have the feeling I didn't really deserve such good fortune. In the course of my career, I've often found myself wishing that I could discuss this or that problem with Lardy.

How did you get on later, when you were working for Pier Luigi Nervi in Paris?

There I was allowed to work on the project for the UNESCO headquarters. There was one very tricky problem that took me a long time to figure out. The floor slab was just 8 centimeters thick, but in one particular place I needed a thickness of at least 14 centimeters. Despairing of ever finding a solution, I turned to my boss for help. He asked me if the added thickness would be visible. When I answered in the negative, he told me to go for 30 centimeters! I was stunned at how casually he took it. Nervi never built any bridges, unfortunately; I would love to have seen how he tackled it.

Now that you yourself are an experienced engineer, how would you help young engineers on their way?

I would advise them not to linger too long over their studies, but to finish their training with respectable grades and then get out into the world as soon as possible. In my day, every young engineer had the chance to go to Othmar Ammann in New York, which is what I planned to do originally, although I never actually got round to it.

DER EINFLUSS VON ROBERT MAILLART UND OTHMAR AMMANN AUF CHRISTIAN MENN
THE INFLUENCE OF ROBERT MAILLART AND OTHMAR AMMANN ON CHRISTIAN MENN

DAVID P. BILLINGTON

Nach dem Symposium (6.–8. November 1930) anlässlich des 75-jährigen Bestehens der Eidgenössischen Technischen Hochschule (ETH) trafen sich Robert Maillart und Othmar Ammann in dem hoch über der Stadt gelegenen luxuriösen Grandhotel Dolder. Dort, mit Blick auf den Zürichsee, tauschten sich die beiden grossen Ingenieure längere Zeit aus. Am 18. August 1930 war im Kanton Graubünden mit der Salginatobelbrücke Maillarts berühmteste Konstruktion eingeweiht worden, während die beiden ersten Arbeiten von Ammann kurz vor ihrer Fertigstellung standen – die George Washington Bridge im Oktober 1931, die Bayonne Bridge im November 1931 – und ihm selbst soeben die Ehrendoktorwürde der ETH verliehen worden war, die ihn als einen der Besten seiner Zunft auswies.[1]

Es wäre sicherlich hochinteressant gewesen, bei dieser Begegnung im Jahr 1930 dabei gewesen zu sein. Sieben Jahre später kam es zu einem weiteren Treffen der beiden, und wie Aufzeichnungen belegen, äusserte sich Ammann während des Gesprächs lobend über die Arbeit von Maillart. Die Bekanntschaft der beiden Männer – wenn auch nur flüchtig – verdankt sich sowohl der Ausbildung, die beide in Zürich erhielten, als auch der Schweizer Staatsbürgerschaft, die beide bis an ihr Lebensende behielten. Jeder der beiden grossen schweizerischen Ingenieure hat mein Verständnis von Ingenieursbaukunst derart radikal verändert, dass ich die Bedeutung der aufsehenerregenden Brücken von Christian Menn sofort erkennen konnte. Und die Erkenntnis, wie eng die Entwürfe von Maillart, Ammann und Menn miteinander verknüpft sind, führte schliesslich zu der Arbeit an meinem Buch *The Art of Structural Design, A Swiss Legacy*.

MAILLART UND MENN

1960 nahm ich eine Assistenzprofessur an der Fakultät für Bauingenieurwesen der Universität Princeton an und ein Jahr später lud man mich ein, an der dortigen Architekturschule eine Vorlesung für fortgeschrittene Studenten zu halten. Nachdem ich diese Vorlesung ein paar Jahre lang gehalten hatte, kamen die Studierenden zu mir und erklärten mir höflich, aber bestimmt, wie sehr sie der Inhalt der Vorlesung langweile. Sie zeigten mir ein dickes Buch mit dem Titel *Raum, Zeit und Architektur*[2] und wiesen mich insbesondere auf ein langes Kapitel mit Abbildungen von eleganten Betonbrücken

Following the 75th Anniversary Symposium (November 6–8, 1930) celebrating the foundation of the Swiss Federal Institute of Technology (ETH), Robert Maillart sat with Othmar Ammann in the luxurious Grand Hotel Dolder high above the city of Zurich. There, overlooking Lake Zurich, these two great engineers conversed at some length. On August 18, 1930 the Canton of Graubünden had opened Maillart's most famous work, the Salginatobel Bridge, while Ammann's first two works, the George Washington Bridge of October 1931 and the Bayonne Bridge of November 1931, were nearing completion, and their designer had already just received an honorary degree recognizing him as being at the very top of the profession.[1] It would have been a remarkable experience to have been present at that encounter in 1930. Seven years later, another meeting of the two engineers did result in a partial record of what was said, including Ammann speaking warmly of Maillart's work. This connection between Maillart and Ammann, however fleeting, does at least attest to the education each received in Zurich as well as to their Swiss citizenship, which both retained their whole life long.

Each of these great Swiss engineers radically changed my own understanding of structural engineering in a way that has enabled me to appreciate all the more the extraordinary bridges of Menn. It was my realization of how closely the bridge designs of Maillart, Ammann, and Christian Menn fit together that led to my book, *The Art of Structural Design, A Swiss Legacy*.

MAILLART AND MENN

In 1960 I joined the Princeton University faculty to teach Civil Engineering students and one year later I was invited to give a lecture to advanced students at the School of Architecture there. After presenting the lecture for a few years, the class came to me and politely but firmly stated that they were bored by the content of the course. Then they showed me a big fat book entitled *Space, Time and Architecture*,[2] from which they proceeded to show me a long chapter with pictures of elegant concrete bridges (all by Maillart), none of which I had ever seen before. They asked me to teach them based on these bridge designs rather than through the diagrams and endless formulas that I had taken from standard textbooks.

In the early 1970s, I was researching Maillart's structures and using some of the results in my course for the architects. In 1972 this

(allesamt von Maillart) hin, von denen ich bis dahin keine einzige gesehen hatte. Sie baten mich, den Unterricht an diesen Konstruktionen auszurichten und nicht an den Diagrammen und ellenlangen Formeln, die ich aus Standardlehrbüchern übernommen hatte.

Anfang der 1970er-Jahre forschte ich über Maillarts Konstruktionen und liess einige meiner Erkenntnisse in die Architekturvorlesungen einfliessen. 1972 organisierten meine Kollegen und ich ein Symposium zu Maillarts Ehren. Wir luden Ingenieure ein, die den Brückenbauer gekannt hatten. Einen besonderen Eindruck auf mich hinterliessen Christian Menn, Felix Candela und Fazlur Khan. Jeder hielt einen sorgfältig ausgearbeiteten Vortrag über seine persönliche Sicht auf die Arbeit von Maillart, wobei insbesondere Menns Präsentation den Zusammenhang zwischen den Konstruktionen von Maillart und den eigenen frühen Brückenentwürfen deutlich machte.[3]

1957 hatte Christian Menn in Chur ein eigenes Büro gegründet; drei seiner ersten Entwürfe wurden kurz darauf verwirklicht: die Crestawaldbrücke (1959) mit einer Spannweite von 71,5 Metern und die Brücke bei Cröt (1959) mit einer Spannweite von 65,8 Metern – zwei durch Fahrbahnplatten versteifte Bogenbrücken – sowie als Drittes die dreigelenkige Letziwald-Bogenbrücke (1959) mit einer Spannweite von 66,4 Metern. Die ersten beiden liessen den Einfluss von Maillarts fahrbahnversteiften Brücken erkennen, während die dritte auf dessen Tavanasabrücke aus dem Jahr 1905 verwies. In den Jahren 1962–1968 entwarf Menn fünf weitere fahrbahnversteifte Bogenbrücken mit Spannweiten von 86 bis 112 Metern, in denen die polygonalen Bögen noch schmaler wirkten. Danach verliess er das Ingenieurbüro in Chur und trat eine Professur an seiner Alma Mater an, der ETH in Zürich. Nun hatte er zwar keine eigene Firma mehr, arbeitete aber als freier Berater und Planer bei einigen grossen Brückenprojekten mit. Zu seinen bekanntesten Arbeiten aus dieser Zeit zählen der Felsenauviadukt (1974) bei Bern, die Ganterbrücke (1980) auf der Strasse zum Simplonpass, die Sunnibergbrücke (1998) in der Nähe von Klosters sowie die Zakim Bunker Hill Memorial Bridge (2002) in Boston, USA. Nach der Fertigstellung repräsentierte jede dieser Arbeiten im weltweiten Vergleich mit ähnlichen Bauwerken eine Neuerung, wobei die letzten drei Brücken Menns Kenntnisse von seilgestützten Konstruktionen eindrücklich belegen. Tatsächlich hätte jede dieser Konstruktionen als Balkenbrücke im Stil des Felsenauviadukts verwirklicht werden können, stattdessen entschied Menn, sie mit einem Stützsystem zu versehen, das oberhalb der horizontalen Fahrbahn sichtbar war. Die Verlagerung des visuellen Schwerpunkts führte zu einer Reihe von wichtigen Entwürfen und brachte Menn an die grossformatigen Brücken heran, die Mitte des 20. Jahrhunderts von den aufsehenerregenden Konstruktionen Othmar Ammanns dominiert worden waren.[4]

AMMANN UND MENN

Wie mir Christian Menn einmal erzählte, wurde die von Ammann entworfene, seilgestützte Bronx-Whitestone Bridge in New York während seiner eigenen Studienzeit in Zürich von den Kommilitonen als eleganteste Konstruktion verehrt.

led to a symposium that my colleagues and I organized to honor the great works of Maillart. We invited engineers who had known the Swiss designer and I was especially impressed by Christian Menn, Felix Candela, and Fazlur Khan. Each had a carefully written account of their views of Maillart and Menn's presentation in particular showed clearly the connection between his early bridges and Maillart's designs.[3]

Menn had founded his own firm in Chur in 1957, and three of his early designs were built soon after in 1959: Two deck-stiffened arch bridges, one at Crestawald spanning 71.5 meters, one at Cröt spanning 65.8 meters, and the third a three-hinged arch at Letziwald spanning 66.4 meters. The first two were influenced by Maillart's deck-stiffened designs, and the third by his Tavanasa Bridge of 1905. Between 1962 and 1968, Menn designed five more deck-stiffened arches with spans ranging from 86 to 112 meters, in which the arches appeared even thinner and had polygonal forms.

Following the concrete arch designs, Menn left his firm in Chur and joined the engineering faculty of his alma mater, the ETH in Zurich. There he had no company but began as an independent consultant and designer of some major bridges. His best known works from that period are the 1974 Felsenau Bridge near Bern, the 1980 Ganter Bridge on the route to the Simplon Pass, the 1998 Sunniberg Viaduct near Klosters, and the 2002 Zakim Bunker Hill Memorial Bridge in Boston, USA. On completion, all of these works represented departures from major designs known elsewhere in the world, and the last three demonstrate Menn's studies of cable-supported forms.

In each case, the structures could well have been designed as girder bridges following Felsenau, but instead Menn chose to design them with crucial supporting elements visible above the horizontal roadway. This change of focus resulted in major designs that in turn brought a change of vision and took him closer to the world of larger-scale bridges, dominated in mid-century by the spectacular structures of Othmar Ammann.[4]

AMMANN AND MENN

Menn once spoke to me about students in Zurich during his undergraduate years who believed Ammann's cable-supported Bronx-Whitestone Bridge in New York City to be the most elegant of structures.

After World War II, Ammann designed four more significant bridge projects ending in 1964 with the opening of his largest design, the Verrazano Narrows Bridge.[5] Its central span of 1298 meters surpassed the 1937 Golden Gate span of 1280 meters, a choice Ammann clearly made not for technical or aesthetic reasons. This last design culminated a personal career of remarkable works. His four greatest bridges, the George Washington, Bayonne, Bronx-Whitestone, and Verrazano Narrows, were all designed between 1931 and 1964. No one engineer before or after has ever created four such extraordinary bridge designs in steel – no one, that is, apart from Christian Menn, whose great designs from 1974 to 2002 have the same quality as those of his illustrious predecessor.

Nach dem Zweiten Weltkrieg entwarf Ammann noch vier weitere bedeutende Brücken, zuletzt die 1964 eröffnete Verrazano Narrows Bridge, seine grösste Konstruktion.[5] Mit 1298 Metern übertraf ihre zentrale Spannweite die 1280 Meter der Golden Gate Bridge (1937) in San Francisco, wenngleich Ammann diese Entscheidung weder aus technischen noch ästhetischen Überlegungen heraus getroffen hatte. Dieser letzte Entwurf Ammanns bildet den krönenden Abschluss einer ganzen Reihe von bemerkenswerten Bauwerken. Seine vier grössten Brücken, die George Washington Bridge, die Bayonne Bridge, die Bronx-Whitestone Bridge und die Verrazano Narrows Bridge, wurden alle zwischen 1931 und 1964 entworfen. Kein zweiter Ingenieur hat jemals vier so herausragende Stahlbrücken konstruiert – wie Christian Menn, dessen bedeutende Entwürfe aus den Jahren 1974 bis 2002 in puncto Qualität mit dem berühmten Vorgänger mithalten können.

Will man Ammann und Menn vergleichen, lohnt sich ein Blick auf ihre Laufbahnen vor der Fertigstellung der ersten grossen Konstruktion: Ammanns erste bedeutende Arbeit war der 1918 veröffentlichte 153-seitige Aufsatz über die Hell Gate Bridge in New York.[6] Die von ihm entworfene George Washington Bridge sowie die Bayonne Bridge wurden erst dreizehn Jahre später fertiggestellt, sodass er 1931 zwar über ein beeindruckendes Fachwissen verfügte, aber noch keinen eigenen Entwurf umgesetzt hatte.[7]

Auch die Laufbahn von Christian Menn lässt sich in zwei Abschnitte unterteilen: Der erste begann mit der Gründung seines eigenen Büros, das auf Betonbrücken wie etwa Konstruktionen aus vorgespannten Balken oder vorgespannten Fahrbahnplatten über schlanken Bögen spezialisiert war, während die zweite Phase mit dem Felsenauviadukt begann, dem die drei seilgestützten Konstruktionen im Gantertal, im Prättigau und in Boston folgten.[8] Beim Felsenauviadukt liess sich Menn von den für Deutschland typischen Konstruktionen mit vorgespannten Hohlkastensegmenten und grossen Spannweiten inspirieren, für die vor allem Ulrich Finsterwalder bekannt war. Hierbei befinden sich die Stahlseile im Inneren von Hohlkästen, die mit einem verschiebbaren Gerüst im freien Vorbau erstellt werden können. Im Falle von grossen Flussüberquerungen bestanden diese Brücken in der Regel aus zwei nebeneinander liegenden Hohlkästen.

Für seine Bauwerke in der Schweiz verwendete Menn ganz bewusst nur einen einzelnen Hohlkasten und schuf breite Kragplatten, die wegen ihrer schlanken Ausbildung in Querrichtung vorgespannt waren. Darüber hinaus versah er den Hohlkasten mit schräg abfallenden Seitenwänden, sodass er in der Feldmitte bei niedrigster Höhe die grösste Breite erreichte, während er über den Pfeilern am schmalsten und höchsten war. Alle genannten Faktoren sorgten in der Untersicht für eine beeindruckende Wirkung. Der Felsenauviadukt war bei seiner Eröffnung im Jahr 1975 die am weitesten gespannte Brücke in der Schweiz. Meiner Meinung nach ist der Viadukt die visuell eindrucksvollste Balkenbrücke, die bis heute erbaut wurde. Darüber hinaus bestach der Entwurf durch seine Wirtschaftlichkeit, was in einem Wettbewerb unter sieben namenhaften Konstrukteuren nicht unerheblich war.

In comparing Ammann to Menn, we can begin with their careers up to their first great designs: Ammann's first major work was his 153-page article on the Hell Gate Bridge published in 1918.[6] His designs for the George Washington and Bayonne Bridges were not completed until thirteen years later, so that by 1931 he had had substantial experience, but no independent designs.[7]

Menn's career was also divided into two parts: the first from the founding of his own company focused on concrete bridges, such as structures with prestressed girders or slender arches beneath prestressed decks, while the second part began with his Felsenau design, followed by three major cable-supported structures in the Ganter Valley, the Prättigau Valley, and in Boston.[8] For the Felsenau Bridge Menn was stimulated by the German long-span, prestressed segmental hollow-box designs famously built by Ulrich Finsterwalder. Here the cables are entirely inside the boxes built without scaffolding below. For major river crossings, these bridges were designed with two boxes side by side. For his Swiss structures, Menn instead consciously chose to use only one box and thus create wide cantilevers that are prestressed laterally within the relatively thin overhanging decks. In addition, the single box is shaped with sloping side walls that enable it to be widest and shallowest at mid-span and narrowest but deepest at the supports. Menn, moreover, put the main spans on a curved plan. All of these factors make for a dramatic view from beneath the structure. Felsenau was the longest spanning bridge in Switzerland when it opened in 1975. In my view this bridge is the most visually engaging girder structure yet built. It was also an economical design, which was clearly a factor of some significance in a competition between seven major designers.

In the same year, 1975, Menn began a study for a new bridge on the Simplon Road over the Ganter Valley.[9] His design represented a new approach in which a major part of the support for a 174-meter span (at that time the longest yet undertaken in Switzerland) was to be above the roadway deck with cables running from the top of the piers to the deck, leaving the middle of the deck supported only through cables inside the flat hollow box. This led to a spectacular profile over two spans with a curved section in the two additional spans at either end.

Once again, as with the German-inspired Felsenau Bridge, Menn found his inspiration for the Ganter design partly in a structure in Germany with very high columns supporting rather closely spaced girders. This design rendered the connections between girders and columns visually insignificant, however, which Menn felt missed an opportunity to accentuate the transfer of loads from the lighter girders to the stronger columns. His actual design led primarily to his goal of a more elegant structure, which is what he achieved. He did regret not dimensioning the cross connection between the tops of the columns more elegantly, but would correct this in his next major work, the Sunniberg Bridge in the Prättigau Valley.[10]

This structure is a major work consisting of tall open piers, low pylons above the deck, a completely curved roadway, and the deck concrete under high forces due to the low cables. The high piers, unlike those of the Felsenau and Ganter Bridge, are visually open, each

1975 begann Menn ausserdem mit den Recherchen für eine neue Brücke, die als Abschnitt der Simplonpassstrasse über das Gantertal führen sollte.⁹ Mit seinem Entwurf wagte er einen völlig neuen Ansatz: Das Tragsystem der Brücke mit einer Hauptspannweite von 174 Metern (damals die längste Spannweite in der Schweiz) befindet sich über der Fahrbahnplatte, während Schrägseile von der Spitze der Pylone bis zu den Fahrbahnträgern verlaufen, sodass die Fahrbahn im Mittelteil nur durch die von flachen Hohlkästen ummantelten Stahlseile getragen wird. Das Ergebnis ist ein spektakuläres Längsprofil mit zwei Hauptfeldern sowie einer Links- und Rechtskurve über den Randfeldern der Brücke.

Wie beim Felsenauviadukt liess sich Menn für die Ganterbrücke von einer Konstruktion aus Deutschland inspirieren, bei der sehr hohe Brückenpfeiler relativ eng gesetzte Balken stützen. Bei diesem Entwurf wurde das Verhältnis von Balken und Pfeiler visuell bedeutungslos und Menn hatte den Eindruck, die Gelegenheit verpasst zu haben, die neue Lastverteilung von den leichteren Balken zu den stärkeren Pfeilern besonders hervorzuheben. Er verfolgte in erster Linie das Ziel, eine elegantere Konstruktion zu schaffen – was ihm in der Tat gelungen ist. Allerdings bedauerte er es, die Querverbindung zwischen den Spitzen der Pfeiler nicht noch eleganter gestaltet zu haben, korrigierte dieses Versäumnis aber in seiner nächsten grossen Arbeit, der Sunnibergbrücke im Prättigau.¹⁰

Das bedeutende Bauwerk besteht aus hohen Pfeilern, flachen Pylonen und einer kurvenförmigen Fahrbahn, wobei der Spannbeton wegen der kurzen Stahlseile unter enormem Druck steht. Im Gegensatz zur Felsenau- und zur Ganterbrücke sind die hohen Pfeiler hier offen; jeder besteht aus zwei seitlich angeordneten schlanken Wandscheiben, die sich nach oben ausweiten und oberhalb der Fahrbahnplatte ohne zusätzliche horizontale Verbindung nach aussen geneigt sind. Die eine Kurve beschreibende Brücke ist sowohl in der Auf- als auch in der Untersicht ein beeindruckendes Bauwerk.

with two carefully shaped columns leading into the verticals above the deck that slope outwards and are free of any horizontal connections between them. The views both below and above the curved deck are equally striking.

Remarkably, there had been a design competition with three companies competing and Menn as part of the jury. He was dissatisfied with the results, described his own plan to the highway department's consulting architect, who in turn advised the building department to accept Menn's design. One of the three competition entrants was chosen to carry out Menn's design, which became the final bridge. Although he got credit for the design, Menn received no fee for the project. His bridge crosses one of the most beautiful valleys in Switzerland and it stands close – by north American standards – to another great design, Maillart's Salginatobel Bridge across a side valley of the Prättigau Valley.

With the Ganter Bridge and the Sunniberg Bridge, Christian Menn showed the power of his concepts and the brilliance of his structures carried by cables supported above the decks. Finally, this part of Menn's career also includes the 2002 Zakim Bunker Hill Memorial Bridge in Boston, which has since become an icon of that city and deserves to be studied in the United States in the same detail as the earlier bridges described in this brief discussion here.¹¹

But it is, I believe, a fair comparison to state that in his recent structures Menn has produced works that conclude the relationship between Maillart, Ammann, and himself. He certainly did not create his later works to be copies of Ammann's major structures. Rather, his later forms reflect a strong desire to express his largest bridges visually. These would use steel elements as forms, whether covered in concrete as in the Ganter Bridge or exposed as in his great bridge designs for Klosters and Boston.

Die Rheinbrücke Tamins ziert das Titelblatt des *American Scientist*, 1984
The Rhine Bridge at Tamins, cover illustration, *American Scientist*, 1984

Interessanterweise hatte zuerst ein Wettbewerb unter drei verschiedenen Büros stattgefunden, dem Menn als Mitglied der Jury beigewohnt hatte. Da er mit den eingereichten Entwürfen jedoch nicht zufrieden war, skizzierte er dem beratenden Architekten der Strassenbaubehörde kurzerhand einen eigenen Entwurf, der diesem so gut gefiel, dass er ihn der Behörde zur Ausführung empfahl. Mit der Umsetzung des Entwurfs wurde dann eines der drei Büros aus dem Wettbewerb betraut. Obwohl Menn als Konstrukteur genannt wurde, erhielt er für das Projekt keinerlei Honorar. Dafür umspannt seine Brücke eines der schönsten Täler der Schweiz und befindet sich – zumindest für nordamerikanische Verhältnisse – ganz in der Nähe eines anderen bedeutenden Bauwerks: Maillarts Salginatobelbrücke, hoch über einem Seitental des Prättigaus.

Mit der Ganter- und der Sunnibergbrücke zeigte Menn die Kraft seines Könnens und die Brillanz seiner seilgestützten Konstruktionen. Zu diesem Abschnitt seiner Karriere gehört schliesslich noch die 2002 fertiggestellte Zakim Bunker Hill Memorial Bridge in Boston, die zu einem Wahrzeichen der Stadt geworden ist und es verdient, in den USA so eingehend studiert zu werden wie die frühen, hier kurz abgehandelten Brücken.[11]

Meiner Meinung nach kann man mit Fug und Recht behaupten, dass es Christian Menn mit seinen letzten Konstruktionen geschafft hat, die Beziehung von Maillart und Ammann zu seinem eigenen Werk zu einem Abschluss zu bringen. Mit seinen späten Arbeiten wollte er ganz bestimmt nicht Ammanns wichtigste Konstruktionen imitieren. Vielmehr zeugen diese Arbeiten von dem Wunsch, seinen grossen Brücken eine unverwechselbare visuelle Gestalt zu geben. Dafür verwendete er Stahlelemente, seien sie von Beton ummantelt wie bei der Ganterbrücke oder freiliegend wie bei seinen grossartigen Brückenkonstruktionen für Klosters und Boston.

---

1 David P. Billington, *Robert Maillart: Builder, Designer, and Artist,* Cambridge, Cambridge University Press 1997, 151 und 282. **2** Sigfried Giedion, *Space, Time and Architecture: The Growth of a New Tradition,* Boston, Harvard University Press 1941. **3** David P. Billington u. a. (Hrsg.), *Maillart Papers,* Princeton, N.J., Dept. of Civil Engineering, 1973. **4** David P. Billington, *The Art of Structural Design: A Swiss Legacy,* Princeton University Art Museum 2003, Kapitel 6. **5** Ibid., Kapitel 3, mit Othmar Ammann. **6** Othmar H. Ammann, «The Hell Gate Arch Bridge and Approaches of the New York Connecting Railroad Over the East River in New York City», in: *Transactions of the American Society of Civil Engineers,* 82 (Dez. 1918), 852–1004. **7** vgl. David P. Billington 2003 (siehe Fussnote 3), Kapitel. 3, mit Othmar Ammann. **8** David P. Billington, «Swiss Bridge Design Spans Time and Distance», in: *Civil Engineering* 51, Nr. 11 (Nov. 1981), 42–44. **9** Ibid, 44–46. **10** Chelsea Honigmann und David P. Billington, «Conceptual Design for the Sunniberg Bridge», in: *Journal of Bridge Engineering,* Bd. 8, Nr. 3, 1. Mai 2003, 122–130. **11** C. J. Pennington, *The Charles River Bridge and Twenty-first Century Signature Design* (Dissertation, Princeton University, 1998), 56–60.

PROJEKTE DES INGENIEURBÜROS 1957–1971
PROJECTS BY CHRISTIAN MENN'S OWN ENGINEERING COMPANY 1957–1971

In den 14 Jahren seiner Karriere als selbstständiger Ingenieur plante und baute Christian Menn rund 90 Brücken; eine kleine, aber repräsentative Auswahl davon wird in der folgenden Zusammenstellung gezeigt. Bei den ersten Projekten im Hinterrhein- und Aversertal sind die Einflüsse von Robert Maillart noch gut zu erkennen (vgl. dazu auch den Beitrag von David P. Billington Seite 29 ff.). Später löste sich Christian Menn von seinem Vorbild, beschäftigte sich aber weiterhin intensiv mit Bogenbrücken, die er konstant weiterentwickelte – fast bis zur Perfektion. Insgesamt baute er 13 Bogenbrücken, darunter so berühmte Exemplare wie die Viamalabrücke und die Rheinbrücke in Tamins.

Als in den 1960er-Jahren in der Schweiz mit Hochdruck der Bau des Autobahnnetzes vorangetrieben wurde, studierte Christian Menn mit Akribie und Hartnäckigkeit die Möglichkeiten der Vorspanntechnik, die es erlaubt, Balkenbrücken mit grossen Spannweiten zu realisieren. Nach einigen Dutzend Balkenbrücken in der ganzen Schweiz fand Menns an der Praxis orientiertes Experimentieren in der über 1100 Meter langen Felsenaubrücke bei Bern einen vorläufigen Höhepunkt.

Die vom Entwerfer selbst verfassten Projektexte sind in zwei Abschnitte gegliedert: Zunächst werden Lage, Aufgabenstellung und das grundlegende konstruktive Konzept erläutert; in einem zweiten Teil widmet er sich mehr den Details und erklärt konkrete technische Probleme und Lösungen.

Christian Menn planned and built around ninety bridges in his fourteen-year-long career as an independent engineer; a small, but representative selection of these is presented in the following section. While the influence of Robert Maillart is still very much in evidence in his first projects in the Hinterrhein Valley and Avers Valley (cf. the essay by David P. Billington, pp. 29 ff.), Menn gradually detached himself from his great role model, even while working tirelessly on developing the art of bridge building—almost to perfection. He built thirteen arch bridges altogether, among them such famous examples as the Viamala Bridge and the Rhine Bridge at Tamins.

In the 1960s, when Switzerland was racing to build a national highway network, Menn applied himself to the in-depth study of prestressed concrete and the possibilities it opened up, among them the construction of beam bridges with very long spans. After several dozen beam bridges built all over Switzerland, his experimentation with this technique culminated in the 1100-m long Felsenau Bridge near Bern, at the time his most daring feat to date.

The project texts written by Menn himself are divided into two sections: The first describes the location, the mission, and the fundamentals of the design concept. The second, more detailed section explains both the specific engineering challenges encountered and the solutions found.

CRESTAWALDBRÜCKE, SUFERS
CRESTAWALD BRIDGE AT SUFERS

1958–1959

Client: Graubünden Department of Transportation
Design and construction: Christian Menn

[01

LOCATION
Sufers
Canton of Graubünden
Switzerland

COORDINATES
749 000 / 159 200

TYPE
Arch bridge

LENGTH
124 m

MAIN SPAN
72.5 m

OPENING
1959

Wo früher eine Naturstrasse durch das Rheinwaldner Tor in den obersten Abschnitt des Hinterrheintals und weiter über die Pässe San Bernardino und Splügen auf die Alpensüdseite führte, steht heute die Staumauer des Sufnersees. Die Autostrasse A13, von der Roflaschlucht her kommend, steigt hier nochmals an und wechselt kurz vor der Staumauer mit der 124 Meter langen und 44 Meter hohen Crestawaldbrücke auf die besonnte Talseite. Der bergwärts reisende Autofahrer sieht die Brücke zunächst frontal, bevor er sie nach einer ansteigenden Kurve überquert. Der 72,5 Meter weit gespannte Bogen fügt sich hier gut in die Umgebung ein. Die Ansicht aus dem Auto auf den eleganten Sichelbogen war entscheidend für die Wahl des Bogentragwerks.

The Sufernsee Dam now stands where a gravel road formerly passed through the entrance to the Rheinwald, heading towards the uppermost section of the Posterior Rhine (Hinterrhein) valley and then on to Splügen, the San Bernardino Pass, and the southern flank of the Alps. At this location, Highway A13 climbs once again on its way up from the Rofla Gorge. As it passes in front of the dam, it is carried over to the north side of the valley by the 124 m long and 44 m high Crestawald Bridge. Motorists traveling towards the pass first see the bridge in a full frontal view before crossing the bridge in a rising curve. The 72.5 m arch span is integrated well into the rocky landscape. The appearance of the bridge as seen by motorists was a decisive factor for the choice of a crescent-shaped arch system for this bridge.

[01] CRESTAWALDBRÜCKE, SUFERS / CRESTAWALD BRIDGE AT SUFERS

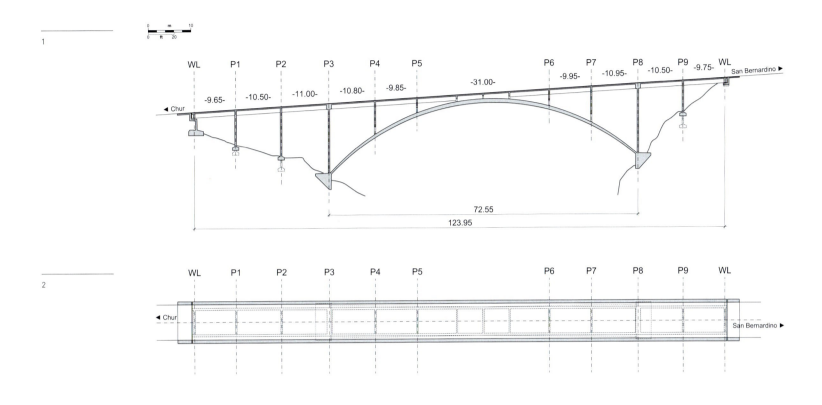

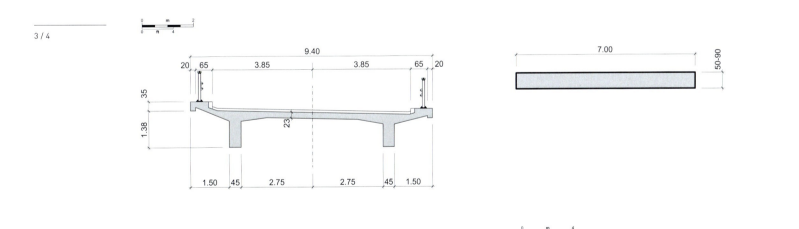

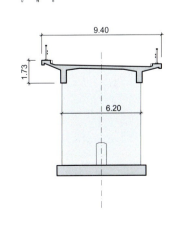

1 Längsschnitt / Longitudinal section
2 Grundriss / Plan
3 Querschnitt / Cross section
4 Bogenquerschnitt / Arch cross section
5 Ansicht Pfeiler 4 / View of column 4

[01 CRESTAWALDBRÜCKE, SUFERS

Das Pfeilverhältnis des Bogens liegt mit l/f = 71,5/14,5 = 4,9 im statisch und visuell günstigen Bereich einer konventionellen Bogenbrücke.

Die 9,6 Meter breite Brückenplatte ragt beidseitig 1,8 Meter über den Bogenrand hinaus. Es stellte sich heraus, dass diese Auskragung zu gering ist – sofern die Bogenoberfläche nicht beschichtet ist: Bei Brücken, die Wind und häufiger Schneeräumung ausgesetzt sind, fällt viel tausalzhaltiger Schnee auf den Bogen.

Über den Kämpferstützen weist die Crestawaldbrücke Dilatationsfugen auf. Es ist nicht gelungen, diese Fugen wasserdicht auszubilden. Salzhaltiges Wasser der Fahrbahn verursachte in der Fuge und an den Kämpferstützen erhebliche Schäden. Bei der Instandsetzung wurden die Fugen geschlossen und beim bergseitigen Endwiderlager, das sich näher beim Bogenscheitel befindet, wurde ein unverschiebliches und beim talseitigen Widerlager ein verschiebliches Trägerauflager eingebaut.

Der Zweigelenkbogen ist im Scheitel 90 Zentimeter und bei den Kämpfern nur 50 Zentimeter dick. Die entsprechende Massenverteilung ergibt eine schöne, parabolische Stützlinie mit der grössten Krümmung im Scheitel und einer Streckung in den Kämpferbereichen. Die Knicke der Bogen-Stützlinie unter den Stützen des Überbaus wurden im Hinblick auf eine fliessende, stetige Krümmung des Sichelbogens ausgeglichen. Diese im Blick auf die Ästhetik des Bogens getroffene Massnahme entspricht allerdings aus drei Gründen nicht ganz der konstruktiven Effizienz: Ein Zweigelenkbogen ist bei felsigem Baugrund nicht erforderlich. Die Biegebeanspruchung des Systems wird grösser als bei einem eingespannten Bogen und das Lehrgerüst mit dem grössten Bogengewicht im Scheitel wird etwas verteuert. Dem empfindlichen Auge des erfahrenen Brückeningenieurs entgehen diese Nachteile kaum. Aber im Hinblick auf das vom Verkehrsteilnehmer gesehene, elegante Erscheinungsbild des parabolischen Sichelbogens, der in der Schrägsicht mit der geringen Dicke und der relativ grossen Breite schalenförmig wirkt, dürfen diese Nachteile in Kauf genommen werden.

[01 CRESTAWALD BRIDGE AT SUFERS

The span to rise ratio of the arch, L/f = 71.5/14.5 = 4.9, lies within a range that is associated with favourable structural behavior and the visual appearance for conventional arch bridges.

The 9.6 m wide deck slab extends 1.8 m beyond the edges of the arch on both sides. The width of the deck slab cantilevers turned out to be insufficient given that no protective coating was provided on the surface of the arch. Wind and frequent snow-plowing brought large quantities of snow containing de-icing salt into contact with the arch.

Expansion joints were originally provided in the girder at the piers over the springing lines. These joints cannot be made completely waterproof. As a result, salt water originating from the deck produced significant damage to the joints and the piers below. These joints were eliminated as part of the repair work. Fixed bearings were provided at the abutment at the north (uphill) end of the bridge, which was closer to the crown of the arch, and expansion bearings were provided at the abutment at the south (downhill) end.

The two-hinged arch is 90 cm thick at the crown and 50 cm thick at the springing lines. The resulting distribution of mass leads to an elegant, parabolic pressure line which has its maximum curvature at the crown and which appears to become straighter towards the springing lines. Angle breaks in the pressure line corresponding to the concentrated loads applied to the arch by the spandrel columns were rounded off to provide a flowing, smooth curvature of the crescent-shaped arch. These measures, which were taken to achieve aesthetic goals, do not however correspond to the most efficient structural system. Two-hinged arches are not necessary when good rock is available for resisting arch reactions. Bending moments in the system as designed are greater than those in a suitable arch with fixed ends, and falsework is somewhat more expensive because the dead load is greatest near midspan. Although these disadvantages will not go unnoticed by the sensitive eyes of experienced bridge engineers, they can nevertheless be accepted, given the elegant appearance of the parabolic crescent arch which by virtue of its thinness appears to motorists as a slim shell.

AVERSERRHEINBRÜCKEN CRÖT UND LETZIWALD, AVERS
CRÖT AND LETZIWALD BRIDGES OVER THE AVERS RHINE AT AVERS

1959

Client: Graubünden Department of Transportation
Design and construction: Christian Menn

[02   [03

Für den Bau der Kraftwerke Hinterrhein wurde die schmale Strasse ins Aversertal von Bärenburg/Andeer bis Juf auf einer Länge von 20 Kilometern ausgebaut und zum Teil neu trassiert. Zur Erschliessung des Hochavers erforderte die neue Linienführung zwei Brücken über den Averserrhein.

Die beiden Brücken – ein Stabbogen beim Weiler Cröt und wenige hundert Meter weiter oben der Dreigelenkbogen der Letziwaldbrücke – sind Hommagen an den grossen Brückeningenieur Robert Maillart. Sie zeigen in aller Deutlichkeit, dass für Maillart der Entwurf eines Tragwerks mit einem möglichst leichten, wirtschaftlichen Lehrgerüst immer ein wichtiges Ziel im Brückenbau war.

For the construction of the Hinterrhein generating station, the narrow road into the Avers valley from Bärenburg/Andeer to Juf was upgraded and partially realigned over a length of twenty kilometers. This development required two bridges over the Avers Rhine: a deck-stiffened arch at the hamlet of Cröt and, a few hundred meters above it, the three-hinged arch Letziwald Bridge.

Both bridges pay homage to the great bridge engineer Robert Maillart. They clearly show that for Maillart, a primary design objective was always to design a structural system that could be built with falsework that was as light and economical as possible.

[02] AVERSERRHEINBRÜCKE CRÖT / BRIDGE OVER THE AVERS RHINE AT CRÖT

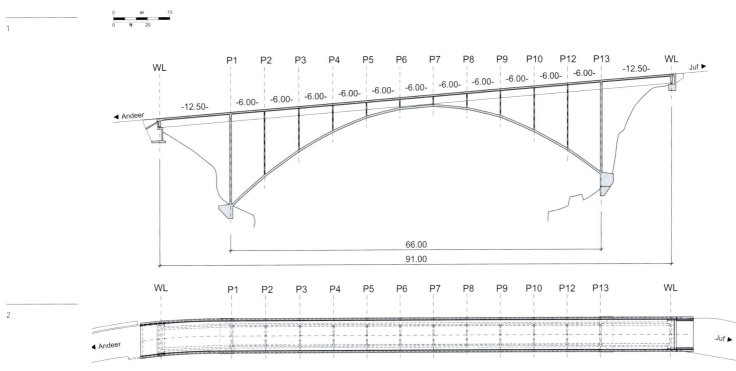

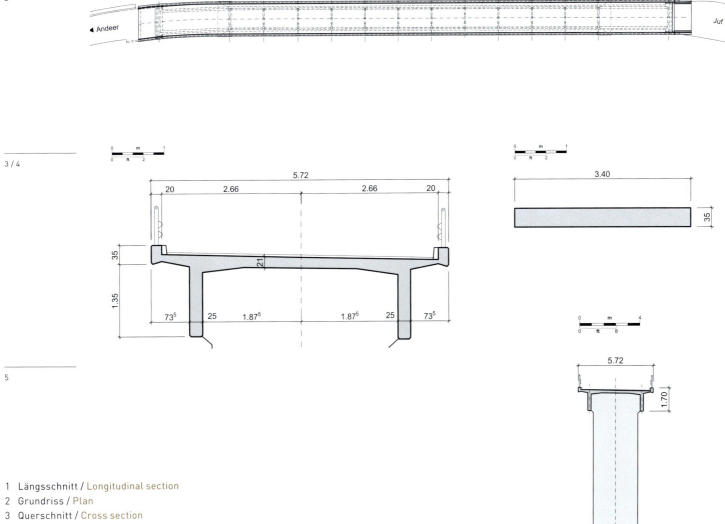

1. Längsschnitt / Longitudinal section
2. Grundriss / Plan
3. Querschnitt / Cross section
4. Bogenquerschnitt / Arch cross section
5. Ansicht Pfeiler 2 / View of column 2

[02

LOCATION
Avers
Canton of Graubünden
Switzerland

COORDINATES
757 400 / 149 350

TYPE
Arch bridge

LENGTH
92 m

MAIN SPAN
66 m

OPENING
1959

[02 AVERSERRHEINBRÜCKE CRÖT

Die Brücke ist 92 Meter lang, hat eine Bogenspannweite von 66 Metern und zwei Randfelder von 13 Metern. Der Versteifungsträger ist auf der ganzen Brückenlänge – insbesondere über den Kämpferstützen – fugenlos durchlaufend und über den Brückenwiderlagern verschieblich. Über dem Bogen betragen die elf Stützenabstände nur 6 Meter, um ein Ausknicken der dünnen Bogensegmente zu verhindern. Das Lehrgerüst wurde nur für das Gewicht des dünnen, leichten Bogens bemessen. Das Gewicht des Aufbaus – bestehend aus Stützen und Versteifungsträger – konnte vom erhärteten Bogen übernommen werden. Das Lehrgerüst diente danach nur noch zur Aufnahme asymmetrischer Lasten beim Betonieren. Ein leichtes Lehrgerüst ist deshalb wirtschaftlich; aber bereits bei einem üblichen Pfeilverhältnis, im vorliegenden Fall l/f = 4,6, ist der Aufwand für die vielen Stützen erheblich. Je flacher der Bogen, umso kürzer die Stützen und umso günstiger ist das Stabbogensystem.

Die kleinmassstäbliche, zierliche Brücke über die beginnende Schlucht hinter dem Dorf fügt sich gut in ihr Umfeld, die paar Häuser von Cröt und das felsige Tobel, ein.

[02 BRIDGE OVER THE AVERS RHINE AT CRÖT

The bridge is 92 meters long, with an arch span of 66 m and two side spans of 13 m. The stiffening girder is continuous over the entire length of the bridge and is supported on expansion bearings at the abutments. Expansion joints are absent at the piers over the springing lines. The eleven girder spans over the arch are only six meters long, to prevent buckling of the thin arch segments. The falsework was dimensioned only for the weight of the thin, light arch. The weight of spandrel columns and stiffening girders was carried by the hardened concrete of the arch, with the falsework serving only to resist asymmetrical load conditions during the placing of concrete for the columns and girders. Although the light falsework was economical, the cost of the large number of columns, given the span to rise ratio L/f of 4.6, was considerable. It follows that the economy of deck-stiffened arch systems increases with an increasing span to rise ratio.

This small-scale, rather delicate bridge spanning the entrance to the gorge behind the town is well integrated into the landscape defined by the handful of houses in Cröt and the rocky gorge.

[03 AVERSERRHEINBRÜCKE LETZIWALD / LETZIWALD BRIDGE OVER THE AVERS RHINE AT AVERS

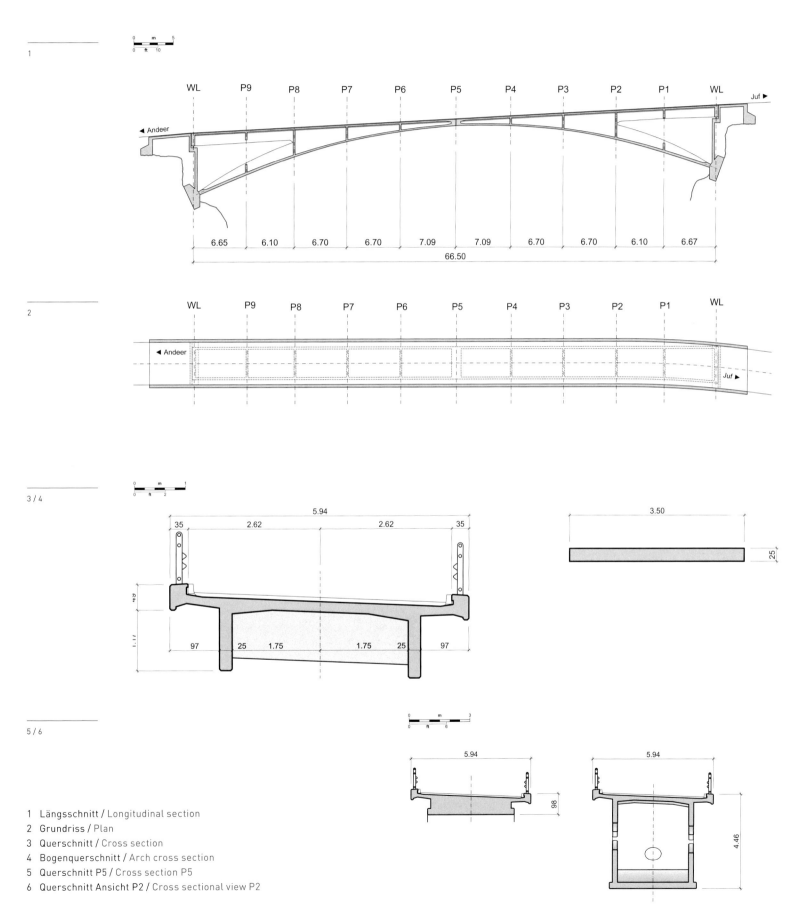

1 Längsschnitt / Longitudinal section
2 Grundriss / Plan
3 Querschnitt / Cross section
4 Bogenquerschnitt / Arch cross section
5 Querschnitt P5 / Cross section P5
6 Querschnitt Ansicht P2 / Cross sectional view P2

LOCATION
Avers
Canton of Graubünden
Switzerland

COORDINATES
757 850 / 149 450

TYPE
Arch bridge

LENGTH
76 m

HEIGHT
85 m

MAIN SPAN
66.5 m

OPENING
1959

[03 AVERSERRHEINBRÜCKE LETZIWALD

Die 76 Meter lange Letziwaldbrücke überquert in 85 Metern Höhe den tief eingeschnittenen Averserrhein am Anfang des Averser Hochtals. Auf der rechten Seite der Schlucht fällt der Fels fast senkrecht bis zum Bergbach ab; auf der linken Seite ist die Flanke ebenfalls sehr steil, aber noch leicht bewaldet. Hier eignete sich am besten das Tragsystem des sehr flachen Dreigelenkbogens mit einem Pfeilverhältnis von etwa l/f = 9,6. So musste nur eine Nische aus dem Fels herausgesprengt werden, in die das Brücken-, Bogen- und Lehrgerüstwiderlager als monolithische Einheit eingebaut werden konnte – mit dem geringsten Risiko für die Arbeiter.

Das Bogenlehrgerüst bestand aus einem leichten, freitragenden Rautenfachwerk aus Holz, das nur für die untere Bogenplatte bemessen wurde. Die erhärtete Bogenplatte übernahm dann das Eigengewicht der Stege des U-förmigen Bogenquerschnitts und des Fahrbahnträgers. Später wurden die Bogengelenke geschlossen beziehungsweise durch Betongelenke ersetzt.

Die Tragwerkskomponenten sind dünn – Bogenplatte 25 Zentimeter, Bogenstege 25 Zentimeter und Fahrbahnplatte 22 Zentimeter –, liessen sich aber bei dem geringen Bewehrungsgehalt von etwa 80 kg/m³ Beton ohne Schwierigkeiten betonieren. Das verwendete Tragsystem zeigt eindrücklich die Effizienz flächiger Konstruktionen bei Betonbauten.

Bezüglich Tragwerk und Abmessungen gleicht die Letziwaldbrücke trotz der komplett unterschiedlichen Topografie der Rheinbrücke Tavanasa, die Robert Maillart 1905 projektierte und die 1927 durch einen Murgang zerstört wurde. Es ist zu bedauern, dass diese erste Dreigelenk-Bogenbrücke mit den von Maillart gestalteten, typischen Öffnungen bei den Widerlagern nicht rekonstruiert wurde. Heute markiert eine Kopie jenes eleganten Tragwerks in 85 Metern Höhe das Tor zum Averser Hochtal mit Juf, der höchst gelegenen, ganzjährig bewohnten Siedlung Europas.

[03 LETZIWALD BRIDGE
OVER THE AVERS RHINE AT AVERS

The 76 meter long Letziwald Bridge stands at the entrance to the Upper Avers Valley, spanning a deep canyon at a height of 85 meters above the Avers Rhine. The right face of the canyon is practically vertical down to the river. The left face, also very steep, is lightly wooded. These conditions were ideal for a very flat three-hinged arch with a span to rise ratio L/f of about 9.6. Its construction required only small recesses to be blasted out of the rock, which enabled the abutments, arch foundations, and foundations for the falsework on a given side to be built as single monolithic units. Minimizing the work on the rock faces in this way greatly increased the safety of workers who built the bridge.

Falsework for the arch consisted of a light, self-supporting timber truss, which was designed to carry only the weight of the bottom slab of the arch. Once the concrete in the slab had hardened, it could span as an arch and thus carry the additional dead load of the webs of the U-shaped arch cross-section and the weight of the deck girder. Temporary hinges provided in the arch for construction purposes were later locked or replaced with concrete hinges.

The structural components are thin: The bottom slab, webs, and deck slab are respectively 25 cm, 25 cm, and 22 cm thick. Due to a relatively low reinforcement ratio of 80 kg/m3 of concrete, however, it was possible to place concrete for these components without difficulty. The structural system used for this bridge is an impressive example of the efficiency of surface structures in concrete.

In spite of completely different topographies, the structural system and primary dimensions of the Letziwald Bridge are very similar to those used at Robert Maillart's Bridge over the Rhine at Tavanasa, which was built in 1905 and destroyed by flooding in 1927. It is unfortunate that this earlier three-hinged arch ridge was not rebuilt with the openings in the spandrel walls as originally designed by Maillart, which are so typical of his work. A copy of Maillart's elegant structural system, however, now stands as an 85 m high gateway to the Upper Avers Valley and the village of Juf, the highest settlement in Europe to be occupied year-round.

GRÜNEBRÜCKE, SPLÜGEN
GRÜNE BRIDGE AT SPLÜGEN

1961

Client: Graubünden Department of Transportation
Design and construction: Christian Menn

[04

LOCATION
Splügen
Canton of Graubünden
Switzerland

COORDINATES
745 750 / 158 050

TYPE
Arch bridge

LENGTH
88 m

MAIN SPAN
49.8 m

OPENING
1961

Zwischen Sufers und Splügen schäumt der Hinterrhein mit der natürlichen, stark variablen Wassermenge eines Gebirgsflusses in einer 30 bis 40 Meter tiefen Schlucht zum letzten Mal. Danach fliesst er in den Stausee von Sufers und wird weiter in die Druckstollen der Kraftwerke Hinterrhein geleitet. Am westlichen Ende der Schlucht überquert die Grünebrücke in einer natürlichen Flusskrümmung mit einem Bogen von 50 Metern Spannweite den Rhein.

Between Sufers and Splügen, the Posterior Rhine (Hinterrhein) flows through a 40 m deep canyon, blubbing for the last time along its length with the natural, highly variable water flows of a mountain river. Beyond this point, the river flows into the lake created by the dam at Sufers and is channelled into the penstocks of the Hinterrhein generating station. At the west end of the canyon, the Grüne Bridge crosses the Rhine at a natural curve in the river with an arch span of 50 meters.

[04 GRÜNEBRÜCKE, SPLÜGEN / GRÜNE BRIDGE AT SPLÜGEN

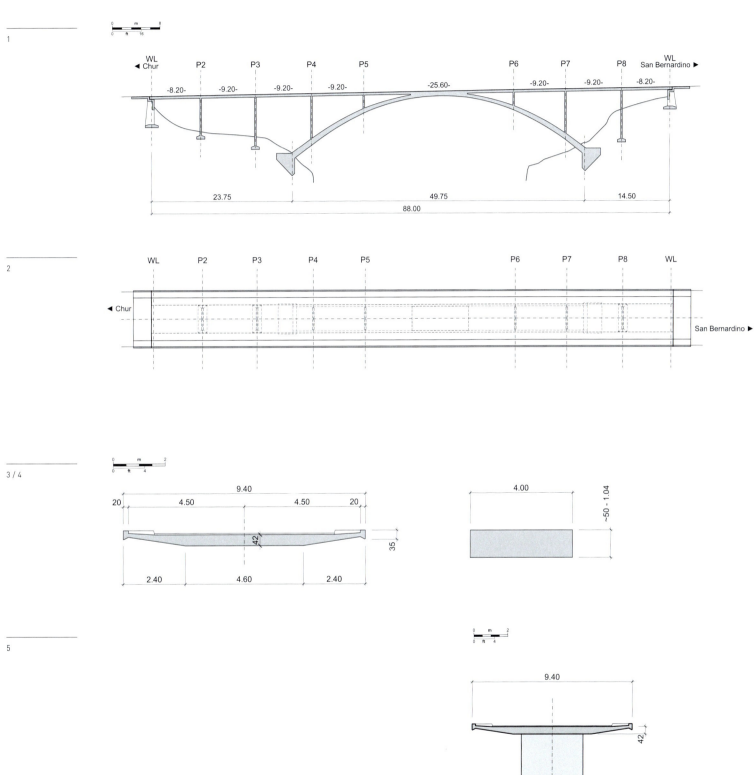

1 Längsschnitt / Longitudinal section
2 Grundriss / Plan
3 Querschnitt / Cross section
4 Bogenquerschnitt / Arch cross section
5 Ansicht Pfeiler 4 / View of column 4

[04 GRÜNEBRÜCKE, SPLÜGEN

Der Brückenträger weist auf der ganzen Länge gleich grosse Spannweiten von 8 Metern auf. Sie sind über dem Bogen symmetrisch angeordnet und da sich die erste und die letzte Stütze über dem Bogen nicht genau über dem Bogenkämpfer befinden, konnte die Überbauspannweite von 9 Metern auch für die östliche, zweifeldrige und die westliche, dreifeldrige Zufahrt beibehalten werden. Die Brücke ist bei den Endwiderlagern verschieblich gelagert; bei den Kämpferstützen wurden keine Dilatationsfugen angeordnet.

Bogen, Stützen und Fahrbahnträger weisen den gleichen plattenförmigen Querschnitt auf und sind monolithisch miteinander verbunden. Die 9,4 Meter breite Fahrbahn ist im Mittelbereich 42 Zentimeter und an den Rändern 24 Zentimeter dick. Der Bogen ist dagegen nur 4 Meter breit und im Scheitel 50 Zentimeter und bei den Kämpfern 1 Meter dick. Bogen und Fahrbahnträger beteiligen sich etwa zu gleichen Teilen am Tragwiderstand des verschieblichen Rahmentragwerks.

Die Brücke fügt sich harmonisch in die Topografie beim westlichen Anfang der Schlucht ein. Das bescheidene, unauffällige Bauwerk wird von den Verkehrsteilnehmern auf der Autostrasse A13 kaum wahrgenommen.

[04 GRÜNE BRIDGE AT SPLÜGEN

The girder has constant spans of 8 meters over the entire length of the bridge. These spans are symmetrically arranged relative to the arch. Since the first and last columns over the arch are not located directly over the springing lines, the girder span of 9 m could be maintained for the two approach spans on the east side and the three approach spans on the west side. The girders can be displaced longitudinally at the abutments. No expansion joints were provided in the girders at the columns over the arch foundations.

The arch, columns, and girder have the same slab cross-section and are connected monolithically to each other. The 9.4 m wide girder is 42 cm thick at its middle and 24 cm thick at its edges. The arch is only 4 m wide. Its thickness varies from 50 cm at the crown to 1 m at the springing lines. The arch and girder each contribute in approximately equal measure to the structural capacity of the flexible frame system.

The bridge fits harmoniously into the topography of the western entrance to the canyon. The modest, unassuming structure is hardly noticed by motorists on Highway A13.

RHEINBRÜCKE, BAD RAGAZ
BRIDGE OVER THE RHINE, BAD RAGAZ

ERSTE BRÜCKE 1961–1962 / ZWEITE BRÜCKE 1971–1972
FIRST BRIDGE 1961–1962 / SECOND BRIDGE 1971–1972

Client: Graubünden Department of Transportation
First bridge: Project in partnership with Weder+Prim, St. Gallen
Second bridge: Project in partnership with Rigendinger/Maag, Chur

[05

LOCATION
Bad Ragaz
Canton of Graubünden
Switzerland

COORDINATES
757 400 / 209 050

TYPE
Beam bridge

LENGTH
198 m

RADIUS
1000 m

MAIN SPAN
82 m

OPENING
1962 / 1972

Im Kanton Graubünden wurde der private Motorfahrzeugverkehr erst mit dem Strassenverkehrsgesetz von 1927 zugelassen. Bis 1962 standen an der Kantonsgrenze zu St. Gallen zwischen dem Wirtschaftszentrum Zürich und Graubünden mit seinen Alpenpässen dem schnell wachsenden Verkehr nur zwei Brücken über den Rhein zur Verfügung: bei Landquart die 1529 erbaute und 1892 erneuerte, einspurige Tardisbrücke (bekannt aus Friedrich Dürrenmatts Roman *Es geschah am hellichten Tag*) – ein schmaler, prismatischer Gitterträger mit innenliegender Fahrbahn – und eine 1885 erstellte, leichte Eisen-Fachwerkbrücke zwischen Bad Ragaz und Maienfeld.
Der Bau der in den 1960er Jahren noch als Nationalstrasse 2. Klasse konzipierten A13 Sargans-Chur-San Bernardino hatte deshalb eine hohe Priorität. 1960 schrieben die Kantone Graubünden und St. Gallen für den vorgesehenen 200 Meter langen Rhein-Übergang bei Bad Ragaz einen Projektwettbewerb aus. Der erstrangierte Entwurf der Arbeitsgemeinschaft Weder+Prim, St. Gallen (Unterbau) und Christian Menn, Chur (Überbau) sah eine dreifeldrige Balkenbrücke in Spannbeton mit Spannweiten von 58, 82 und 58 Metern vor.

In the Canton of Graubünden, private motor vehicle traffic was first allowed afer the Highway Traffic Act of 1927. This resulted in rapid growth in travel between Zurich, Switzerland's economic centre, and Graubünden's alpine passes. Until 1962, however, there were only two crossings of the Rhine at the boundary between St. Gallen and Graubünden, a key link along this route. The first was the one-lane Tardis Bridge at Landquart, which was built in 1529 and renovated in 1892 as a narrow, prismatic lattice girder with internal deck. (This bridge figured in Friedrich Dürrenmatt's novel *Es geschah am hellichten Tag (It Happened in Broad Daylight)*.) The second crossing was a light iron truss linking Bad Ragaz and Maienfeld, built in 1885. The construction of Highway A13 linking Sargans, Chur, and San Bernardino (which in the 1960s had been designated a second class National Highway) thus had a high priority. In 1960, the cantons of Graubünden and St. Gallen held a design competition for a 200 m long crossing of the Rhine at Bad Ragaz. The prize-winning design, submitted by the joint venture Weder+Prim of St. Gallen (substructure) and Christian Menn of Chur (supertructure), was a three-span prestressed concrete girder bridge with spans of 58, 82, and 58 m.

[05 RHEINBRÜCKE, BAD RAGAZ / BRIDGE OVER THE RHINE, BAD RAGAZ

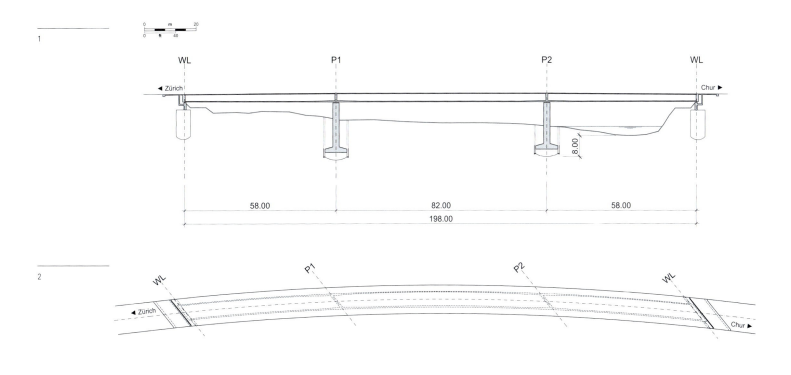

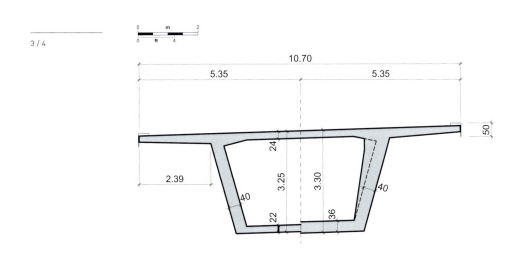

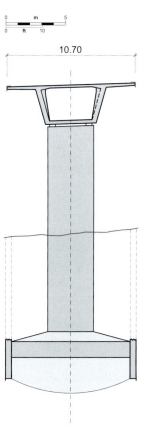

1 Längsschnitt / Longitudinal section
2 Grundriss / Plan
3 Querschnitt / Cross section
4 Ansicht Pfeiler 2 / View of column 2

[05 RHEINBRÜCKE, BAD RAGAZ

Die Brückenachse ist gekrümmt (Radius = 1000 Meter) und der Brückenträger entsprechend der Krümmung und der im Mittel 40 Grad schrägen Flussüberquerung leicht unterschiedlich schief gelagert. Die Pfeilerfundation besteht aus oben offenen Senkkästen, die 7 Meter unter die Flusssohle des Rheins reichen.

Der Brückenträger ist 10,7 Meter breit und weist Spannweiten von 58,82 und nochmals 58 Metern auf. Die Trägerhöhe ist variabel, sie beträgt bei den Widerlagern 2,85 Meter, über den Pfeilern 3,30 Meter und in Brückenmitte 3,25 Meter, was einer üblichen Schlankheit (Verhältnis Länge zu Höhe) von 25 entspricht. Mit der sorgfältig gewählten Variation der Trägerhöhe erreichten wir die Reduktion der visuellen Trägermasse bei den Uferwegen und eine elegante Perspektive beim Blick entlang der Brücke. Der Trägerquerschnitt besteht aus einem einzelligen Kasten mit leicht geneigten Stegen.

Für das Lehrgerüst wurden Holz-Fachwerkträger verwendet, die auf einreihigen Holz-Pfahljochen gelagert waren. Der Umstand, dass sich die Pfähle nicht exakt rammen liessen, und die komplizierte, gekrümmte Brücken-Geometrie hatten äusserst heikle und gefährliche Probleme bezüglich der Auflager-Zentrierung der Fachwerkträger zur Folge.

Das Betonieren des Trägers erfolgte in zwei Phasen: Zunächst wurde der Trog und danach die Fahrbahnplatte erstellt. Die hohen, etwas geneigten und mit kräftigen Spannkabeln bewehrten Stege waren nicht einfach zu betonieren. Der Belag bestand aus einer acht Zentimeter starken Betonschicht, die sich, abgesehen von den unnötigen Fugen, gut bewährte, später aber durch ein Abdichtungs-Asphalt-System ersetzt wurde.

1971/72 erfolgte der Bau der Zwillingsbrücke für den vierspurigen Querschnitt der Nationalstrasse 1. Klasse. Das Grundkonzept und die meisten konstruktiven Abmessungen wurden beibehalten.

Die Rheinbrücke Bad Ragaz stellt ein würdiges Brücken-Tor zum Kanton Graubünden dar. Die Sicht von der Bahn aus auf das elegant-kräftige Bauwerk wird heute leider durch eine etwas banale Rohrbrücke beeinträchtigt.

[05 BRIDGE OVER THE RHINE, BAD RAGAZ

The alignment of the bridge in plan follows a circular curve with a radius of 1000 m. Due to the curve and the angle formed by the highway and the river, the supports are skewed, with an average angle of 40 degrees. The piers are founded in open cofferdams which extend 7 m below the bed of the Rhine.

The girder is 10.7 m wide and has three spans of 58, 82, and 58 m. The depth of the girder varies from 2.85 m at the abutments to 3.30 m at the piers and 3.25 m at the midpoint of the central span. The ratio of main span length to depth of girder at midspan is about 25, a rather common value. By carefully varying the depth of the girder, it was possible to reduce the visual bulk of the girder when viewed from pathways along the river banks present an elegant perspective when the bridge was viewed along its length. The girder cross-section consists of a single-cell box with lightly inclined webs.

The falsework consisted of timber trusses, which were supported on single-row timber pile bents. Because the piles could not be driven with precision, and due to the rather complex curved bridge geometry, centering the supports of the timber trusses was an extremely tricky and dangerous operation.

Concrete for the girder was placed in two stages: first the bottom slab and the webs, and then the deck slab. Placing concrete in the webs was not easy due to their height, inclination, and the presence of large prestressing tendons. An 8 cm thick concrete wearing surface was provided. Apart from the joints provided in the wearing surface, which were not necessary, this component performed well. It was later replaced with a membrane and asphalt system.

In 1971/72, a twin parallel bridge was constructed to increase traffic capacity to four lanes as required for a first class National Highway. The overall concept and most of the primary dimensions and details of the first bridge were retained.

The bridge over the Rhine at Bad Ragaz is a worthy gateway to the Canton of Graubünden. The view from the railway of this elegant and strong structure has unfortunately been marred by the nearby presence of a rather banal pipeline bridge.

RHEINBRÜCKE, TAMINS
BRIDGE OVER THE RHINE AT TAMINS

1963

Client: Graubünden Department of Transportation
Design and construction: Christian Menn

[06

LOCATION
Tamins
Canton of Graubünden
Switzerland

COORDINATES
750 800 / 188 250

TYPE
Arch bridge

LENGTH
158 m

MAIN SPAN
100 m

OPENING
1963

Die 158 Meter lange Rheinbrücke bei Tamins führt die Bündner Hauptstrasse H19 unmittelbar nach der Abzweigung von der Bernardinoroute A13 in einer Höhe von etwa 28 Metern über den vereinigten Vorder- und Hinterrhein. Die Flusslandschaft beim Schloss Reichenau im beginnenden Staugebiet des Emser Kraftwerks ist von aussergewöhnlicher und faszinierender Schönheit. In dieses Umfeld fügt sich die ausgewogene, traditionell wirkende Brücke mit ihrer Leichtigkeit und Transparenz des Tragwerks und den sorgfältig abgestuften Spannweiten des Überbaus harmonisch ein. Auf beiden Seiten des Rheins fällt das Terrain gleichmässig zum Fluss hin ab; die Bogenbrücke mit einer Spannweite von 100 Metern, deren Widerlager nur wenige Meter neben und über dem Wasserspiegel liegen, passt sich optimal in die vorhandene Topografie ein.

This 158 meter long structure carries carries Graubünden Highway H19 over the Rhine. It is located immediately after H19 branches away from the Bernardino Highway A13 and just downstream from the confluence of the Rhine's Anterior (Vorderrhein) and Posterior (Hinterrhein) tributaries. The highway is at a height of about 28 m above the water. The river landscape, near Schloss Reichenau and at the beginning of the artificial lake created by the Emser hydro-electric generating station, is one of extreme beauty. The balanced, traditional form of the bridge, the lightness and transparency of its structure, and the carefully chosen sequence of span lengths over the arch all enable the bridge to integrate itself harmoniously into this environment. At this location, both banks of the Rhine slope down towards the river at roughly equal gradients. The arch bridge, with a span of 100 meters, and with springing lines only a few meters above the water, fits perfectly into this topography.

[06   RHEINBRÜCKE, TAMINS / BRIDGE OVER THE RHINE AT TAMINS

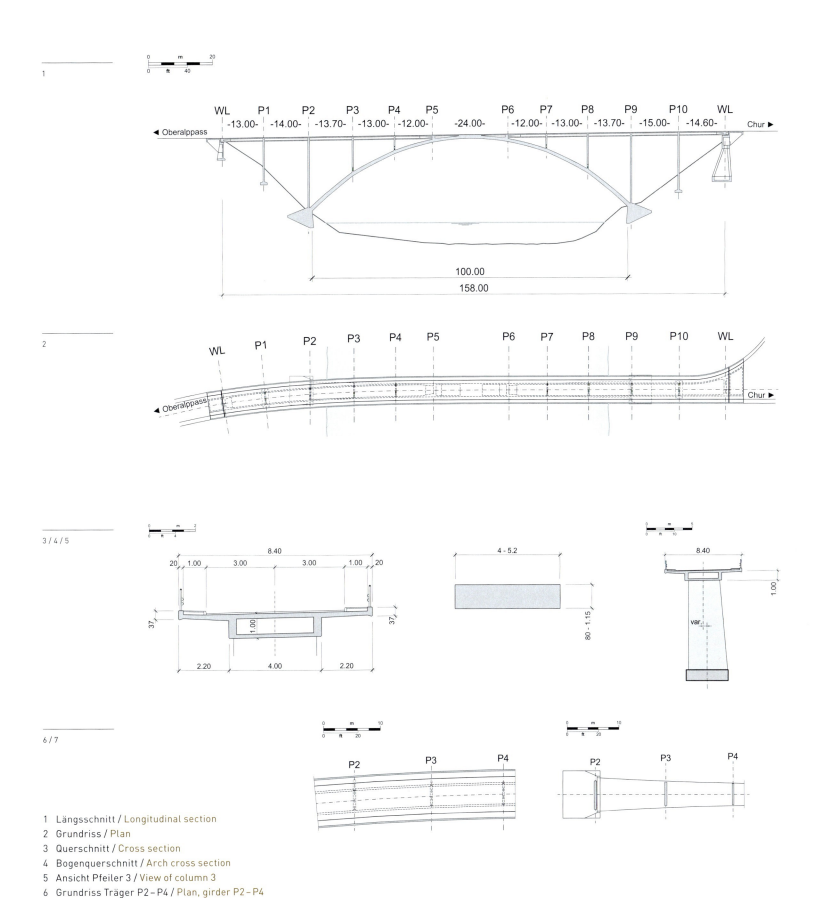

1 Längsschnitt / Longitudinal section
2 Grundriss / Plan
3 Querschnitt / Cross section
4 Bogenquerschnitt / Arch cross section
5 Ansicht Pfeiler 3 / View of column 3
6 Grundriss Träger P2–P4 / Plan, girder P2–P4
7 Grundriss Bogen P2–P4 / Plan, arch P2–P4

[06 RHEINBRÜCKE, TAMINS

Die Rheinbrücke Tamins besteht aus teilweise vorgespanntem Beton und weist verschiedene Neuerungen auf. Die Bogenform entspricht genau der Stützlinie und die kleinen Knicke unter den Stützen des Überbaus sind nicht ausgerundet. Der Betrachter empfindet diese Unstetigkeit in der Bogenkrümmung – wie eine kleine Überhöhung bei einem Balken – als erwünschte Tragreserve. Bogen und Fahrbahnträger weisen in etwa die gleiche Biegesteifigkeit auf. Damit können über dem Bogen ähnliche Spannweiten wie bei den Zufahrten erreicht werden. Der relativ schlanke Bogen erforderte jedoch ein nicht allzu schweres, teures Lehrgerüst.

Das Tragwerk ist statisch und konstruktiv als kohärentes System konzipiert. Bei fast allen zuvor erbauten Bogenbrücken wurde der Bogenbereich über den Kämpferstützen mit Bewegungsfugen von den Zufahrtsbereichen getrennt; oft mit kräftigen Kasten- oder Doppelstützen. Der Brückeningenieur der SBB-Generaldirektion Ad. Bühler verwendete bei der SBB-Lorrainebrücke in Bern sogar Gerberträger in den ersten Bogenfeldern. Bei der Rheinbrücke Tamins konnte diese konstruktiv unvorteilhafte Ausbildung vermieden werden: Bewegungsfugen sind nur auf den Widerlagern angeordnet. Unter Verkehrslast zeigen Bogen und Fahrbahnträger ein ähnliches, effizientes Verformungsverhalten.

Wahrscheinlich war die Rheinbrücke Tamins weltweit die erste teilweise vorgespannte Bogenbrücke. Die Vorspannung des Trägers wirkt im Nutzungszustand versteifend, was im Hinblick auf die Verformung zweiter Ordnung günstig ist. Nach der Bildung eines Risses lässt jedoch diese Wirkung der Vorspannung nach. Der Einfluss zweiter Ordnung – die Systemverformung – darf bei schlanken, verschieblich gelagerten Bogenbrücken wie derjenigen in Tamins nicht vernachlässigt werden. Er lässt sich aber beträchtlich reduzieren, wenn nach ein paar Jahren die Systemverschiebung blockiert wird.

[06 BRIDGE OVER THE RHINE AT TAMINS

The Bridge over the Rhine at Tamins is a partially prestressed structure which incorporates several innovative features. The shape of the arch corresponds exactly with the pressure line. At the intersection of arch and spandrel columns, therefore, the small angle breaks corresponding to the concentrated vertical load applied at this location were maintained rather than rounded off. Observers of the bridge generally regard this discontinuity in the curvature of the arch as evidence of a desirable reserve of structural capacity, similar to the case of beams with slight upward camber.

The arch and girder have approximately the same bending stiffness. This enables the spans over the arch to be of similar length to the spans on the approaches. Because the arch is relatively slender, the weight and cost of its falsework were not excessive.

The bridge was conceived as a single coherent system with regard to both structural behaviour and overall design. Almost all previously constructed arch bridges were separated from their approach spans through the provision of expansion joints in the girder over the springing lines, a measure which was invariably associated with excessively thick hollow columns or twin columns over the springing lines. (At the Lorraine Bridge, completed in 1941 in Berne, this separation is accomplished by a drop-in girder (Gerber system) in the first spans over the arch). By contrast, at the Bridge over the Rhine at Tamins, these problematic details were avoided by making the girder continuous over its entire length, with expansion joints provided only at the abutments. Under live load, arch and girder exhibit similar and efficient deformation behavior.

It is likely that the bridge over the Rhine at Tamins is the world's first partially prestressed arch bridge. The prestressing in the girder provides stiffness under service conditions, which helps to minimize second-order deformations. This effect is however reduced after the formation of cracks. In this type of slender arch bridge on flexible supports, second-order effects cannot be neglected. They can, however, be significantly reduced by blocking the system against longitudinal displacement, which will generally be possible a few years after construction is complete.

NANIN- UND CASCELLABRÜCKE, MESOCCO
NANIN AND CASCELLA BRIDGES AT MESOCCO

1966–1968

Client: Graubünden Department of Transportation
Design and construction: Christian Menn

[07

LOCATION
Mesocco
Canton of Graubünden
Switzerland

COORDINATES
737 700 / 141 700
737 650 / 141 850

TYPE
Beam bridges

LENGTH
192 m / 173 m

MAIN SPAN
112 m / 96 m

OPENING
1968

Die unterste Talstufe des San-Bernardino-Passes von Mesocco nach Pian San Giacomo weist eine Höhendifferenz von etwa 400 Metern auf. Die alte Kantonsstrasse verläuft hier auf der orografisch rechten Seite mit zahlreichen Haarnadelkurven den bewaldeten Abhang entlang. Auf der linken Seite steigt die kahle, mit Geröll, Bachgräben und Lawinenzügen durchsetzte Talflanke steil zu den Bergspitzen bis auf 3000 m.ü.M. an. Zwischen den beiden unterschiedlichen Talflanken befindet sich eine landwirtschaftlich genutzte Zone mit vielen kleinen Rustici, die die Autostrasse A13 im oberen, besonders steilen Abschnitt mit grosszügigen Schleifen und dem maximal zulässigen Gefälle von 8 Prozent überwindet. Das Flüsschen Moesa wird dabei einmal mit einer kleinen Balkenbrücke und weiter oben zweimal kurz nacheinander mit über 60 Meter hohen Bogenbrücken überquert. Die beiden filigranen Bogenbrücken sind im ganzen Bereich der Talstufe sichtbar: Sie markieren und beleben die Passstrasse, fügen sich spektakulär in das Landschaftsbild ein und sind ein Wahrzeichen der San-Bernardino-Südseite.

The Moesa valley undergoes a rapid change in elevation of 400 meters between Mesocco and Pian San Giacomo as it rises towards the San Bernardino Pass. At this location, the old cantonal highway climbs along the forested slopes of the west side of the valley with many hairpin curves. On the east side, the valley slope is mostly bare and interspersed with debris, gullies, and avalanche tracks, and climbs steeply towards 3000 meter high peaks above. Between these two very different flanks of the valley lies an agricultural area and many small rustici (the typical farmhouses of this area). This is surmounted by the newer Highway A13 that passes through this particularly steep section with generous looping curves and the maximum allowable gradient of 8 percent. Highway A13 crosses the Moesa creek three times, first by means of a small girder bridge and, farther above this, twice again in quick succession with two 60 meter high arch bridges. These two bridges are visible from any point in this area. They enliven and give distinction to the highway rising towards the pass, are integrated spectacularly into the landscape, and are a landmark of the south side of the San Bernardino.

[07 NANINBRÜCKE, MESOCCO / NANIN BRIDGE AT MESOCCO

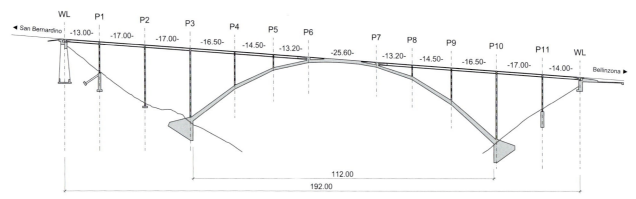

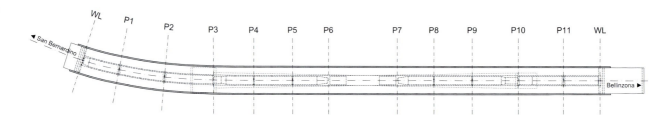

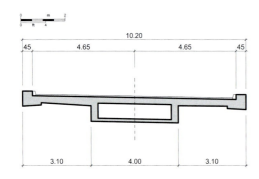
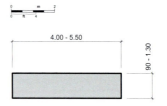

1 Längsschnitt / Longitudinal section
2 Grundriss / Plan
3 Querschnitt / Cross section
4 Bogenquerschnitt / Arch cross section
5 Ansicht Pfeiler 4 / View of column 4

[07 CASCELLABRÜCKE, MESOCCO / CASCELLA BRIDGE AT MESOCCO

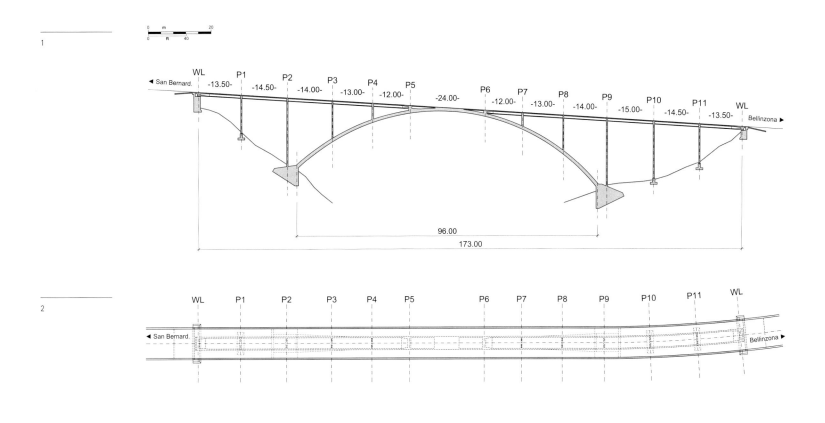

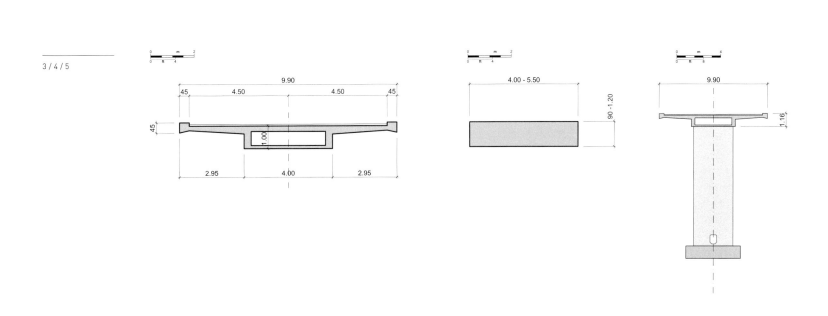

1 Längsschnitt / Longitudinal section
2 Grundriss / Plan
3 Querschnitt / Cross section
4 Bogenquerschnitt / Arch cross section
5 Ansicht Pfeiler 3 / View of column 3

[07] NANIN AND CASCELLA BRIDGE AT MESOCCO

The Nanin Bridge is 192 m long and has an arch span of 112 m. Its span to rise ratio L/f is 4.6. The Cascella Bridge is 173 m long and has an arch span of 96 m, which corresponds to a span to rise ratio of 4.8. The width of both bridges is 10.2 m. Both bridges share the same structural concept and details as the bridge over the Rhine at Tamins. The arch, which consists of a 4 meter wide slab cross-section, is stiffened by a 1 meter deep prestressed concrete box girder. Three girder spans are provided on each side of the arch crown. These spans are approximately the same length as the approach spans, two or three of which are provided at either end of both bridges. The bridges thus convey an appearance of extreme lightness and transparency.

There are important differences, however, in the design of these two bridges and that of the bridge over the Rhine at Tamins. These arise primarily as a result of differing geotechnical conditions and roadway grade. At the site of the Nanin and Cascella bridges, soils consist of scree containing moraine. After accounting for long-term settlement, the natural slopes at the site of this material have a relatively low level of safety which, in conjunction with the heavy rainfalls that can occur on the southern flank of the Alps, presented a risk that could not be underestimated. The slope of the approach curves for Nanin, the lower of the two bridges, was therefore loaded with several meters of additional fill. This measure, together with the horizontal arch reactions of 23 000 kN at the Cascella Bridge and 30 000 kN at the Nanin Bridge, produced a small but worthwhile increase in the stability of the slopes.

At both ends of the bridges, the girders were originally supported on expansion bearings. Given the steep roadway gradient of 6 percent, the acceleration and braking of trucks produced significant longitudinal and transverse vibrations in the structures. After most of the deformations due to creep and shrinkage had occurred, therefore, the supports at the lower ends of both bridges were changed to fixed bearings. This measure greatly reduced the vibrations and also significantly increased the margin of safety of the two structures.

SALVANEIBRÜCKE, MESOCCO
SALVANEI BRIDGE AT MESOCCO

1968–1969

Client: Graubünden Department of Transportation
Design and construction: Christian Menn

[08

LOCATION
Mesocco
Canton of Graubünden
Switzerland

COORDINATES
736 250 / 144 650

TYPE
Beam bridge

LENGTH
168 m

RADIUS
130 m

MAIN SPAN
60 m

OPENING
1969

Etwa drei Kilometer südlich des Dorfes San Bernardino quert die Autostrasse A13 hoch oben, von Westen nach Osten sinkend die Geländekammer von Pian San Giacomo. Unmittelbar vor dem Erreichen des östlichen Talabhangs befindet sich vor dem Wasserfall eines kleinen Seitenbachs der Moesa die Salvaneibrücke an einem exponierten, landschaftlich sehr schönen Standort. Die Brücke ist 168 Meter lang, 13,5 Meter breit und im Grundriss relativ stark gekrümmt (Radius = 130 Meter). Sie überquert die Kantonsstrasse und den kleinen Bach und ist an ihrer spektakulären Lage bereits vom weit unten liegenden Talboden aus deutlich zu erkennen.

In der licht bewaldeten, landschaftlich einzigartigen Talstufe des San-Bernardino-Passes war ein schlankes, elegantes Bauwerk beabsichtigt. Die Brücke ist aber leider auf der Ostseite um eine Randspannweite zu kurz; die hohe, damals noch aufgelöste Stützmauer war deutlich wirtschaftlicher als das entsprechende Brückenfeld.

Approximately three kilometers south of the village of San Bernardino, Highway A13 passes high above the catchment area of Pian San Giacomo as it heads down from west to east. The Salvanei Bridge stands immediately before the highway reaches the eastern slope of the valley in front of a waterfall on a small tributary of the Moesa. This is an exposed and beautiful setting. The bridge is 168 m long, 13.5 m wide, and, with a radius of 130 m, relatively sharply curved in plan. The bridge crosses the cantonal road and the little brook, and is clearly recognizable in its spectacular location from the bottom of the valley far below.

For this lightly wooded, unique and very steep landscape of the San Bernardino Pass. A slender, elegant structure was required for this lightly wooded, unique and very steep landscape of the San Bernardino Pass. The bridge is unfortunately one span too short on the east side. The tall retaining wall provided instead was certainly more economical than a bridge span but far less pleasing visually.

[08 SALVANEIBRÜCKE, MESOCCO / SALVANEI BIDGE AT MESOCCO

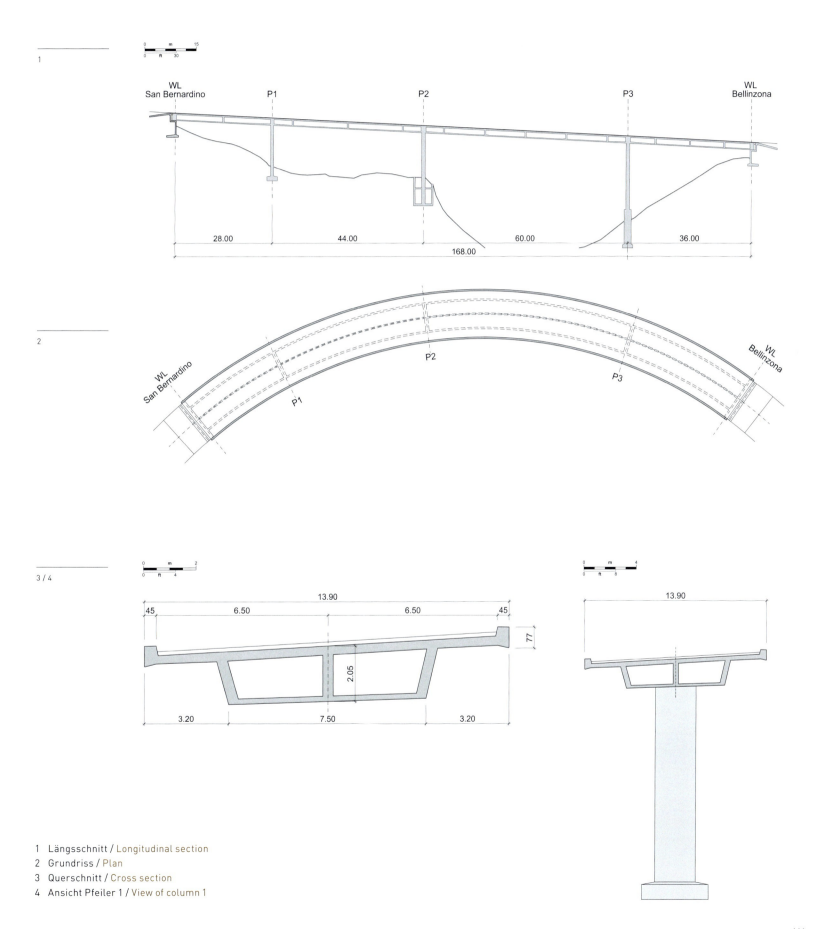

1 Längsschnitt / Longitudinal section
2 Grundriss / Plan
3 Querschnitt / Cross section
4 Ansicht Pfeiler 1 / View of column 1

[08 SALVANEIBRÜCKE, MESOCCO

Der 2.1 Meter hohe Brückenträger weist vier Spannweiten von 28–44–60–36 Metern auf; die maximale Schlankheit beträgt l/h = 28,5. Berechnung und Konstruktion des Tragwerks sind im Wesentlichen konventionell. Besondere Aufmerksamkeit erforderte die Torsion infolge der Trägerkrümmung im Grundriss. Das Drehmoment (tordierendes Moment) entsteht durch die Umlenkung der Normalkräfte aus der Trägerbiegung. Die Einleitung dieser (oberen und unteren) Umlenkkräfte erzeugt je nach Biegesteifigkeit des Kastenträgers (in Querrichtung) mehr oder weniger Umlauftorsion oder Biegung in den Kastenplatten um die Vertikalachse.

Die Konstruktion ist einfach und pragmatisch und wirkt im Landschaftsbild nicht störend; der Ersatz des östlichen Randfeldes durch eine hohe Stützmauer ist jedoch ein Mangel in der Balance von Ästhetik und Wirtschaftlichkeit.

[08 SALVANEI BIDGE AT MESOCCO

The 2.1 m deep bridge girder has four spans of length 28 m, 44 m, 60 m, and 36 m. The maximum slenderness ratio (span to depth L/h) is 28.5. Analysis and detailing of the structure proceeded for the most part in a conventional manner. Torsion due to the curve of the girder in plan did, however, required special attention. Torques are produced by deviation of normal forces that provide the couple resisting bending in the girder. The introduction of these upper and lower deviation forces creates, depending on the transverse bending stiffness of the box girder, a combination of pure torsion and transverse bending in the cross-section components about a vertical axis.

The design is simple and pragmatic, and does not disturb the visual landscape. The replacement of the eastern span with a tall retaining wall is nevertheless a deficiency in the balance of aesthetics and economy.

VIAMALABRÜCKE, ZILLIS
VIAMALA BRIDGE AT ZILLIS

1966–1967

Client: Graubünden Department of Transportation
Design and construction: Christian Menn

[09

LOCATION
Zillis-Reischen
Canton of Graubünden
Switzerland

COORDINATES
753 900 / 169 300

TYPE
Arch bridge

LENGTH
180 m

MAIN SPAN
96 m

OPENING
1967

Von Thusis her kommend, etwa 700 Meter oberhalb der historischen Viamalabrücken, wechselt die San-Bernardino-Route A13 in einer S-Kurve etwa 60 Meter über dem Hinterrhein von der orografisch linken auf die rechte Seite der Schlucht. Die Brücke ist 180 Meter lang, die Bogenspannweite beträgt 96 Meter. Etwa 12 Meter unter der Fahrbahn fällt der Fels auf der linken Hangseite steil ab und ist schwer zugänglich. Das Bogenwiderlager wurde deshalb oben, auf der Hangschulter angeordnet; daraus ergab sich ein flacher, eleganter Bogen. Zunächst überquert die Brücke die Kantonsstrasse und dann mit ausgewogenen, sorgfältig abgestuften Trägerspannweiten ohne Rücksicht auf die Lage der Bogenwiderlager die Viamala-Schlucht. Visuell besteht kein Bezug zwischen Bogen undAufbau und es entsteht so der Eindruck, dass der Bogen zur vorhandenen Geländetopografie gehört.

Coming from Thusis, about 700 m above the historical Viamala Bridges, the San Bernardino Highway A13 changes from the left to the right side of the canyon in an S-curve about 60 m above the Posterior Rhine (Hinterrhein). The bridge is 180 m long with an arch span of 96 m. About 12 m below the deck, the rock drops off steeply on the left side which makes for difficult access. The arch foundations were therefore located above this level on the shoulders of the slope. This led to a flatter and more elegant arch. The bridge first crosses the cantonal road and then the Viamala Canyon with well-balanced, carefully arranged girder spans, chosen without consideration of the location of the arch foundations. The lack of visual relation between the arch and the structure it supports creates the impression that the arch actually belongs to the existing topography.

[09 VIAMALABRÜCKE, ZILLIS / VIAMALA BRIDGE AT ZILLIS

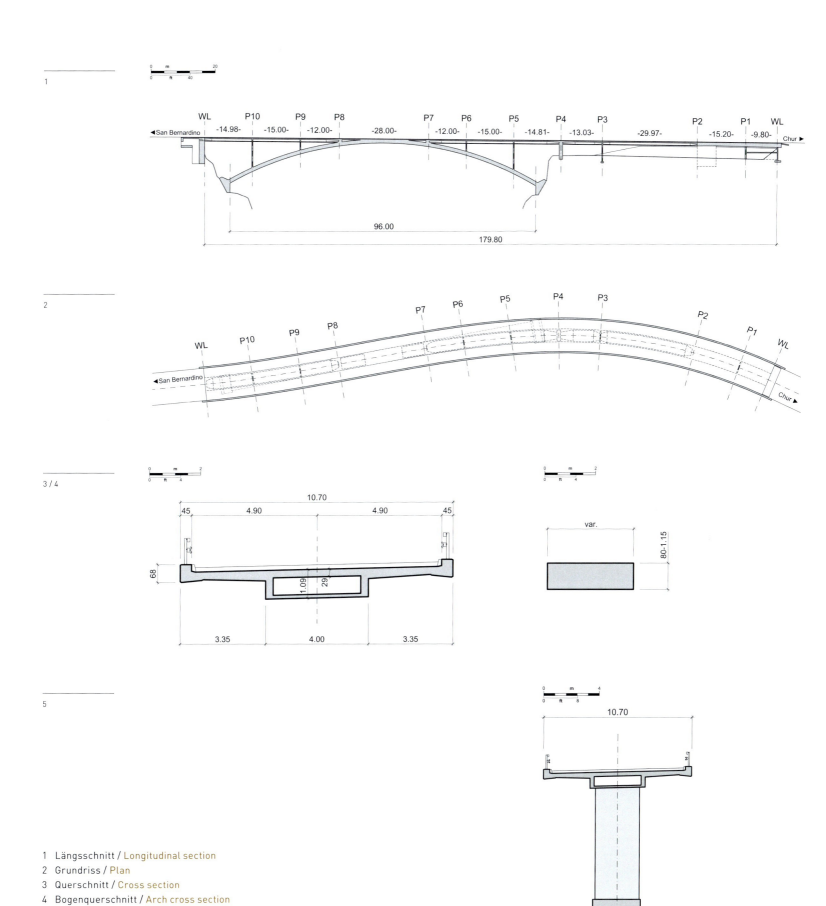

1 Längsschnitt / Longitudinal section
2 Grundriss / Plan
3 Querschnitt / Cross section
4 Bogenquerschnitt / Arch cross section
5 Ansicht Pfeiler 10 / View of column 10

[09 VIAMALABRÜCKE, ZILLIS

Die Brücke besteht aus zwei Abschnitten: aus der dreifeldrigen, 68 Meter langen Zufahrt auf der linken Talseite und dem 112 Meter langen Bogenbereich. Beide Abschnitte sind nach der Überquerung der Kantonsstrasse mit einer Dilatationsfuge über einer Doppelstütze voneinander getrennt. Das Bogentragwerk ist verschieblich gelagert und wurde entsprechend berechnet.

Die Spannweite des Versteifungsträgers über dem Bogen beträgt 112 Meter; sie ist somit 2 x 8 Meter länger als die Bogenspannweite und weist nicht die möglichst kleine zum Bogen affine Spannweite auf. Der damit verbundene Verlust an Tragwerkseffizienz wird im vorliegenden Fall bewusst in Kauf genommen.

Die geometrische Gestaltung der Viamala-Bogenbrücke, deren Fahrbahn in einer S-Kurve liegt, basierte auf folgenden Überlegungen: Die Fahrbahnachse ist entsprechend der vorgeschriebenen Linienführung definiert; auf der Unterseite des Trägerquerschnitts ist die Achse wegen des Quergefälles und der Querschnittshöhe leicht verschoben; vertikal darunter verläuft die gerade Achse des Bogens, der im Bogenscheitel die gleiche Breite aufweist wie der Trägerkasten. Die Bogenbreite ist symmetrisch zur Bogenachse und auf der Kurveninnenseite befindet sich der Bogenrand immer vertikal unter dem unteren Trägerrand. Das bedeutet, dass der Rand der scheibenförmigen Stützen auf der Innenseite der Kurve vertikal und auf der Aussenseite geneigt ist. Die komplexe Tragwerksgeometrie mit den drei Achsen ist nicht ohne Weiteres erkennbar, vermittelt aber eine optimale statische Effizienz und ein natürliches, harmonisches Aussehen.

Auf der rechten Seite der Schlucht mündet die Strasse direkt in einen Tunnel. Wäre das Portal als vorspringendes, schräg abgeschnittenes Tunnelprofil ausgeführt worden, hätte es wahrscheinlich das Erscheinungsbild des flachen Bogens und der beschwingten Linienführung noch unterstrichen.

Die Viamalabrücke war geometrisch wegen der S-Kurve der Fahrbahn mit dem wechselnden Quergefälle über dem achsgeraden Bogen relativ kompliziert zu konzipieren. Die saubere Lösung befriedigt jedoch in statischer, konstruktiver und ästhetischer Hinsicht.

[09 VIAMALA BRIDGE AT ZILLIS

The bridge consists of two sections, the first of which is the 68 m long approach on the left side of the canyon, and the second of which is the 112 m long arch proper. Both sections are separated by an expansion joint located after the span crossing the cantonal road. The arch structure is thus flexibly supported and was analyzed accordingly.

The span of the stiffening girder above the arch is 112 m, which is 2 x 8 m longer than the arch span. Although this is not the shortest possible girder span in relation to the arch span length, the corresponding loss of structural efficiency was considered in this case to be acceptable.

The geometrical aspects of the design of the Viamala Bridge, the deck of which follows an S-curve, were based on the following considerations: (1) The axis of the deck is defined by the prescribed highway alignment, (2) at the underside of the girder cross-section, the centreline of the cross-section is slightly offset from the axis of the highway due to the cross-slope and the depth of the cross-section, (3) directly below this is the straight axis of the arch, which at the crown must have the same width as the box girder. The width of the arch is symmetrical about the arch axis. On the inner side of the curve, the edge of the arch is always directly under the lower edge of the girder. This implies that the edge of the wall-shaped piers must be vertical on the inner side of the curve and inclined on the outer side. Although this complex structural geometry defined by three separate axes is not easily recognizable, it enables ideal static efficiency and a natural, harmonious appearance. On the right side of the canyon, the highway enters directly into a tunnel. If the portal had been designed to protrude from the rock with inclined surfaces, it would have given further visual emphasis to the flat arch and the changing alignment.

The Viamala Bridge was relatively complex to design given the S-curve of the roadway and the variable cross-slope over the straight arch. The neat solution that resulted, however, embodies a highly satisfactory combination of structural behaviour, design, and aesthetics.

ISOLABRÜCKE, MESOCCO
ISOLA BRIDGE AT MESOCCO

1964–1965

Client: Graubünden Department of Transportation
Design and construction: Christian Menn

[10

LOCATION
Mesocco
Canton of Graubünden
Switzerland

COORDINATES
734 600 / 146 100

TYPE
Arch bridge

LENGTH
72 m

MAIN SPAN
49.5 m

OPENING
1965

Eine verborgene, bescheidene Bogenbrücke über stillem Wasser im Bergwald und Heidelbeerkraut. Der Verkehrsteilnehmer auf der Strasse sieht von der Brücke nichts, nur ein paar Wanderer gelangen zu einem der wenigen Standorte, von denen aus die kleine Brücke überraschend ins Blickfeld rückt.

The Isola Bridge is a concealed, unassuming arch bridge over still water in a setting of alpine forest and blueberry bushes. Motorists traveling along Highway A13 will see nothing of this bridge. Only hikers may be able to find one of the few locations from which this small bridge surprisingly comes into view.

[10 ISOLABRÜCKE, MESOCCO / ISOLA BRIDGE AT MESOCCO

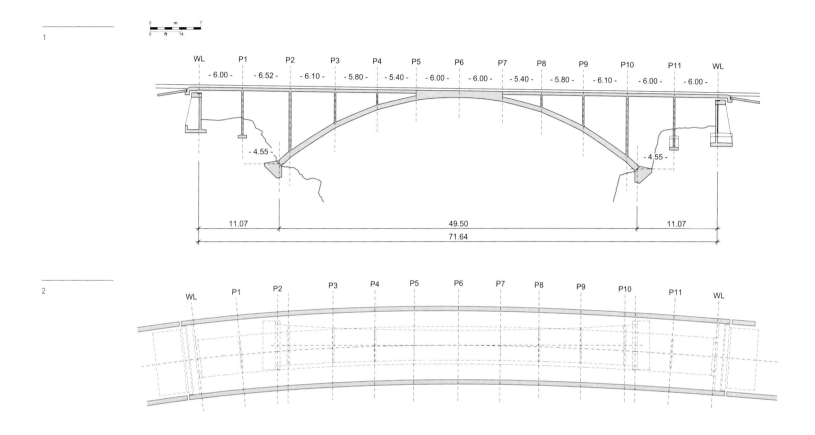

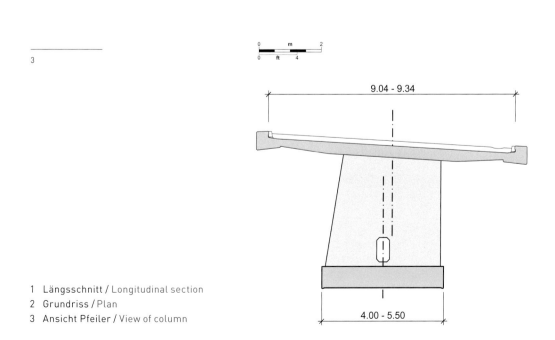

1 Längsschnitt / Longitudinal section
2 Grundriss / Plan
3 Ansicht Pfeiler / View of column

[10 ISOLABRÜCKE, MESOCCO

Vom Stausee Isola erstreckt sich seitlich wie ein Fjord die Staufläche bis zum Dorf San Bernardino. Die Autostrasse A13 überquert diesen Fjord an der engsten Stelle unmittelbar vor seiner Einmündung in den tiefblauen See. Die Brücke ist 72 Meter lang. Als Tragsystem wurde eine symmetrische Bogenbrücke mit einer Bogenspannweite von 50 Metern gewählt, mit je zwei Trägerfeldern über dem Bogen und beidseits je einem Feld für die Zufahrten. Bogen, Stützen und Fahrbahnträger weisen den gleichen Plattenquerschnitt auf. Diese Homogenität des Tragwerks spiegelt die Ruhe der umgebenden Landschaft wieder.

Die Brücke ist auf beiden Widerlagern verschieblich gelagert; heute könnte man zur Erhöhung des Tragwiderstandes und der Dauerhaftigkeit den Träger auf einem der Widerlager fixieren und dadurch eine Dilatationsfuge eliminieren. Das Lehrgerüst bestand aus einem hölzernen, dreiteiligen Rautenfachwerk, das rasch montiert werden konnte. Die Baukosten für die Bogenbrücke und das vergleichbare Sprengwerk waren etwa gleich hoch. In der idyllischen Landschaft wurde schliesslich dem kleinen, nostalgischen Bogen der Vorzug gegeben.

[10 ISOLA BRIDGE AT MESOCCO

The man-made Isola Lake stretches like a fjord from the Isola Dam to the village of San Bernardino. Highway A13 crosses this fjord at its narrowest location right before it opens up into the lake proper. The bridge is 72 m long and a symmetrical arch bridge with an arch span of 50 m was chosen, with two girder spans on either side of the crown and one approach span on either side of the arch. The same slab cross-section is used for the arch, columns, and girder. This unity of the structural system reflects the peacefulness of the surrounding landscape. The bridge is supported at both abutments with expansion bearings. Nowadays, fixed bearings could be provided at one end, which would increase the structural capacity of the bridge and increase durability through the elimination of one expansion joint. The falsework consisted of a timber truss in three sections, which could be quickly erected. The construction costs for the arch bridge and a comparable inclined-leg frame were about the same. In the end, the small, somewhat nostalgic arch bridge was the preferred choice for this idyllic site.

PREGORDABRÜCKE, MESOCCO/SOAZZA
PREGORDA BRIDGE AT MESOCCO/SOAZZA

1971–1973

Client: Graubünden Department of Transportation
Project in partnership with Rigendinger/Maag, Chur

[11

LOCATION
Mesocco Soazza
Canton of Graubünden
Switzerland

COORDINATES
737 800 / 137 850

TYPE
Beam bridge

LENGTH
604 m

MAIN SPAN
40 m

OPENING
1973

Ein paar hundert Meter unterhalb von Mesocco verengt sich die Talsohle fast zu einer Schlucht. Hier steht auf einer erhöhten, markanten Geländeschulter das im 13. Jahrhundert erbaute Castello di Mesocco, eine der grössten und gut erhaltenen Burganlagen der Schweiz. Bergseits unter dem Castello verlaufen eng nebeneinander die alte Kantonsstrasse und die Autostrasse A13. Die Pregordabrücke, die neben dem Burghügel ihr Endwiderlager hat, ist zur Zeit mit einer Länge von 604 Metern die längste Brücke im Kanton Graubünden.

A few hundred meters below Mesocco, the bottom of the Moesa valley becomes so narrow it could more aptly be called a canyon. The Castello di Mesocco stands on a high promontory at this location. Built in the thirteenth century, it is one of the largest and best preserved castles in Switzerland. Below and to the north of the Castello, Highway A13 and the cantonal road run side by side. The Pregorda Bridge, which has its abutment beside the hill on which the castle stands, is currently the longest bridge in the Canton of Graubünden with a total length of 604 m.

[11   PREGORDABRÜCKE, MESOCCO / PREGORDA BRIDGE AT MESOCCO

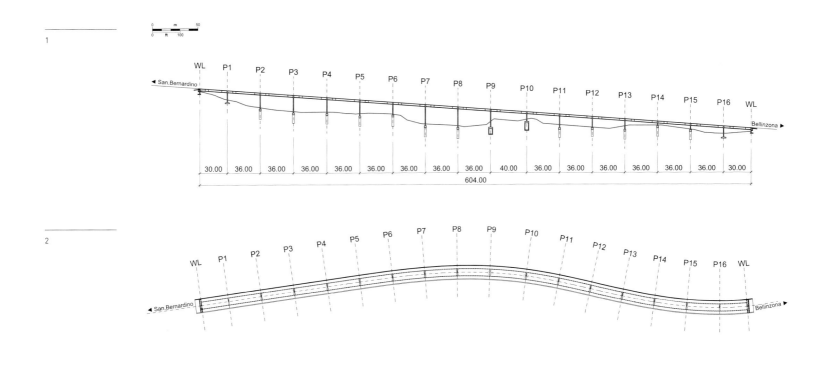

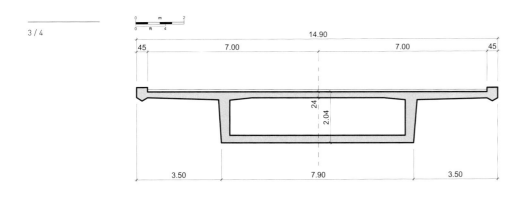

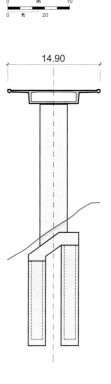

1 Längsschnitt / Longitudinal section
2 Grundriss / Plan
3 Querschnitt / Cross section
4 Ansicht Pfeiler 7 / View of column 7

[11 PREGORDABRÜCKE, MESOCCO

Die Pregordabrücke führt als typische Lehnenbrücke in relativ geringer Höhe, aber tief und solide fundiert den steilen Abhang aus Bergschutt entlang und überquert auf halber Länge die Kantonsstrasse. An dieser Stelle sind verstärkte Stützen biegesteif monolithisch mit dem Brückenträger verbunden. Damit wird die Brücke in Längsrichtung stabilisiert.

Die Regelspannweite beträgt 36 Meter, die Fahrbahn ist 14.9 Meter breit. Damit bei den vielen Stützen auch in der Schrägsicht – von der parallel verlaufenden Kantontrasse aus – Transparenz und Leichtigkeit erhalten bleiben, sind die Stützen nur 4 Meter breit, etwa ein Viertel der gesamten Brückenbreite. Die lange Pregordabrücke führt unauffällig den bewaldeten Abhang entlang; auch von weiter unten im Tal, wo die A13 die Moesa überquert, fügt sich das konstruktiv einfache und klare Bauwerk optimal in die Geländetopografie ein.

[11 PREGORDA BRIDGE AT MESOCCO

The Pregorda Bridge is a low bridge that follows the contours of the steep valley slope. It rests on deep and solid foundations in the scree. It crosses the cantonal road approximately midway between its abutments. At this location, the piers have been made stronger and are connected monolithically to the girder, to longitudinally stabilize the bridge.

The typical span length is 36 m and the deck is 14.9 m wide. To maintain visual transparency and lightness of appearance of the bridge when viewed by motorists on the cantonal road, the piers were made only 4 meters wide, i.e. about one quarter of the overall bridge width. This long structure runs unobtrusively along the wooded slope. Even from farther below in the valley, where the A13 crosses the Moesa, this simple and clearly defined structural system is ideally integrated into the topography.

VALSERRHEINBRÜCKE, UORS / SURCASTI
VALSERRHEIN BRIDGE BETWEEN UORS AND SURCASTI

1962

Client: Graubünden Department of Transportation
Design and construction: Christian Menn

[12

LOCATION
Lumnezia
Canton of Graubünden
Switzerland

COORDINATES
733 300 / 173 550

TYPE
Arch bridge

LENGTH
142 m

MAIN SPAN
86 m

OPENING
1962

Surcasti – auf Deutsch «über der Burg» – ist ein kleines Dorf, das isoliert auf einem fast hundert Meter hohen Geländevorsprung oberhalb des Zusammenflusses von Valserrhein und Glenner liegt. Auf der alten Verbindungsstrasse zwischen den beiden Dörfern Surcasti und Uors musste eine relativ grosse Höhendifferenz überwunden werden. 1961 beschloss der Kanton Graubünden, die beiden Dörfer mit einer 142 Meter langen und 60 Meter hohen, aber nur 4,6 Meter breiten Brücke zu verbinden. Am besten eignete sich dafür eine Bogenbrücke mit einer Bogenspannweite von 86 Metern. Das ausserordentlich schmale Tragwerk quer über den tief eingeschnittenen Valserrhein, das immer wieder starken Föhnstürmen ausgesetzt ist, wurde mit einfachen gestalterisch-konzeptionellen Massnahmen stabilisiert. Die filigrane Brücke passt sich sehr gut in die rustikale Umgebung mit dem massiven Turm der ehemaligen Burg ein. Die verwendeten Beton-Zuschlagstoffe zeigten an ein paar Stellen im Fahrbahnträger Alkalireaktionen. Die entsprechenden Bereiche wurden nach etwa vierzig Jahren repariert.

Surcasti, which in English means above the castle, is a small village located on an isolated promontory that lies almost one hundred meters above the confluence of the Valserrhein and the Glenner Rivers. Traveling along the old road linking the villages of Uors and Surcasti required overcoming a relatively large difference in elevation. In 1961, the Canton of Graubünden decided to connect the two villages with a bridge that would be 142 m long, 60 m high, and only 4.6 m wide. An arch bridge with an arch span of 86 m was best suited for this situation. Because the narrow valley of the Valserrhein channels the frequent and strong foehn winds, the extremely narrow structure spanning high over the valley required stabilization, which was accomplished by design measures. The delicate bridge fits in well with the rustic environment and the massive tower of the former castle.

[12 VALSERRHEINBRÜCKE, UORS / SURCASTI / VALSERRHEIN BRIDGE BETWEEN UORS AND SURCASTI

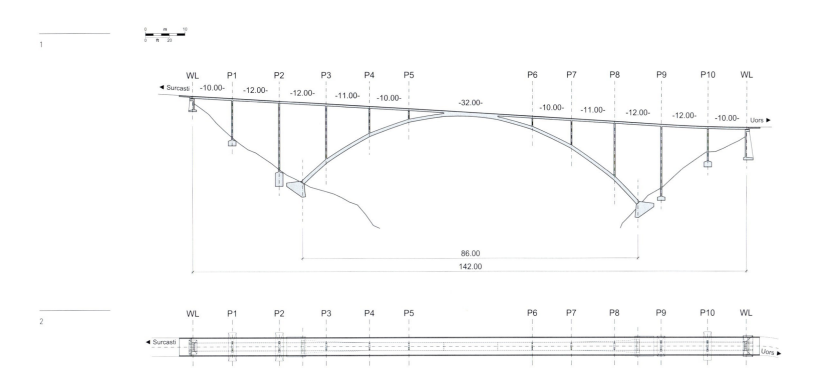

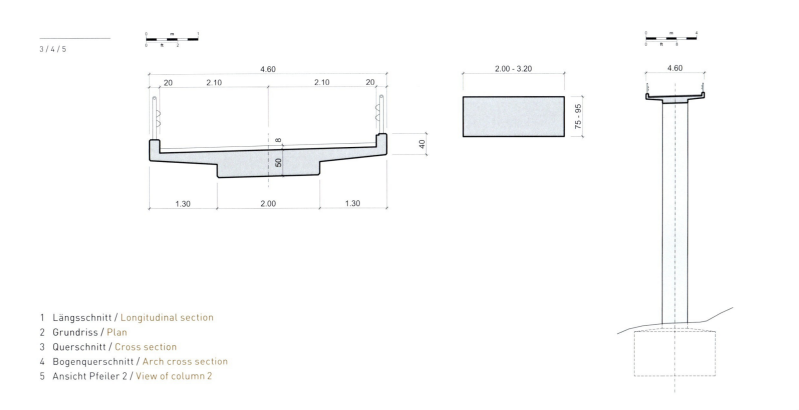

1 Längsschnitt / Longitudinal section
2 Grundriss / Plan
3 Querschnitt / Cross section
4 Bogenquerschnitt / Arch cross section
5 Ansicht Pfeiler 2 / View of column 2

[12 VALSERRHEINBRÜCKE, UORS / SURCASTI

Die Brücke ist in Bezug auf den 86 Meter weit gespannten Bogen und die beiden 22 Meter langen, zweifeldrigen Zufahrten symmetrisch. Bei den Widerlagern ist sie verschieblich gelagert. Die Kämpferstützen sind gegenüber dem Fusspunkt der Bogenachse um 6 Meter zurück verschoben, bleiben aber dennoch mit dem Bogenfundament monolithisch verbunden. Der Tragwiderstand der heute über fünfzig Jahre alten Brücke liesse sich durch Blockieren der Verschieblichkeit eines der Lager erhöhen.

Den in dieser Region starken Winddruck leitet die schmale Brücke einerseits über den Bogen auf die Bogenfundamente und andererseits über den Fahrbahnträger vor allem auf die Kämpferstützen und von diesen ebenfalls auf die schweren Bogenfundamente ab. Deshalb sind die Stützen im unteren Teil entsprechend dem Kraftfluss merklich verbreitert – eine einfache, wirtschaftliche Massnahme, die auch der Ästhetik der Brücke zugute kommt. Beispielhaft zeigt sich hier, dass die Erhöhung der Tragwerkseffizienz meistens mit der natürlichen Ästhetik korreliert.

[12 VALSERRHEIN BRIDGE BETWEEN UORS AND SURCASTI

The bridge is symmetrical, with an 86 m arch span and two 22 m long two-span approaches. The bridge can displace longitudinally at both abutments. The columns above the arch foundations have been shifted back 6 m from the true springing lines of the arch, but remain monolithically connected to the arch foundations. The structural capacity of the bridge, now over fifty years old, was increased by the provision of fixed bearings at one of the abutments.

The strong prevailing winds apply high loadings to the structure. These are carried to the arch foundations of this narrow bridge in part by the arch directly and in part by the girder to the columns above the springing lines, and then by these columns down to the arch foundations. The lower ends of these columns are thus noticeably widened to correspond with this flow of forces. This simple and economical measure that also benefits the visual appearance of the bridge is an example of how increasing structural efficiency is usually correlated with natural aesthetics. The aggregates used for the concrete in this bridge caused alkali-silica reactions at a few locations in the girder. These areas were repaired about forty years after construction.

SBB-ÜBERFÜHRUNG, BUCHS
SWISS FEDERAL RAILWAYS OVERPASS AT BUCHS

1968–1969

Client: St.Gallen Department of Transportation
Design and construction: Christian Menn

[13

LOCATION
Buchs
Canton of St.Gallen
Switzerland

COORDINATES
754 700 / 225 950

TYPE
Beam bridge

LENGTH
232 m

MAIN SPAN
32 m

OPENING
1969

Die Rheintal-Autobahn A13 verläuft bei Buchs zwischen dem Rhein und den Bahngleisen. Der Anschluss der A13 östlich des Bahnhofs erfolgte an die bestehende Verbindung von Buchs über die Rheinbrücke nach Schaan im Fürstentum Liechtenstein. Der Verkehr ab der Autobahn erforderte eine neue Einfahrt nach Buchs: eine 232 Meter lange Brücke über die Gleisanlagen, unmittelbar südlich des Bahnhofs. Besonders problematisch war die Überwindung des Niveauunterschieds zwischen dem Bahnhofsplatz und dem erforderlichen Lichtraum für die Bahn. Auf relativ engem Raum gelang schliesslich die Entwicklung einer ausgezeichneten Lösung mit einem spiralförmigen Brückenende zu einem beispielhaft gestalteten Kreisel und einem leistungsfähigen Parkplatz.

At the town of Buchs, the Rhine Valley Freeway A13 runs between the Rhine and the tracks of the Swiss Federal Railway station. Connection of the A13 east of the station was based on the existing link from Buchs over the Rhine to Schaan in the Principality of Liechtenstein. Traffic exiting the freeway required a new access to Buchs, which would be provided by a 232 meter long bridge over the railway tracks, immediately to the south of the station. It was particularly difficult to overcome the difference in elevation between the station plaza and the required vertical clearance for the railway. In spite of the relatively tight space, it was possible to develop an excellent solution that incorporated a spiral shaped end to the bridge, a traffic circle, and an efficient parking lot.

[13 SBB-ÜBERFÜHRUNG, BUCHS / SWISS FEDERAL RAILWAYS OVERPASS AT BUCHS

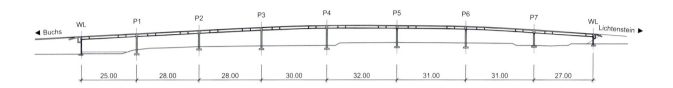

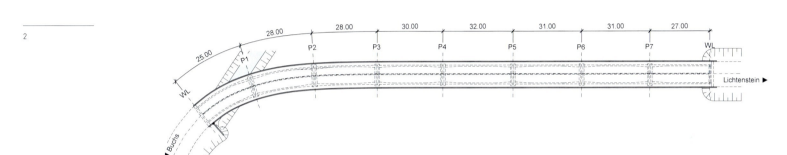

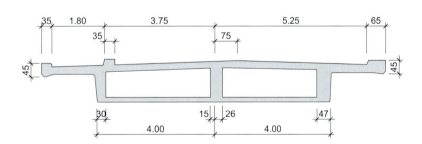

1 Längsschnitt / Longitudinal section
2 Grundriss / Plan
3 Querschnitt / Cross section

[13   SBB-ÜBERFÜHRUNG, BUCHS

Die Brücke ist 232 Meter lang und in acht Felder von durchschnittlich 30 Metern Spannweite unterteilt. Die Gleise, die im Bereich der Brücke mehrere Weichen aufweisen, werden mit einem Feld von 32 Metern Spannweite überquert. Schlanke Doppelstützen lassen das Bauwerk leicht und transparent erscheinen. Der Querschnitt des 11,8 Meter breiten, vorgespannten Brückenträgers besteht aus einem doppelzelligen Kasten mit einer Höhe von 1,37 Metern; dies entspricht einer Schlankheit (l/h) von 23. Im Umfeld der zahlreichen Oberleitungsmasten fallen die kurzen Feldweiten mit den vielen Stützen nicht auf; die Brücke fügt sich sehr gut in das von den Bahnanlagen geprägte Umfeld ein.

[13   SWISS FEDERAL RAILWAYS
OVERPASS AT BUCHS

The bridge is 232 meters long and is divided into eight spans, the average length of which is 30 meters. The railway tracks, which include several switches near the bridge, were crossed with a single span of 32 m. Slender twin columns give the bridge a light and transparent appearance. The cross-section of the 11.8 m wide, prestressed concrete girder consists of a two-cell box with a depth of 1.37 m. This corresponds to a slenderness ratio (span to depth) of 23. The large number of columns required for the short spans fit in well with the many masts used by the railway, helping the structure to be successfully integrated into the railway environment.

VIADUKT MÜHLE RICKENBACH, WIL
MÜHLE RICKENBACH VIADUCT AT WIL

1964–1965

Client: St. Gallen Department of Transportation
Design and construction: Christian Menn

[14

LOCATION
Wil
Canton of St. Gallen
Switzerland

COORDINATES
721 850 / 256 750

TYPE
Beam bridge

LENGTH
257 m

MAIN SPAN
57 m

OPENING
1965

Südlich von Wil, unmittelbar vor dem Anschluss an die Autobahn A1, überquert die Hauptstrasse H16 aus dem Toggenburg in einer Höhe von etwa 18 Metern eine parkähnliche Senke mit einem Weiher. Im Mittelbereich der Brücke war das Terrain ursprünglich noch einige Meter tiefer; es wurde bei der Parkgestaltung mit sandig-lehmigem Material bis auf das Niveau des Weihers aufgefüllt. Die Brückenstützen in der Aufschüttung mussten deshalb mit Bohrpfählen auf der tief liegenden Nagelfluh fundiert werden. Der Spannbeton-Viadukt ist 257 Meter lang, 10,9 Meter breit und weist auf der ganzen Länge eine konstante Trägerhöhe von 2,4 Metern auf. Die grösste Spannweite über dem Weiher, die stützenfrei bleiben musste, beträgt 57 Meter.

South of Wil, on its way from the Toggenburg and just before it connects with the A1 freeway, Highway H16 crosses a hollow at a height of about 18 m. The hollow was developed as a park and was therefore filled with several meters of sandy material to create a pond. The bridge piers located in this fill must therefore be founded using piles drilled down to the deep conglomerate bedrock. This prestressed concrete viaduct is 257 meters long, 10.9 meters wide, and has a constant depth of 2.4 m over its entire length. The longest span, 57 m, is over the pond where piers could not be located.

[14 VIADUKT MÜHLE RICKENBACH, WIL / MÜHLE RICKENBACH VIADUCT AT WIL

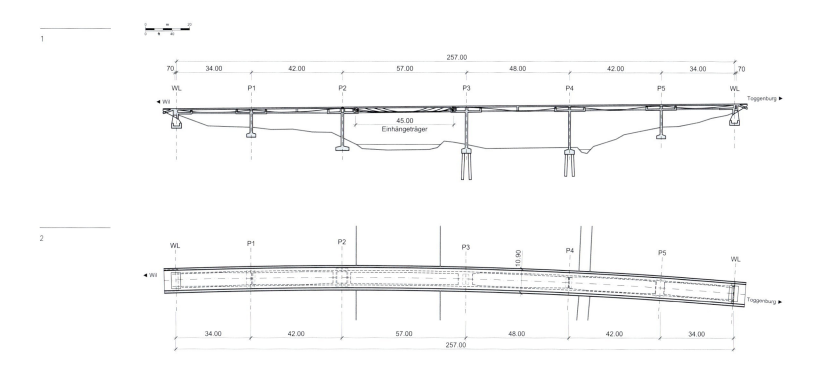

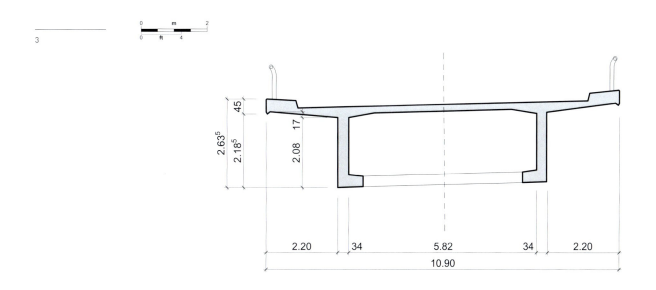

1 Längsschnitt / Longitudinal section
2 Grundriss / Plan
3 Querschnitt / Cross section

[14 VIADUKT MÜHLE RICKENBACH, WIL

Der Brückenträger überspannt sechs Felder von 34 – 42 – 57 – 48 – 42 – 34 Metern. Im Hinblick auf einen rationellen Bauvorgang und jeweils durchgehende Kabelstränge in den beiden nördlichen und den drei südlichen Feldern wurde in der 57 Meter langen Hauptspannweite über dem Weiher ein Gerberträger eingebaut. Bei den Gelenken des Gerberträgers wurde die Fahrbahnplatte ohne Fuge durchgezogen. Obwohl der relative Knickwinkel zwischen Kragarm und Einhängeträger sehr klein ist, entstanden im Gelenk wegen der kinematischen Unverträglichkeit Zwängungen, die im Beton und in der Abdichtung kleine wasserführende Risse zur Folge hatten. Die Risse in der Abdichtung und die daraus folgenden Schäden im Gelenk wären vermeidbar gewesen, wenn die Abdichtung über dem Gelenk auf einer Breite von ca. 40 Zentimetern nicht mit der Fahrbahnplatte verklebt oder (noch besser) wenn die Verbindung zwischen Fahrbahnplatte und Stegen über der Gelenkfuge auf einer Länge von ca. 40 Zentimetern unterbrochen worden wäre.

Die einfache, relativ schlanke Brücke (l/h = 23,7) dominiert die Senke mit dem Weiher nicht; Bauwerk und Umfeld sind miteinander im Gleichgewicht.

[14 MÜHLE RICKENBACH VIADUCT AT WIL

The girder is divided into six spans of 34 m, 42 m, 57 m, 48 m, 42 m, and 34 m. The 57 m span was built as a Gerber system to enable a rational construction method and permit the use of continuous post-tensioning tendons in the two northern and three southern spans. The deck slab was made continuous at the hinges of the Gerber beam. Although the relative angle of rotation between cantilever and suspended girders is very small, small cracks formed in the concrete and the deck slab waterproofing, which allowed water to penetrate. The cracks in the waterproofing and the resulting damage to the hinge could have been prevented, however, if the waterproofing had been left unbonded from the deck slab for a length of about 40 cm centered on the hinges. Even better would have been not to connect the deck slab to the girder webs over a length of about 40 cm. The simple, relatively slender bridge (L/h = 23.7) does not dominate the hollow and the pond. The structure and environment are in mutual equilibrium.

LIMMATBRÜCKE, WÜRENLOS
BRIDGE OVER THE LIMMAT AT WÜRENLOS

1967–1970

Client: Aargau Department of Transportation
Design and construction: Christian Menn

[15

LOCATION
Würenlos
Canton of Aargau
Switzerland

COORDINATES
669 100 / 254 200

TYPE
Beam bridge

LENGTH
168 m

MAIN SPAN
60 m

OPENING
1970

Im Bereich der Gemeinde Würenlos folgt die sechsspurige Autobahn A1 der Limmat und dank einer geschickten Trassierung überquert sie den Flusslauf in einer kleinen Biegung, sodass Schiefe und Länge der Brücke reduziert werden konnten. Die Brückenlänge beträgt mit drei Spannweiten von 54 – 60 – 54 Metern insgesamt 168 Meter. Die Breite misst 29,5 Meter und der Winkel zwischen Brücken- und Flussachse beträgt ca. 30 Grad. Ein Streifen zwischen Autobahn und Limmat mit Buschwerk und einem Spazierweg am Wasser blieb erhalten und ein kleiner Fachwerksteg auf der Baustelle, der Würenlos mit dem Bahnhof Killwangen verband, wurde mit Pontons etwa 50 Meter flussaufwärts transportiert und dort wieder eingebaut.

Der Baugrund im Bereich der Limmatquerung stellte bezüglich Konzeption und Bau der Brücke besondere Anforderungen. Die Baustelle befindet sich im Einzugsgebiet einer Grundwasserfassung. Bei der Brücke liegt der Grundwasserspiegel unter der durch das Limmatwasser verschlammten, nahezu wasserdichten Flusssohle. Eine Verletzung der dichtenden Schlammschicht liess sich nicht ganz vermeiden, war aber am geringsten bei einer Pfahlfundation. Die Anzahl der Pfähle musste jedoch so klein wie möglich gehalten werden.

Near the town of Würenlos, the six lane A1 freeway follows the Limmat River and crosses it at this location on a slight curve, which enables both the skew and the length of the bridge to be reduced. The bridge has a total length of 168 m, divided into three spans of 54 m, 60 m, and 54 m. Its width is 29.5 m and the angle between the axis of the bridge and that of the river is 30 degrees.

A strip of land, containing a footpath and brush, was maintained between the freeway and the Limmat. A small truss bridge, which linked Würenlos to the Killwangen railway station during construction, was floated on pontoons 50 m upstream where it was installed as a permanent bridge.

The soil at the site posed significant challenges for the design and construction of the bridge. The site is in a catchment area for groundwater. The water table lies below the bed of the Limmat, which is underlain by a layer of silt that is practically impermeable. Although it was not possible to prevent all intrusions into this layer of silt, the number of piles needed to be as small as possible.

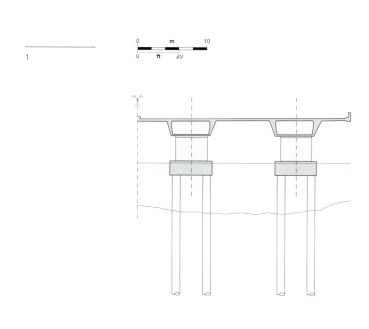

1

[15 LIMMATBRÜCKE, WÜRENLOS / BRIDGE OVER THE LIMMAT AT WÜRENLOS

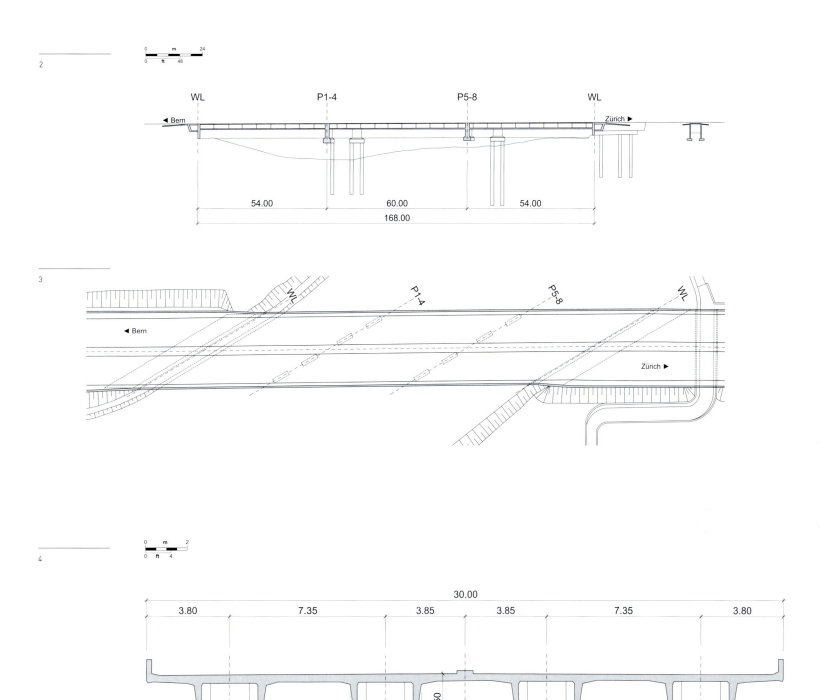

1 Ansicht Pfeiler P1 und P2 / View of columns P1 and P2
2 Längsschnitt / Longitudinal section
3 Grundriss / Plan
4 Querschnitt / Cross section

[15 LIMMATBRÜCKE, WÜRENLOS

Der Überbau der aussergewöhnlich breiten Limmatbrücke besteht aus vier Kastenträgern, die auf schief scheibenförmigen Stützen gelagert sind. Die Stützen sind mit je zwei Bohrpfählen fundiert. Zwischen den einzelnen Stützen wurden während der Bauzeit die Pfahlbankette für die Verschiebebahn der Kastenträger provisorisch miteinander verbunden. Nach der Fertigstellung des Überbaus wurden die Verbindungselemente ausgebaut und versenkt.

Die Kastenträger weisen nur geringe Wandstärken auf und die Kabel der Vorspannung wurden nachträglich im Kasteninnern extern, also seitlich an den Kastenwänden eingebaut. Zur Einsparung der Gerüstpfähle wurde nur für einen einzigen Kastenträger ein schmales, leichtes Lehrgerüst erstellt. Nach dem Aufbringen der Vorspannung konnte der Kastenträger seitlich in seine endgültige Lage verschoben werden, und Lehrgerüst und Schalung dienten ohne jede Änderung für den nächsten Träger. Die Verschiebung der Kastenträger bereitete anfänglich einige Schwierigkeiten, weil sich die Träger bei Sonneneinstrahlung in der Horizontalebene krümmten und die Verschiebeplatten wegen der starken Schiefe dazu tendierten, aus der Verschiebebahn zu gleiten. Die Trägerverschiebung durfte deshalb nur nachts durchgeführt werden. Der anspruchsvolle Bauvorgang prägte den Brückenentwurf massgeblich. In Verbindung mit der vorsichtigen Pfahlfundation konnte zum einen die Anzahl der Lehrgerüstpfähle um etwa 75 Prozent reduziert werden, zum anderen resultierten daraus beträchtliche Kosteneinsparungen. Die Brücke wurde kürzlich beidseits um eine Fahrspur verbreitert. Die Einzelpfähle am Brückenrand gehörten nicht zum ursprünglichen Konzept. Die Brücke fügt sich technisch und visuell sehr gut in den Limmatraum von Würenlos und Killwangen ein.

[15 BRIDGE OVER THE LIMMAT AT WÜRENLOS

The superstructure of this unusually wide bridge is composed of four box girders, which are supported on skew wall-shaped piers. Each pier is founded on two drilled piles. During construction, the pilecaps were temporarily connected to each other to support a track for moving the box girders for the superstructure. After construction of the superstructure, the components used to connect the pilecaps were detached and sunk into the river.

The box girders have thin walls. Post-tensioning tendons were installed inside the cavity of the boxes and installed into the walls of the boxes. To save on piles for the falsework, a simple scaffolding that supported only a single box was constructed. After it was prestressed, a given box was displaced laterally into its final location, and the same scaffolding and formwork were then used without modification to cast the next box girder. The displacement of the box girders at first presented some difficulties, since the girders became curved in the horizontal plane due to uneven warming by the sun, and the sliding plates tended to glide off their tracks due to the sharp skew. The displacement of the girders was henceforth performed only at night.

The challenging construction sequence had a significant impact on the design of the bridge. The careful design of the pile foundations enabled the number of falsework piles to be reduced by about 75 percent, which resulted in considerable cost savings. Recently the bridge has been widened on both sides by a new lane. Therefore the necessary single piles at the edges of the bridge didn't belong to the original concept. The bridge fits technically and visually very well into the Limmat valley from Würenlos to Killwangen.

FELSENAUBRÜCKE, BERN
FELSENAU BRIDGE AT BERNE

1972–1974

Client: Bern Department of Highway Construction
Project in partnership with Emch+Berger, Bern
and Rigendinger/Maag, Chur

[16

LOCATION
Bern
Canton of Bern
Switzerland

COORDINATES
600 700 / 202 050

TYPE
Beam bridge /
Cantilever construction

LENGTH
1116 m

HEIGHT
60 m

RADIUS
800 m

MAIN SPAN
156 m

OPENING
1974

Rund um Bern fliesst die Aare in einem 30 bis 40 Meter tiefen Einschnitt und beschreibt dabei zahlreiche Schlaufen. Die Möglichkeiten günstiger Aareübergänge nördlich der Stadt sind dadurch stark eingeschränkt. Für die Autobahn A1 wurde in erhöhter Lage, 60 Meter über dem Fluss, ein idealer, aber relativ schmaler Korridor genutzt. Im Osten des Übergangs münden die A6 Thun–Bern und im Westen die A12 Fribourg–Bern in die A1; ausserdem ist beidseits das städtische Verkehrsnetz an die Brücke angeschlossen. Die Felsenaubrücke sitzt deshalb wie eine Spinne in einem Netz. Sie ist 1116 Meter lang und mit je drei Spuren für beide Fahrrichtungen (die heute dem Verkehr kaum mehr genügen) 26,2 Meter breit.

Die markante Felsenaubrücke dominiert den Blick vom Felsenauquartier flussaufwärts zu den Alpen im Hintergrund. Ein möglichst transparentes Tragwerk mit grossen Spannweiten und schmalen Stützen war aus diesem Grund erwünscht. Deshalb wurden im Projektwettbewerb für den Aarebereich grosse Spannweiten, ein einziger, einzelliger Trägerquerschnitt mit weit ausladenden Fahrbahnkonsolen und nur 7 Meter breiten Stützen vorgeschlagen. Für die beiden weniger kritischen Zufahrtsviadukte wurden bei einer viel geringeren Höhe kürzere, wesentlich wirtschaftlichere Spannweiten gewählt. Mit dieser Zielsetzung konnte die immer noch wuchtige Brücke mit ihrem kleinmassstäblichen, vorstädtischen Umfeld einigermassen in ein Gleichgewicht gebracht werden.

The Aare River flows around Berne in a valley that lies 30 to 40 m below the surrounding land and makes many sharp bends. The possibilities for suitable crossings of the Aare north of the city are therefore severely limited. For the A1 freeway, an ideal but relatively narrow corridor, elevated 60 m above the river, was selected. At the east end of the crossing, there is an interchange with the A6 Thun-Bern freeway; in the west an interchange with the A12 Fibourg-Bern freeway. City streets also connect to the A1 at both ends of the bridge. The Felsenau Bridge thus sits like a spider in the centre of a web. The bridge is 1116 m long and carries three lanes of traffic in both directions (which are now barely sufficient to handle current traffic), for a total width of 26.2 m.

The Felsenau Bridge is a prominent structure and dominates views from the Felsenau district up the river towards the Alps in the background. A structure of maximum transparency with the longest possible spans and narrow piers was therefore desirable. For the submission to the bridge design competition, long spans were proposed for the portion of the bridge in the immediate vicinity of the Aare, with a single-cell girder cross-section, wide deck slab cantilevers, and piers of only 7 m in width. For approach viaducts, which are less critical than the main spans, shorter and significantly more economical spans were chosen. In this way, this massive bridge could be brought in some measure into balance with its small-scale, suburban environment.

[16 FELSENAUBRÜCKE, BERN / FELSENAU BRIDGE AT BERN

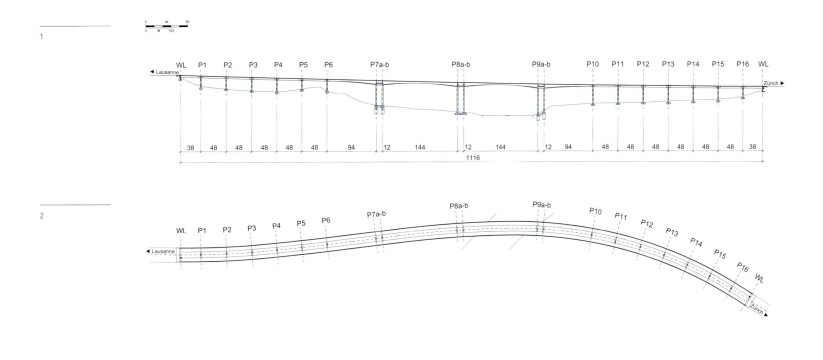

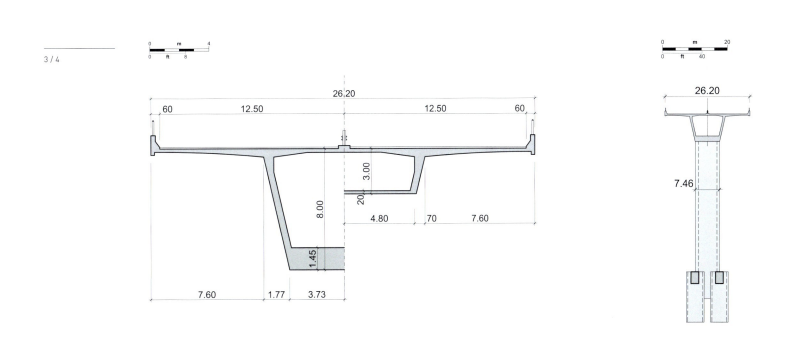

1 Längsschnitt / Longitudinal section
2 Grundriss / Plan
3 Querschnitt / Cross section
4 Ansicht Pfeiler 7a / View of column 7a

[16 FELSENAUBRÜCKE, BERN

Die Felsenaubrücke ist 1116 Meter lang und 26,2 Meter breit. Sie überquert in 60 Metern Höhe und im Grundriss leicht gekrümmt (Radius 800 Meter) das Aaretal. Die beiden 156 Meter überbrückenden Hauptspannweiten und die sechs- beziehungsweise siebenfeldrigen Zufahrtsviadukte auf der West- beziehungsweise Ost-Seite mit Regelspannweiten von 48 Metern entsprechen unterschiedlichen Tragsystemen. Beide beruhen aber auf dem gleichen, grundlegenden Prinzip, dass jedes hergestellte Tragelement so rasch wie möglich als tragender Systemteil für die Herstellung des nächsten Tragelements genutzt werden soll. Für die Hauptspannweiten eignete sich am besten der freie Vorbau. Dabei werden beidseits einer Doppelstütze auf einem verschiebbaren Gerüst 3 bis 4 Meter lange Trägersegmente hergestellt, die kurz nach dem Betonieren mit Spannkabeln an das bereits vorhandene Trägerteil angepresst werden. Die Spannkabel werden in der Regel auf der ganzen Länge des bereits betonierten Trägers in leere Hüllrohre eingezogen oder -gestossen und im angefügten Segment verankert und gespannt.

Entscheidend bei einem Freivorbau ist die Konzeption eines sorgfältigen Rasters für alle Aussparungen und Verankerungen des Vorbauwagens, für die Kabelanordnung, die Bewehrungsabstände und die Schalungs-, Bewehrungsstege und die Lücken in den Kastenstegen für das Einbringen und Verdichten des Betons. Zu beachten ist auch ein ausreichender Kabelabstand in der Fahrbahnplatte im Hinblick auf die horizontalen Schubspannungen sowie die erforderliche Vertikalverbügelung der Platte. Die Trägerüberhöhung beim Vorbau kann mit einer einfachen Berechnung ermittelt werden.

Die Herstellung der Zufahrtsviadukte mit den kürzeren Spannweiten erfolgte feldweise auf einem Lehrgerüst in mehreren Etappen: Zuerst wurde der Trägertrog betoniert, dann – nach der Vorspannung des Trogs – die obere Kastenplatte und schliesslich mit einem auskragenden, fahrbaren Gerüst in Längen von 8 Metern die Kragplatten des Querschnitts. Das Lehrgerüst musste nur für das Gewicht des Trogs bemessen werden; das Gewicht der oberen Kastenplatte wurde vom inzwischen vorgespannten und tragfähigen Trog übernommen.

Die Brücke war ausserordentlich wirtschaftlich; sie kostete inklusive Projekt und Bauleitung 33 Millionen Franken, oder umgerechnet 1140 Franken pro Quadratmeter. Das ist etwa gleich viel wie die 15 Jahre zuvor erbaute Weinland-Brücke bei Andelfingen, die 1050 Franken pro Quadratmeter kostete. Heute kosten mittlere Brücken in der Regel mehr als 2500 Franken pro Quadratmeter. Die signifikante Preissteigerung ist allerdings nicht nur auf die Teuerung zurückzuführen, sondern grösstenteils auf die wesentlich höhere Ansprüche an Sicherheit, sparsamen Unterhalt und Dauerhaftigkeit.

Angesichts des im Stadt- und Landschaftsraum exponierten Standorts der Felsenaubrücke wären ein paar gestalterische Verbesserungen in der Grössenordnung von 1 bis 2 Prozent der Gesamtkosten durchaus vertretbar gewesen, etwa für Einzel- statt Doppelpfeiler und für eine profilierte Querschnittsform der Pfeiler.

[16 FELSENAU BRIDGE AT BERN

The Felsenau Bridge is 1116 m long and 26.2 m wide. It crosses the Aare valley at a height of 60 m along a slight curve (radius 800 m) in plan. The two main spans of 156 m and the approach spans (six at the west end and seven at the east) with a typical span of 48 m correspond to different structural systems. Both are based, however, on the same fundamental principle, namely that each structural component must be able to carry load within the structural system as soon as possible, to enable it to be used for the production of subsequent components.

For the main spans, cantilever construction was the most suitable method of construction. Girder segments with lengths of 3 to 4 meters were produced on both sides of a twin-legged pier. Shortly after concrete was placed for these segments, they were attached to the previously completed portion of the girder using post-tensioning tendons. These tendons were normally pulled or pushed into empty ducts that extended over the entire length of the previously constructed girder and then anchored and stressed in the newly built segment.

Of critical importance in cantilever construction is the careful layout of an arrangement for all openings and the anchorages for the travelers, for the arrangement of tendons, the spacing of reinforcement, and gaps in the box girder webs for the placement and consolidation of concrete. Sufficient spacing of the tendons in the deck slab must also be provided, in consideration of horizontal shear stresses and the required vertical stirrups in the slab. Girder camber during cantilever construction can be calculated using simple methods.

The construction of the approach viaducts with shorter spans was done span by span on falsework in multiple steps. First, concrete was placed for the bottom slab and webs. This U-shaped partial girder was then prestressed and the middle portion of the top slab was constructed. Finally, the deck slab cantilevers were constructed using a traveler in 8 m long segments. In this way, the falsework needed to be designed only for the weight of the U-shaped partial girder, since the weight of the top slab was carried by the prestressed and thus structurally functional U-shaped girder.

The bridge was extremely economical. Its cost, including design and construction management, was 33 million Swiss francs, or 1140 francs per square meter. This is about the same as the Weinland Bridge in Andelfingen, built 15 years prior, which cost 1050 francs per square meter. Nowadays, average bridges normally cost more than 2500 francs per square meter. The significant increase in cost cannot all be attributed to inflation. Rather, most if it is due to significantly higher demands for safety, the low cost of maintenance, and durability.

In consideration of the exposed location of the Felsenau Bridge within the urban landscape, a few improvements to the visual aspects of design would have been feasible, since they would have increased the total cost by only one or two percent. Single leg piers with a more suitable shaping, for example, would have been preferable to the double leg piers with rectangular cross-sections that were built.

BRÜCKENBAU AUS DER SICHT DES POLITIKERS
BRIDGE BUILDING FROM THE POLITICIAN'S PERSPECTIVE

LUZI BÄRTSCH

Im symbolischen Sinn verbinden Brücken Menschen, Kulturen und Länder, konkret überqueren sie als Bauwerke Gewässer, Schluchten und Täler. In der Politik hat der Brückenbau – die Kunst des Verbindens – ebenfalls grosse Bedeutung. Die Politik muss Brücken bauen, den Ausgleich finden zwischen Partnern mit gegensätzlichen Interessen. Vollständige Wunscherfüllung ist dabei kaum möglich, weil sich die im Einzelnen berechtigten Anliegen oder Forderungen oft widersprechen. Auf der einen Seite wünschen wir zum Beispiel Vollbeschäftigung, andererseits weniger Wirtschaftswachstum aus Gründen des Umweltschutzes. Auf der einen Seite wird volle, grenzenlose Personenfreizügigkeit gewünscht, andererseits kein Landschaftsverbrauch für neue Wohngebiete. Es gilt, zwischen sich widersprechenden Einzelinteressen und unterschiedlichen Positionen Kompromisse zu schliessen, die ein sinnvolles Ganzes ergeben. Dabei muss ein dauerhafter Kompromiss mehrere Anforderungen erfüllen: Mehrwert für alle Beteiligten und umsetzbare, auf Dauer tragfähige und wirtschaftliche Lösungen. Für gesunde, nachhaltige Kompromisse braucht es Verstand, Mut und Fantasie für bessere Alternativen.

ÜBER 2000 BRÜCKEN

Zwischen dem Brückenbau im übertragenen Sinn und der Kunst des konkreten Brückenbaus sind Parallelen unübersehbar: bei beiden geht es um eine Optimierungsaufgabe. Auch der Brückenbauer muss sich widersprechende Anforderungen zu einem sinnvollen Ganzen fügen. Christian Menn umschreibt das wie folgt: «Neben der verkehrstechnischen Funktionalität sind die wichtigsten Entwurfsziele im Brückenbau die normgemässe Tragsicherheit, eine ausreichende Dauerhaftigkeit und dem Standort und der Bedeutung der Brücke entsprechend eine optimale Balance von Wirtschaftlichkeit und Ästhetik.»[1]

In der Schweiz, im Alpenraum und dort insbesondere im Kanton Graubünden hat der Brückenbau einen hohen Stellenwert. Im dünn besiedelten Alpenkanton hat das Strassen- und Bahnnetz für die Erschliessung der Talschaften, den Tourismus und den Transitverkehr eine herausragende Bedeutung. Die Verkehrspolitik und der Strassenbau gehören seit Jahrhunderten zu den grossen Staatsaufgaben im Kanton Graubünden. Verkehrspolitik war im Kanton der 150 Täler stets auch Regionalpolitik; sie gehörte immer zu den

Bridges cross rivers and straits, valleys and ravines. Viewed symbolically, they connect people, cultures, and countries. As the art of connecting, bridge building is also of the utmost importance in the world of politics. After all, balancing the needs of parties with opposing interests is also a form of bridge building. Universal satisfaction is rarely possible, if only because some concerns and demands simply cancel each other out, no matter how legitimate they may be in isolation. Full employment, for example, is considered desirable; but for the sake of the environment so is less growth. Freedom of movement is another principle that most would subscribe to; but no one wants to see yet more land being sacrificed to new housing. So politicians have to find compromises that take account of conflicting interests without becoming so watered-down as to be meaningless. Any compromise that is to last must meet several requirements: It must rest on feasible, economically viable, long-term solutions that offer some sort of gain for all parties. Healthy, sustainable compromises call for a cool head, courage, and the ability to imagine better alternatives.

MORE THAN 2000 BRIDGES

The parallels between bridge building in the metaphorical sense and bridge building in the literal sense are obvious. Both are about optimization. The bridge builder, too, has to reconcile contradictory demands and combine these in a meaningful whole. Christian Menn describes this as follows: "The most important objectives when designing a new bridge, alongside its functionality for a specific means of transport, are structural safety in compliance with the relevant norms, adequate durability, and the best possible balance between affordability and aesthetics for that particular bridge and location."[1]

Bridge building is very important in Switzerland, especially in mountainous regions like the Canton of Graubünden. Switzerland's easternmost canton is thinly populated and heavily reliant on its road and rail network for development, tourism, and transit traffic. Transport and road building have therefore long counted among the key tasks incumbent on policymakers there. And because so many of Graubünden's 150 valleys are remote and separated by high mountains, transport policy has always been about development, too, which is one of the most difficult – and most remarkable – chap-

schwierigsten und bemerkenswertesten Kapiteln der bündnerischen Geschichte. Nicht umsonst heisst es: Die Geschichte Graubündens sei weitgehend die Geschichte seiner Pässe und Verkehrslinien. Dementsprechend wurde mit grossen Opfern ein weit verzweigtes Bahn- und Strassennetz erstellt. Die topografischen Verhältnisse erfordern im Verkehrsnetz des Alpenkantons unzählige Kunstbauten, davon über 2000 Brücken. Sie sind die prägenden Bauten aller Verkehrsanlagen. Sie geniessen ausserordentliche Beachtung, «denn sie zeigen den Ort, wo der Mensch auf Hindernisse stiess und sich doch nicht aufhalten liess, sondern sie überwand und sie überbrückte, wie er es eben vermochte, je nach seiner Auffassung, seinem Geschmack und den Verhältnissen, von denen er umgeben war». (Ivo Andrić, serbokroatischer Autor und Literatur-Nobelpreisträger 1961 in seinem Meisterwerk *Die Brücke über die Drina*.)

ERFINDUNGEN KÜHNER MÄNNER

Und so werden seit Urzeiten Brücken gebaut. Möglicherweise römischen Ursprungs sind die wohl ältesten noch bestehenden Steinbogenbrücken in Promontogno im Bergell und in Curaglia an der Lukmanierstrasse. Herausragende Meilensteine im Brückenbau wurden im 19. Jahrhundert mit dem Bau der Commerzialstrassen und des Bahnnetzes gesetzt. Mit den Commerzialstrassen für den Transitverkehr erlebte der Strassenbau im Kanton Graubünden einen ersten grossen Aufschwung. Es entstanden dabei bedeutende Brücken aus Holz, Stein und Eisen. Der Ausbau des Bahnnetzes ermöglichte den Ingenieuren den Bau einer ganzen Reihe imposanter Natursteinbrücken. Die Viadukte bei Filisur, Wiesen und Solis sind die bekanntesten Bauwerke einer Anlage, die auch als Ganzes unsere Bewunderung verdient. Der Historiker Georg Thürer hat im Schulbuch *Von Bündner Volk und Bündner Land* im Jahre 1958 unter dem Titel «Technische Wunderwerke» seine Begeisterung zum Ausdruck gebracht: «Im Gebirgskanton Graubünden gibt es herrliche Brückenbauten, von denen manche unsere Täler nicht nur erschliessen, sondern auch schmücken. Kühne Männer ersannen sie […] Wer ein solches Wundergebilde aus Stein erdenken, solche Pfeiler türmen und solche Bögen wölben konnte, der war ein Held in unseren Knabenaugen. Er konnte sich neben Drachentötern, Tell und Winkelried sehen lassen.»

Während der Naturstein-Brückenbau in Graubünden seine Blüte erlebte, wurde der Baustoff Eisenbeton erfunden, mit dem grundlegende Neuerungen im konstruktiven Ingenieurbau ermöglicht wurden. Mit weiteren Entwicklungsschritten unter den Stichwörtern Spannbeton, Verbundbrücken, Hängebrücken und Schrägseilbrücken konnten grössere Spannweiten realisiert werden. Bezogen auf die Wirtschaftlichkeit und die Gestaltung wurden dadurch die Spielräume erweitert. Aus Sicht der Verkehrs-, der Finanz- und der Umweltpolitik waren das willkommene Entwicklungen: Die grösseren Spannweiten bieten mehr Freiheit bei der Trassierung, tiefe Erstellungskosten sind finanzpolitisch erwünscht und ästhetische Qualität und hohe Verträglichkeit mit dem Umfeld sind umweltpolitische Anliegen.

ters in its history. Not by chance is it often said that Graubünden's history is largely the history of its passes, roads, and railways. This road and rail network was built at great human cost. The topography is daunting and calls for countless feats of engineering. The most striking of these are its 2000 and more bridges – structures that command extraordinary respect, "because they show the place where humankind encountered an obstacle and did not stop before it, but overcame and bridged it the way humankind could, according to understanding, taste, and circumstances," as Ivo Andrić, the Yugoslav Nobel laureate and author of *The Bridge over the Drina*, once wrote.[2]

INVENTIONS OF BOLD MEN

And so bridges have been built since time immemorial. The oldest stone arch bridges still standing in Graubünden – in Promontogno in the Bregaglia Valley and on the road to the Lukmanier Pass in Curaglia – are thought to date from Roman times; but the really great milestones all date from the nineteenth century, when the first commercial roads and railways were built. The arrival of transit traffic ushered in the first major upswing in cantonal history and saw the building of still more bridges made of wood, stone, and iron. The expansion of the rail network, moreover, gave engineers an opportunity to build ever more ambitious structures out of local stone. The viaducts near Filisur, Wiesen, and Solis are only the best known of these and form part of a larger whole that is fully deserving of our admiration. In an essay called "Technische Wunderwerke" written for the 1958 textbook *Von Bündner Volk und Bündner Land*, the historian Georg Thürer went into raptures over these feats of civil engineering: "There are some magnificent bridges in the mountain Canton of Graubünden, some of which not only open up our valleys, but actually adorn them. These were the inventions of bold men… Whoever could dream up such wonderworks in stone, could build such towering piers, could span such lofty arches – in the eyes of us boys he was no less a hero than the great dragon-slayers, Tell and Winkelried."[3]

Stone bridges were still in their heyday in Graubünden when the invention of reinforced concrete provided a material that before long would give rise to some fundamental innovations in civil engineering. Further developments such as prestressed concrete, composite bridges, suspension bridges, and cable-stayed bridges allowed even larger spans to be overcome as well as broadening the bridge builder's scope with regard to both economics and design. From the point of view of transport, financial, and environmental policy, these were all welcome developments. Larger spans translate into a wider choice of routes; lower construction costs mean less pressure on the public purse; and aesthetic quality combined with topographical compatibility meet two key environmental criteria.

It was thanks largely to these technological and conceptual developments that the Canton of Graubünden acquired so many fascinating bridges. My own personal favorites are the following three: The Salginatobel Bridge near Schiers by Robert Maillart, built in 1930 on the road from Schiers to Schuders and described by Ameri-

Gestützt auf die technologischen und konzeptionellen Entwicklungen sind im Kanton Graubünden eine Vielzahl faszinierender Brücken entstanden. Meine persönlichen Favoriten sind die drei folgenden, herausragenden Brückenbauwerke: die Salginatobel-Brücke bei Schiers, 1930 erbaut von Robert Maillart an der Verbindungsstrasse Schiers–Schuders. Gemäss dem amerikanischen Ingenieurhistoriker David. P. Billington war es «im Jahre 1928 die wohl fortschrittlichste Bogenbrücke»[2]. Christian Menn sieht darin «eine Brücke von höchster ästhetischer Qualität. Maillart fügte seine Brücke perfekt in ihr wildes Umfeld und die spezielle örtliche Topografie ein. Das Tragwerk ist aus einem Guss, man kann nichts hinzufügen und nichts hinwegnehmen.»[3] 1991 wurde die Salginatobelbrücke von der American Society of Civil Engeneers als World Monument ausgezeichnet.

Die «Zwillinge» Nanin- und Cascellabrücke im Misox, 1967/68 erbaut von Christian Menn als Betonbogenbrücken, sind von ausserordentlicher Eleganz. Der grosse deutsche Bauingenieur Jörg Schlaich äusserte sich dazu mit grosser Begeisterung: «Robert Maillart kämen die Tränen, Freudentränen, wenn er das Brückenpaar an der Südseite des San Bernardino oder die 100 Meter weit gespannte Rheinbrücke Reichenau sehen könnte. Bogen und Träger sind ausgewogen, Brücke und Landschaft eins!»[4]

Die Sunnibergbrücke bei Klosters, 2004 erbaut nach dem Entwurf von Christian Menn und dem Projekt von Bänziger & Partner. Die Brücke überquert vor dem Nordportal des Gotschnatunnels auf 60 Metern Höhe die Landquart. Das Konzept der Schrägkabelbrücke wurde international bekannt, mehrfach preisgekrönt und in der ganzen Welt unzählige Male übernommen. Die Sunnibergbrücke ist das markanteste Bauwerk an der Prättigauerstrasse: kühn, elegant und transparent. Vom emeritierten ETH-Professor für Rechtswissenschaften Martin Lendi stammt die Formel: «Christian Menn ist in Klosters in einen Dialog mit dem Lebensraum getreten.»

AUSDRUCK DER BAUKULTUR
Ab Mitte des 20. Jahrhunderts nahmen der Motorfahrzeugbestand und damit der Strassenverkehr progressiv zu. Der Bau des Nationalstrassennetzes wurde beschlossen und der Ausbau der Kantonsstrassen mit voller Kraft vorangetrieben. Der Brückenbau in Beton boomte. In dieser Zeit sind herrliche Betonbrücken von hoher Qualität entstanden, aber auch andere. Aus verkehrs- und finanzpolitischen Gründen forderte das Gemeinwesen kurze Bauzeiten, schnelle Inbetriebsetzung und möglichst tiefe Erstellungskosten. Zeitlicher und wirtschaftlicher Druck hatten negative Auswirkungen. Der Ausbaustandard wurde zum Teil gesenkt und die Qualitätssicherung vernachlässigt. Zudem nahmen die Fahrzeuglasten, die Verkehrsfrequenzen und die Schneeräumung mit Salz zu. Die Kombination der erhöhten Anforderungen mit bautechnischen Mängeln ergab vielerorts massive Schäden bei den Betonbrücken. Ab den 1990er Jahren wurden die Schäden überdeutlich und umfangreiche Instandsetzungsmassnahmen mit entsprechenden Kostenfolgen waren zwingend notwendig. Aufgrund dieser negativen Erfahrungen setzte bei Behörden und in der Politik eine Rückbesin-

can engineering historian David P. Billington as "the most advanced arch bridge designed by 1928."[4] Christian Menn sees it as "a bridge of the highest aesthetic quality. Maillart's bridge blends in perfectly with its wild surroundings and the special topography of its setting. The load-bearing structure is of a piece; nothing can be added and nothing taken away."[5] The American Society of Civil Engineers in 1991 declared it a World Monument.

The "twin" Nanin and Cascella Bridges by Christian Menn, built in 1967/68 in the Misox Valley, are concrete arch bridges of exceptional elegance. Catching his first glimpse of them, the great German civil engineer Jörg Schlaich was thrilled by what he saw: "Robert Maillart would shed tears of joy if he could see this pair of bridges on the southern side of the San Bernardino or the 100-meter-wide Rhine Bridge at Reichenau. The arches and piers are so perfectly balanced, the bridge and landscape one!"[6]

The Sunniberg Bridge near Klosters was built in 2004 to a design by Christian Menn in collaboration with the civil engineers Bänziger & Partner. The bridge crosses the Landquart River at a height of 60 meters in front of the northern portal of the Gotschna Tunnel. The concept of the cable-stayed bridge became internationally famous, won several prizes, and was emulated all over the world. The Sunniberg Bridge is the most striking structure in the Prättigau Valley being at once bold, elegant, and transparent. Martin Lendi, emeritus professor of law at the Swiss Federal Institute of Technology (ETH) in Zurich, summed it up perfectly when he said: "At Klosters, Christian Menn entered into a dialogue with our habitat."

ATTESTATIONS OF BUILDING CULTURE
Starting in the mid-twentieth century, a rapid increase in car ownership led to ever larger volumes of motorized traffic. While work commenced on a national highway network, there was a massive drive to upgrade the country's cantonal roads. Concrete bridge building boomed and while some of the bridges dating from this period are superb, many others were built too fast and too cheaply. Budgetary constraints and the presumed urgency of each new bridge often had a negative impact on the outcome. Standards were actually lowered in some instances, and quality assurance all too often neglected. Meanwhile, maximum loads, traffic volumes, and the use of salt to clear snow were on the rise. Ever greater wear and tear combined with shoddy engineering left many a bridge in a woeful state of disrepair. By the nineteen-nineties, the problem could no longer be ignored and numerous restoration projects were initiated, for which funds naturally had to be made available. Chastened by this negative experience, policymakers recalled what, 2000 years earlier, the Roman engineer Vitruvius had hailed as the three salient qualities of all good architecture, namely utility, durability, and beauty. They realized that what was needed was a holistic view that after addressing the economic and engineering issues would also give durability and design their due. Merely minimizing construction costs is neither sustainable nor even good value in the long run. The focus must rather be on optimizing the sums invested over the whole lifetime of the whole structure.

nung ein auf das, was der römische Ingenieur Vitruv vor mehr als 2000 Jahren als Qualität eines Bauwerkes bezeichnete: «Die Kombination von Funktionalität, Beständigkeit und Schönheit ist anzustreben.» Erwartet wird eine ganzheitliche Betrachtung: Neben den wirtschaftlichen und den statisch-konstruktiven Belangen ist insbesondere der Dauerhaftigkeit und der Gestaltung gebührende Beachtung zu schenken. Allein die Minimierung der Erstellungskosten ist nicht nachhaltig und nicht werthaltig. Im Vordergrund muss die Optimierung der eingesetzten Mittel über den ganzen Lebenszyklus des gesamten Bauwerkes stehen.

Brückenbauwerke sind untrennbare Bestandteile unseres Lebensraumes. Sie sind nicht nur Merkmale der technischen Entwicklung, sondern auch Ausdruck der Baukultur. Bei guter Gestaltung können sie über den Zweck hinaus zu Wahrzeichen werden, ihrer Umgebung eine neue Identität verschaffen oder ganze Landschaften prägen. Der Brückenbauer muss sich darum ausdrücklich mit der Frage befassen, wie die Brücke im Raum wirken, wie sich das Bauwerk in der Landschaft präsentieren soll. Er muss also nicht nur eine bautechnische und wirtschaftliche, sondern auch eine gestalterische Aufgabe lösen. Er hat damit einen gesellschaftspolitischen Auftrag zu erfüllen. Darum ist Bauen letztlich ein kultureller Akt.

Unter Berücksichtigung der genannten Aspekte hat die Regierung des Kantons Graubünden im Jahre 1991 Christian Menn als erstem Bauingenieur den Bündner Kulturpreis verliehen. Dies in Würdigung seines umfassenden, praktischen und wissenschaftlichen Werkes als Brückenbauer in- und ausserhalb des Kantons Graubünden und in Anerkennung seines unermüdlichen Einsatzes für die Förderung des Schweizerischen Ingenieurwesens.

Brückenbauten prägen in hohem Masse die Landschaft, den öffentlichen Raum. Daher hat die Bevölkerung ein Recht auf dauerhafte und anspruchsvolle Brückenbauten. Die Behörden sowie die Politik sind verpflichtet, gute Rahmenbedingungen für intelligente Lösungen zu schaffen. Angesprochen sind dabei auch die Bildungspolitik, die Ausbildung von innovativen und von ihrer Aufgabe begeisterten ETH-Bauingenieuren, der Wettbewerb, die Auftragsvergabe, die Auszeichnung von beispielhaften Bauten und die Anerkennung von herausragenden Ingenieurleistungen.

Es ist zu wünschen, die Politik könnte mit guten Rahmenbedingungen dazu beitragen, dass neben der Sicherung einer bedarfsgerechten Verkehrserschliessung der Brückenbaukanton Graubünden mit weiteren Brückenkunstwerken bereichert und geschmückt wird.

Bridges, after all, are inseparable from our habitat. They are more than just badges of technical sophistication; they are attestations of our building culture, too. If designed well, they can become landmarks with a reach extending far beyond their actual span, lending their environs and perhaps even whole landscapes a new identity. Bridge builders thus have to engage explicitly with the question of how a particular bridge should look, not just in the space it occupies but as part of a larger landscape. The creation of a new bridge, in other words, is not just an engineering and economic challenge, but also a design challenge. Bridge building is thus a social mission that has a bearing on society as a whole; which is why building is ultimately a cultural act.

In 1991, taking account of the aforementioned aspects, Graubünden's cantonal government awarded the Bündner Kulturpreis to Christian Menn, the first civil engineer ever to receive it. In doing so, it honored Menn's wide-ranging practical and conceptual work as a bridge builder both in Graubünden and elsewhere, as well as his indefatigable efforts to promote Swiss engineering.

Bridges are a defining aspect of the landscapes we inhabit and hence of the public space. The population therefore has a right to bridges that are solidly engineered, durable, and pleasing to look at. It is up to us public administrators and policymakers to create the conditions needed for intelligent solutions to be found. It is a huge task that must involve those responsible for education policy and the training of innovative and enthusiastic civil engineers at the ETH as well as those in charge of competition, contracting, the awarding of prizes to exemplary structures, and public recognition of outstanding engineering achievements.

By creating favorable conditions, or so it is hoped, we politicians can help safeguard a road and rail infrastructure that fulfills the needs of all those who use it, while at the same time enriching a canton already famed for its bridges with still more stunning examples of the art of bridge building.

---

1 Christian Menn, «Die Kunst des Brückenbaus», in: Schweizerische Akademie der Wissenschaften SATW (Hg.), *Technoscope* 3/2000. **2** David P. Billington, *Robert Maillart und die Kunst des Stahlbetonbaus*, Zürich/München, Artemis 1990, S. 49. **3** Christian Menn, *Erfahrungen im Schweizer Betonbrückenbau,* Forschungsauftrag Astra 2012, S. 41. **4** Jörg Schlaich, Laudatio bei der Verleihung der Ehrendoktorwürde an Prof. Dr. Christian Menn durch die Universität Stuttgart am 2. Februar 1996.

1 Christian Menn, "Die Kunst des Brückenbaus", in Schweizerische Akademie der Wissenschaften SATW (ed.), *Technoscope* 3/2000. **2** Andrić, Ivo, "Bridges", quoted here from the translation by Amela Kurtović in *Spirit of Bosnia* Vol. 1, No. 1, 2006. **3** The reference is to William Tell and Arnold Winkelried, whose legendary self-sacrifice at the Battle of Sempach secured victory for the Old Swiss Confederacy against the Habsburgs. **4** David P. Billington, *Robert Maillart and the Art of Reinforced Concrete,* New York 1990, p. 49. **5** Christian Menn, *Erfahrungen im Schweizer Betonbrückenbau,* study for the Swiss Federal Roads Office, Bern 2012, p. 41 **6** Jörg Schlaich, laudatory speech at the awarding of an honorary doctorate to Prof. Christian Menn by the University of Stuttgart on February 2, 1996.

HARMONIE UND ELEGANZ AUS KALKÜL UND ÖKONOMIE
AN IDEAL BALANCE OF HARMONY AND ELEGANCE

WERNER OECHSLIN

Dass die Baukunst zum Glück und zur guten Lebensführung ganz wesentlich beitrage, schreibt Leon Battista Alberti am Anfang seines *De re Aedificatoria* (1452). Damit sind insbesondere Ingenieurwerke, Felsdurchbrüche, Flusskorrekturen und auch die Brücken gemeint. Wo immer man erfolgreich Brücken über Flüsse schlug, um Menschen und Kulturen miteinander zu verbinden, fand dies grösstes Lob und Anerkennung. Der neapolitanische Poet Jacopo Sannazzaro lobte seinen Freund Fra Giovanni Giocondo, der in Paris gerade eine Brücke über die Seine gebaut hatte, in doppeldeutiger Anspielung als *pontefice*. Und der, der diesen Titel trug, Papst Julius II., beauftragte Fra Giocondo kurz darauf mit einem Projekt für St. Peter. Brücken galten als Meisterleistungen und wurden wie Weltwunder – oder wie in Fischer von Erlachs *Historischer Architektur* (1721) in gleichem Atemzug mit ihnen – gepriesen. Carl Christian Schramm benutzte 1735 den Neubau der Elbbrücke in Dresden als Anlass, um ein Panorama des Brückenbaus «aus allen vier Theilen der Welt» im Sinne eines «historischen Schauplatzes» zu entwerfen. Brücken gehören zu den bedeutendsten und deshalb auch am meisten bewunderten Leistungen menschlicher Kultur. «Er ging noch weiter fort, als sich ein Mensch getraut…», lobt Schramm den kurz zuvor verstorbenen König August den Starken, weil er mit der Brücke zwischen Dresden und der Neustadt seine Kirch- und Schlossbauten noch übertroffen habe.

Als Paul Bonatz und Fritz Leonhardt für die populären *Blauen Bücher* den Band *Brücken* herausgaben und ihn mit zahlreichen Abbildungen versahen, von einer Schwebebrücke im Himalaja bis zur Golden Gate Bridge in San Francisco, stand auch dies im Zeichen der «Tatkraft der Menschen» und öffnete zugleich den Blick auf die Schönheit technischer Bauten, was sie denn auch gleich als «Eigenschönheit der Technik» – ganz im Sinne einer modernen Errungenschaft – herausstellten. Als ob hier eine alle Kulturen betreffende menschliche Leistung ihren Höhepunkt erreicht hätte! So sah es auch Le Corbusier, wenn er provokativ den Ingenieur auf den aufsteigenden und den Architekten auf den absteigenden Ast der Kulturentwicklung setzte, um dann doch beides, «deux choses solidaires», in ein Ganzes zusammenzuführen. Es ist die «esthétique de l'ingénieur», die für ihn im Vordergrund steht. Der Architekt und der Ingenieur finden in der gemeinsamen Wertschätzung der Geometrie zusammen. «Géométrie, géométrie», ruft er aus und

In the preface to his *De re Aedificatoria* of 1452, Leon Battista Alberti explains architecture's crucial contribution to human happiness and "convenience". Significantly, his definition of architecture includes what these days would count as engineering: "rocks cut, mountains bored through… rivers turned, their mouths cleared, bridges laid over them." All bridges built across rivers to connect the people and cultures on either side have reaped praise and recognition in their time. Deliberately punning on the two meanings of pontifex, the Neapolitan poet Jacopo Sannazzaro hailed his friend Giovanni Giocondo, builder of the Pont Notre-Dame across the Seine in Paris of 1507, as a *pontifice*. Another holder of the title, Pope Julius II, decided to commission the same Fra Giocondo with a project for St. Peter's just a short while later. Bridges were regarded as extraordinary feats and extolled as wonders of the world – or at any rate mentioned in the same breath as them, which is what Fischer von Erlach does in his *Historische Architektur* of 1721. When a new bridge across the River Elbe in Dresden was built in 1735, Carl Christian Schramm marked the occasion by publishing a series of engravings of "scenes of history" in the form of bridges "from all four corners of the world". Bridges do indeed rank among civilization's most significant and hence most widely admired accomplishments. "He ventured further than any man had yet dared…" wrote Schramm of the recently deceased Augustus the Strong, King of Saxony, in reference to the bridge linking Dresden to the Neustadt, which to his mind outshone all his many churches and palaces.

A book about bridges published by Paul Bonatz and Fritz Leonhardt in 1951 as part of the popular *Blaue Bücher* series – and richly illustrated with everything from a rope bridge in the Himalayas to the Golden Gate Bridge in San Francisco – also falls under the general heading of "humanity's heroic exploits". Part of its purpose was to make readers more appreciative of what the authors describe as the "inherent beauty of engineering" as one of the great achievements of the modern age. As if here the sum of all human endeavor had reached its apogee! This is certainly how Le Corbusier saw it, when he provocatively cast engineering and architecture as, "two things that march together and follow one from the other – the one at its full height, the other in an unhappy state of retrogression." It is the "aesthétique de l'ingénieur" to which Le Corbusier gives prominence. For what the architect and engineer have in common,

stellt sie wirksam als Antipoden der Poesie in den Vordergrund. Und Le Corbusier lässt Élie Faure, «un lyrique», fragen: «‹Pourquoi les ponts sont-ils si émouvantes?› Parce qu'au milieu de l'incohérence apparente de la nature ou des villes des hommes, un pont est un lieu de géométrie, un lieu où règne une effective mathématique.»

Gebaute und ästhetisch wirksame Mathematik! Das ist der Stoff, aus dem all die bewundernden Beschreibungen moderner und waghalsiger Brücken gemacht sind: «Miracolous elegance!» Für viele – Legenden beschwören es – sind Brücken Teufelswerk, ebenso wie Niccolò Paganinis Violinmusik. Hier spielt man Risiko und hält doch alles durch zuverlässige, dem Laien nur Staunen abverlangende Berechnung zusammen. Das steigert die Faszination. Es lässt umgekehrt verstehen, dass der Brückenbauer sich ungern für einen blossen Rechner halten lässt. Wie aber geht dies alles zusammen, das souveräne Spiel mit Linien und Formen und das sichere Kalkül? Robert Maillart, in dessen Werk Sigfried Giedion «science and the methods of art» vereinigt sah, ist dafür berühmt geworden, dass seine Brücken gleichsam aus der Intuition entstanden und erst hinterher berechnet worden seien. Dahinter verbirgt sich ein alter philosophischer Streit, der danach fragt, ob die *contemplatio* der *actio* vorausgeht oder ihr nicht vielmehr nachfolgt und sich in ihr vollendet. Le Corbusiers Überlegungen berühren durchaus solche Gedanken: Wie erfüllt sich, was der Mensch vollbringt, als seine Ordnung oder als Vollzug göttlicher Harmonie!

Hinter *calcul* und *économie* verbirgt sich noch eine ganz andere «kulturelle» Wirklichkeit, die Condillac in seiner *Langue des Calculs* (1798) darlegt. Er geht von der Einheit des Symbols – hier der Zahl – mit der bezeichneten Sache aus, sodass wir die abstrakten Vorstellungen «sehen» können. Weiter gedacht, wir erkennen, was wir womöglich noch gar nicht begreifen: «C'est la simplicité qui donne du prix à tout.» Die Einfachheit ist es, die ins Auge springt und die «d'un coup d'œil» erfasst wird. Auf diese Weise – und nicht kraft Einsicht in ein kompliziertes Zahlenwerk – hat auch Charles-Étienne Briseux 1752 die eleganten Proportionen der Palastfassaden Palladios erkannt. In der Tat ist es Eleganz, die auf diese Weise, als plausible und unmittelbar erkennbare Formqualität aufgefasst werden kann. Oder anders: Zahlen werden einem ästhetischen Ganzen und einem ganzheitlichen Eindruck zugeführt.

Folgt man der *Encyclopédie,* so ist der Begriff Eleganz von *eligere* (auswählen) abgeleitet, beruft sich also durchaus auf einen Vorgang der Selektion, aus dem resultiert, was die Eleganz ausmacht: «un résultat de la justesse & de l'agrément». Weil das *elegans signum,* ein (äusseres) Zeichen von Eleganz, so etwa eine entsprechende Linie und Kontur, mit im Spiel ist, verwies man in der *Encyclopédie* schnell auf die – dafür zuständige – Kunst. Und dort wird man schnell weiterverwiesen auf die Schönheit und die «délicatesse de l'exécution». Am Ende ist die Formgebung bis in jeden Linienzug und jeden Farbton hinein entscheidend dafür, dass die Eleganz – als eine ästhetische Qualität – wahrgenommen werden kann.

Der moderne Ingenieur hat zwar die neuesten technischen Mittel zur Verfügung, aber in seinem Tun und seiner darüber hinausweisenden Absicht steht er in einer langen Tradition, gemäss der er

he argues, is their shared love of geometry. "Géométrie, géométrie" he proclaims – and presents it as the very antithesis of poetry. It is Le Corbusier, moreover, who has the lyrically inclined Élie Faure ask: "'Pourquoi les ponts sont-ils si émouvantes?'" And then answers him as follows: "Parce qu'au milieu de l'incohérence apparente de la nature ou des villes des hommes, un pont est un lieu de géométrie, un lieu où règne une effective mathématique."

There we have it again: built, aesthetically pleasing mathematics! This is the stuff of which all the admiring descriptions of today's most hair-raising bridges are made: "Miraculous elegance!" For many, so legend would have it, bridges are the work of the Devil, rather like Niccolò Paganini's violin music. They are inherently risky undertakings held together by mathematical calculations that the uninitiated among us can only marvel at. This greatly adds to their fascination. And it also explains why bridge builders do not relish being regarded as mere number crunchers. But how does all this hang together – the assured modeling of lines and forms on the one hand and the sums underpinning them on the other? Robert Maillart, whose work, said Sigfried Giedion, united "science and the methods of art", became famous for creating bridges by intuition, as it were, and leaving the sums until later. Lurking behind this is the ancient philosophical debate of which comes first, *contemplatio* or *actio.* Le Corbusier's musings touch on much the same ideas: How is what man accomplishes actually fulfilled? Is it an order of his own creation or rather the consummation of divine harmony?

Hidden behind the words *calcul* and *économie* is a very different "cultural" reality, described by Étienne Bonnot de Condillac (1714–1780) in his *Langue des Calculs* of 1798. Condillac attributes our ability to "see" abstract ideas to the unity of the symbol – in this case the digit – with the thing it describes. Take this a stage further and we will no doubt recognize something that is perhaps beyond our ability to understand: "C'est la simplicité qui donne du prix à tout." What strikes us most forcefully, the "coup d'œil" in other words, is *simplicity.* It was this rather than any insight into the mathematics that enabled Charles-Étienne Briseux, writing in 1752, to appreciate the elegant proportions of Palladio's palace façades. For elegance can indeed be grasped as a plausible and instantly recognizable formal quality. Or to put it another way, numbers can indeed coalesce into an aesthetic whole and thus be subsumed in an overall impression.

Following the *Encyclopédie,* the term "elegance" is derived from *eligere,* meaning "to choose", and thus rests on the notion of selection, the outcome of which is what makes elegance so distinctive: "un résultat de la justesse & de l'agrément". Because *elegans signum,* an outward sign of elegance such as a particular line or shape, also has a role to play, the *Encyclopédie* wastes no time in referring readers to the entry for Art as the field responsible for such things. There, we are in turn referred to Beauty and the "délicatesse de l'exécution". What we are left with in the end is form, for it is form, down to every last line and color, that decides whether or not elegance as an aesthetic quality can be perceived.

dank Intelligenz und Scharfsinn *(argutezza)* einen Höchstgrad von zu überwindenden Schwierigkeiten mit spielerischer Eleganz vereinigt. Und weil er dabei jenseits von Zufälligkeit und Willkür *calcul* und *économie* einer Harmonie zuführt, ist er letztlich der *formgiver* universaler Gesetzmässigkeiten. Es ist in der Tat die «esthétique de l'ingénieur», die den Formwillen der Moderne, die über all die neuen technischen Möglichkeiten in zuvor nie erreichtem Ausmass verfügte, am besten zum Ausdruck gebracht hat. Und keiner hat dies mehr verkörpert als der Brückenbauer, in dessen Werk Können, Harmonie und Eleganz in idealer Weise zusammenfinden.

While today's engineers have cutting-edge technologies at their disposal, their actions and the intentions informing them are part of a long tradition of using intelligence and acuity *(argutezza)* to unite maximum difficulty with playful elegance. And because their work entails harmonizing *calcul and économie* in a way that is anything but arbitrary, they are ultimately the ones who lend shape to universal laws. For it is indeed the "esthétique de l'ingénieur" that, for all the unprecedented technical possibilities now open to us, best lends expression to Modernism's will to form. And no one epitomizes this more truly than the bridge builder whose work constitutes an ideal balance of harmony and elegance.

ZUR ARCHITEKTUR IM BRÜCKENBAU
ON ARCHITECTURE IN BRIDGE BUILDING

JOSEPH SCHWARTZ

«Es ist noch kein Meister vom Himmel gefallen.» Das altbekannte Sprichwort trifft auf den Entwurf von Brücken im Allgemeinen und auf die Mitwirkung von Architekten im Brückenbau ganz besonders zu. Die Frage nach der Zusammenarbeit von Ingenieur und Architekt stellte sich überhaupt erst nach der Aufspaltung des Berufs des Baumeisters, das heisst nach der Trennung der Disziplinen Architektur und Bauingenieurwesen im Laufe des 18. Jahrhunderts. Die Konsequenz dieses epochalen Schrittes wird besonders deutlich bei der Betrachtung des Tragwerksentwurfs als einen Prozess, der sich im Spannungsfeld zwischen gestalterischer Freiheit und physikalischer Notwendigkeit abspielt, mäandrierend zwischen den Aspekten der architektonischen Idee, der Tektonik des Lastens und der Tektonik des Fügens.

EMPIRIE UND WIRTSCHAFTLICHKEIT

Von der Antike bis zur Zeit der Industrialisierung waren Technik und Gestaltung im Bauwesen und somit auch im Brückenbau untrennbar miteinander verbunden. Sowohl die Einpassung in die Umgebung als auch die Anwendung von Stilen oder Ornamentik basierten auf intuitiven Prinzipien, beeinflusst vom Gefühl oder vom Zeitgeist der jeweiligen Epoche. Bereits die antiken Kulturen brachten sehr mutige und harmonische Bauwerke hervor, darunter auch Brücken – mit den Materialien und den Mitteln ihrer Zeit. Als Qualitätskriterien galten, wie es Vitruv, der grosse römische Baumeister und Schriftsteller bereits im 1. Jahrhundert vor Christus beschrieb, Robustheit, Nützlichkeit und Schönheit. Gefühl und Erfahrung waren die zur Verfügung stehenden Mittel. Die gestalterischen Belange im Brückenbau waren vergleichbar mit denjenigen des Hochbaus. Architektur entstand dabei auf natürliche Art und Weise im Sinne Vitruvs.

Nach der Trennung der Disziplinen Architektur und Bauingenieurwesen verlieh die in der zweiten Hälfte des 18. Jahrhunderts einsetzende Industrialisierung im 19. Jahrhundert dem Ingenieurberuf ungeahnten Aufschwung. Im Gleichschritt mit der Entwicklung der Baustatik wurde der Entwurf der Brückenbauwerke immer stärker von den Ingenieuren dominiert. Der Ausbau der Eisenbahnnetze machte eine Vielzahl von Brücken in grossem Massstab erforderlich, zuerst in Guss- und dann in Schmiedeeisen. Zeitgleich wurde der Stahlbeton entwickelt. Die Entwicklung des Brückenbaus

"No master ever fell from heaven," or so the saying goes. This is certainly true of bridge design in general and even more so of the involvement of architects in bridge building. The question of how engineers and architects might profitably collaborate did not arise at all until the eighteenth century, when the work of the masterbuilder split into two distinct disciplines: architecture and civil engineering. The consequences of that groundbreaking development are especially apparent in the perception of structural design as a process that steers a path between creative license at one extreme and physical necessity at the other, meandering along between architectural conceptualization and the tectonics of load-bearing structures and joints.

EMPIRICISM AND ECONOMICS

From Antiquity to the age of industrialization, engineering and design were inextricably linked in the business of construction, and hence in the business of bridge building, too. The molding of structures to their surroundings and application of specific styles or ornaments rested on intuitive principles, which in turn were influenced by the mood or zeitgeist of the period. Even ancient civilizations produced some very bold and harmonious structures – among them several bridges – using the materials and methods of their times. As the great Roman masterbuilder and writer Vitruvius explained as early as the first century B.C., utility, durability, and beauty were the three key criteria for measuring these, even if the only gauges available were intuition and experience. The design challenges posed by bridges were comparable with those posed by buildings. Architecture thus happened of its own accord, just as Vitruvius believed it should.

Industrialization, which began after the great schism between architecture and civil engineering in the second half of the eighteenth century and gathered pace in the course of the nineteenth, brought about an unprecedented boom in engineering. Paralleling developments in the structural design of buildings, bridge design became increasingly dominated by engineers. The expansion of the railway networks necessitated the construction of a number of very large bridges, made first of cast iron and then of wrought iron. Reinforced concrete was developed at around the same time. Bridge building thus developed in parallel to building generally, with iron

verlief parallel zum Hochbau: neben Stein- und Holzbauten waren Eisen und Beton zu salonfähigen Baumaterialien geworden. Die architektonischen Einflüsse der klassischen Moderne Anfangs des 20. Jahrhunderts wurden im Brückenbau mit weniger Widerstand aufgenommen als im Hochbau. Spielte das Ornament bei den Brücken des 19. Jahrhunderts noch eine wichtige Rolle, so rückte im 20. Jahrhundert die Konstruktion immer stärker in den Vordergrund.

Mit dem Fortschritt im theoretischen Wissen und der technischen Weiterentwicklung der Materialien sowie der Verbindungstechnologien ging sowohl im Beton- als auch im Stahlbau ein kontinuierlicher Fortschritt in den Bauweisen einher, der neben den Tragwerken selbst auch deren Bauvorgang betraf. So führte die Weiterentwicklung des Stahl- und Spannbetons im Zusammenspiel mit der Wirtschaftlichkeit der Gerüste und Schalungen zu Tragwerken mit immer flächigeren Bauteilen, namentlich Scheiben, Platten und Schalen. Nachdem über sehr lange Zeiträume Intuition, Empirie und Überlieferung von Erfahrung die Grundlage gebildet hatten beeinflussten erst in den letzten beiden Jahrhunderten zunehmend theoretische Hilfsmittel, die Erforschung der Baustoffe und die Wirtschaftlichkeit den Brückenbau. Eine immer wichtigere Rolle spielt seither das Verhältnis von Material- zu Lohnkosten.

PHYSIK UND ABSTRAKTION

Die Tatsache, dass diese Schwerpunkte primär im Arbeitsfeld der Ingenieure liegen, führte dazu, dass das Mitwirken der Architekten im Brückenbau vollständig in den Hintergrund rückte, was nicht nur in der Praxis, sondern auch in der Lehre seinen Niederschlag fand. So beschäftigen sich Architekturstudierende fast ausschliesslich mit Hochbauten; mit dem Brückenbau kommen sie dagegen, wenn überhaupt, nur ganz am Rande in Berührung. Die Bauingenieurstudierenden hingegen setzen sich weder mit der Frage des gebauten Raumes auseinander, noch haben sie Gelegenheit, die Werkzeuge des Entwerfens kennenzulernen. Soll das Tragwerk bei Hochbauten gezielt als Mittel zur Stärkung der architektonischen Idee eingesetzt werden – was selbstverständlich kein Kriterium für gute Architektur sein muss –, so ist die fruchtbare Zusammenarbeit zwischen Architekt und Ingenieur eine Grundvoraussetzung. Entscheidend ist dabei beider Haltung zum Entwurf: Gegenseitiges Verständnis und ein Öffnen über die Grenzen der eigenen Disziplin hinaus sind unumgänglich. Da bei Hochbauten der Bauingenieur nur einen Teil des Bauwerks, nämlich den Rohbau, entscheidend mitprägt, liegt die Leitung bei der Realisierung beim Architekten. Die wenigen Hochbauten, bei denen das Tragwerk als architektonisches Element gekonnt thematisiert wird, sodass nach Fertigstellung des Bauwerks tatsächlich nicht erkennbar ist, ob der architektonische Entwurf oder das Tragwerk zuerst vorhanden war, bleiben leider Ausnahmen beziehungsweise Glücksfälle.

Eine Brücke wird, wie jeder Hochbau auch, in eine Umgebung gesetzt, mit der sie in einen Dialog tritt. Proportionen, Materialisierung und Tektonik spielen ebenfalls eine wesentliche Rolle bei der Gestaltung der Brücke. Zwei Aspekte unterscheiden jedoch das Brückenbauwerk massgeblich vom Hochbau: Zum einen hat der In-

and concrete gaining widespread acceptance as materials alongside stone and timber. In the early days of the twentieth-century, moreover, bridge building proved more receptive to the architectural influences of Modernism than did construction generally. If ornamentation had played an important role in bridge building even as late as the nineteenth century, design increasingly took center stage as the twentieth century progressed.

The advances made both at the theoretical level and in the development of materials and joining technologies brought a steady stream of advances in concrete and steel construction affecting not just load-bearing structures themselves, but also the construction process. The further development of steel and prestressed concrete in conjunction with the economic advantages of frames and formwork led to load-bearing structures with ever flatter elements, specifically slabs, plates, and shells. After centuries in which intuition, empiricism, and the legacy of previous generations had provided the fundamentals, only in the last two hundred years have theoretical models, materials science, and economic factors had a role to play in bridge building. Since then, the ratio of material to labor costs has also become an increasingly important factor.

PHYSICS AND ABSTRACTION

The fact that these concerns fall primarily within the remit of the engineer has largely eclipsed the involvement of architects in bridge building and this has inevitably had knock-on effects in academia, too. Thus, students of architecture are almost exclusively preoccupied with buildings and come into contact with bridge building only tangentially, if at all. By the same token, few civil engineering students are required to address the question of built-up space, nor do they have an opportunity to acquaint themselves with design tools. If, for example, the load-bearing structure of a building is to be instrumentalized in support of a specific architectural concept—which is not of itself a criterion of good architecture of course—then fruitful cooperation between the architect and engineer is essential. The crucial factor is how the two stand in relation to the design; they must be on the same wavelength and have to be receptive to what lies beyond the bounds of their own discipline. As the civil engineer has a formative influence only on part of a given building, specifically the shell, responsibility for seeing the project through to completion lies with the architect. Those few buildings that succeed in making the load-bearing structure an aspect of the architecture so that on completion of the building, it is in fact impossible to say which came first, the architectural design or the load-bearing structure, unfortunately remain the exception rather than the rule – or are perhaps just a stroke of good luck.

Bridges, like buildings too, are placed in a larger context with which they enter into dialogue. Proportions, materials, and tectonics also play a crucial role in bridge design. Bridges nevertheless differ from buildings in two crucial respects: First, the inside of a bridge plays almost no role at all, and second, the load-bearing structure, how it is built, and all the related design aspects are *the* defining parameter for the design. Here, we see very clearly how

nenraum kaum eine Bedeutung, zum anderen wird das Tragwerk und dessen Bauvorgang, kombiniert mit den unzertrennlich damit zusammenhängenden konstruktiven Aspekten, zum wichtigsten, alles bestimmenden Entwurfsparameter. Genau hier wird erkennbar, dass ein Architekt in der Regel nicht in der Lage sein kann, im Brückenbau federführend aktiv zu werden. Das liegt nicht daran, dass er diese Aufgabe grundsätzlich nicht erledigen könnte, sondern dass ihm häufig die Ausbildung und die Erfahrung dazu fehlen.

Aber auch Bauingenieure können nur in Ausnahmefällen den Entwurf einer Brücke ganzheitlich angehen und die Aspekte der gestalterischen Freiheit und der physikalischen Notwendigkeit bewusst und gezielt ausspielen – im oben erwähnten Spannungsfeld zwischen der architektonischen Idee, der Tektonik des Lastens und der Tektonik des Fügens. Im Brückenbau wird unweigerlich die physikalische Notwendigkeit in Kombination mit der Tektonik des Tragens und des Konstruierens zu den treibenden Entwurfselementen. Quantifizierbar sind dabei lediglich die physikalischen Faktoren, wenn auch nur in Teilaspekten. Alle anderen Elemente sind wie bei jedem architektonischen Entwurf weder mess- noch optimierbar. Nur sehr wenigen Menschen ist die Gabe geschenkt, die nötige Sensibilität für die Tektonik des Tragens aufzubringen.

Wie soll aufgrund der Prinzipien der Stabstatik entworfen werden, wenn alle Stäbe zu Linien abstrahiert werden und deren wichtigste formgenerierende Dimension (die Querschnittsfläche und insbesondere deren Variation über die Stablänge) von Anfang an nicht in Erscheinung tritt? Wie soll entworfen werden, wenn der Einfluss der Form der einzelnen Tragelemente nicht veranschaulicht werden kann? Wie soll eine Parametervariation stattfinden können, wenn ausgehend von einem gewählten System Berechnungen durchgeführt werden, die undifferenziert und digital die alles entscheidenden Antworten geben sollen? Die Entwicklung der klassischen Baustatik ist in den letzten Jahrhunderten insofern ungünstig verlaufen, als dass die baustatischen Methoden eine zu absolute analytische und abstrakte Form angenommen haben.

Ein Ausweg aus dieser Situation könnte darin liegen, vermehrt Methoden anzuwenden, die den Verlauf der inneren Kräfte visualisieren. Auf einfache Art kann so der qualitative Einfluss der Form des Tragwerks auf den Verlauf und die Intensität der inneren Kräfte erkannt und damit eine Lösung entwickelt werden, bei der die Kräfte auf dem direkten Weg abgeleitet werden. Es wird dann auch möglich, einen Entwurfsprozess betreffend Zusammenspiel von Tragwerk und Umgebung einer Brücke durchzuspielen. Die grundlegende Konzeptidee des Entwurfes ist das Entscheidende, die statische Berechnung kann in dieser wichtigen Projektierungsphase in den Hintergrund treten, wichtig ist in erster Linie die Effizienz des Tragwerks und nicht nur das physikalische Gleichgewicht der inneren Kräfte, sondern vor allem auch das Gleichgewicht zwischen der Brücke und der Landschaft.

FEINGEFÜHL UND TEKTONIK
So folgen zwei zu den Frühwerken von Christian Menn zählende Brücken, die Letziwaldbrücke bei Avers und die Crestawaldbrücke

an architect cannot, as a rule, be the person in charge of a bridge-building project. Not because he or she would lack the wherewithal needed to do the job, but because in most cases he or she has not had the necessary training or gained the necessary experience.

Having said that, it is also true to say that only in exceptional cases can a civil engineer handle every aspect of bridge design, steering a path between creative license at one extreme and physical necessity at the other. After all, physical necessity combined with the tectonics of load bearing and design are bound to be the key driving factors in bridge building. But only physical factors are quantifiable, and then only in certain respects. The other elements, as in architectural design, are neither measurable nor can they be optimized. Sensitivity to the tectonics of load bearing is a gift with which very few are endowed.

How are we to follow the principles of the statics of rods when these same rods are abstracted to lines and their most important formative dimension (their cross-sectional area and how it varies over the length of the rod) is not apparent right from the start? How are we to design when the influence of the form of individual load-bearing elements cannot be visualized? How is there to be parameter variation when the calculations made on the basis of the system chosen to deliver all-important answers are undifferentiated and digital? To the extent that its methods have taken on an excessively absolutist analytical and abstract form, classical structural design can be said to have taken an unfavorable turn over the past few centuries.

One way out of this predicament could be the increased use of methods that visualize the flow of inner forces. This would allow the qualitative influence of the form of the load-bearing structure on the flow and intensity of these inner forces to be identified, which in turn would enable the development of solutions that divert the said forces by the most direct route. Dry runs of the design process to ascertain how the load-bearing structure of a bridge might interact with its surroundings would then be possible. The decisive factor is the underlying concept; getting the structural design right is not quite so important at this stage of the project. What counts most is the efficiency of the load-bearing structure – meaning not just the physical equilibrium of inner forces but also, and above all, the equilibrium of the bridge in the landscape.

SENSITIVITY AND TECTONICS
Two bridges that count among the early works of Christian Menn, namely the Letziwald Bridge near Avers and the Crestawald Bridge near Sufers, follow the same structural design principles as arched bridges. Because of differences in the topography, however, the two load-bearing structures are formulated in a radically different way. Whereas the influence of Robert Maillart's Salginatobel Bridge is especially apparent in the deck-stiffened arch of the Letziwald Bridge, the point of reference for the uprights supporting the roadway of the Crestawald Bridge was undoubtedly Maillart's Valtschiel Bridge. Both were designed with the utmost care and the visual outcome of the underlying concepts is impressive indeed. The concentrated

bei Sufers, den gleichen statischen Prinzipien der Bogenbrücken. Aufgrund der unterschiedlichen topografischen Gegebenheiten werden die beiden Tragwerke jedoch gegensätzlich formuliert. Bei der Letziwaldbrücke erfolgt die Aussteifung in Anlehnung an die Salginatobelbrücke von Robert Maillart vor allem durch den Bogen, bei der Crestawaldbrücke hingegen in Anlehnung an Maillarts Valtschielbrücke mit Hilfe des Fahrbahnträgers. Beide Brücken sind sorgfältig konstruiert, und das visuelle Resultat aus der konsequenten Umsetzung der Konzepte ist beeindruckend: Die Letziwaldbrücke erfährt eine angespannte Konzentriertheit, wie eine Wildkatze im Sprung überwindet sie die steil abfallende Schlucht, sodass der mutige Brückenschlag im schwierigen Gelände unterstrichen wird. Die Crestawaldbrücke besticht durch ihre grosse Transparenz und betont dadurch die Öffnung des Tals, indem sie entspannt in der Landschaft ruht.

Ganz anders verhalten sich die beiden späteren Werke Ganterbrücke und Sunnibergbrücke, als Schrägseilbrücken im Freivorbau erstellt. Hier wird das Konzept der Brücken nebst dem Einfügen in die Landschaft aus zwei sich aus den statischen Gegebenheiten ergebenden Erfordernissen abgeleitet: Ist es bei der Ganterbrücke der Kriechhang, auf den mit einer äusserst steifen Rahmenkonstruktion reagiert wird, so beeinflusst bei beiden Werken die Krümmung im Grundriss den Entwurf in entscheidender Weise. Aus einer physikalischen Notwendigkeit heraus wurden bei der Ganterbrücke die im Grundriss gekrümmt verlaufenden Schrägseile in Scheiben einbetoniert, sodass das Mittelfeld der Brücke als auf den Kopf gestellte Letziwaldbrücke in Erscheinung tritt. Bei der Sunnibergbrücke bestimmten die horizontalen Temperaturverformungen des fest mit den Widerlagern verbundenen Brückenträgers die Form der Stützen sowie das Gesamtkonzept der Brücke. Konnte die raue Ganterschlucht mit einem massiveren Bauwerk konfrontiert werden, so standen bei der Umfahrung Klosters Leichtigkeit und Transparenz zur Einfügung der Brücke in die Umgebung im Vordergrund. Beide Bauwerke sind tektonisch meisterhaft bearbeitet und die Entscheide in Bezug auf Proportionen und Gestaltung sind, basierend auf einer starken, durch Tragwerksüberlegungen beeinflussten Konzeptidee, mit viel Feingefühl erfolgt und ergeben sich keineswegs aus einem naturwissenschaftlichen Optimierungsprozess.

Selbstverständlich kann bei diesen vier Bauwerken die Intensität, mit der die Konzeptidee das ausgeführte Bauwerk ästhetisch beeinflusst, aus Sicht des bewussten Betrachters kontrovers diskutiert werden. Genau hier liegt die gestalterische Freiheit des Entwerfers, und es sind nicht zuletzt diese Entscheide, die den Brücken ihren einzigartigen Charakter verleihen. Die Beispiele belegen aber auch schön, welche Rolle die Architektur im Brückenbau spielt und wie schwierig es ist, diese Zusammenhänge in der Lehre zu vermitteln. Meister kann hier nur werden, wer sein Handwerk als Bauingenieur hervorragend beherrscht, ausserordentliches gestalterisches Gefühl mitbringt und sich so für die Belange des Gestaltens öffnet. Hier schliesst sich der Kreis: Es ist eben doch kein Meister vom Himmel gefallen. Wer sich nicht über eine längere Zeit ausdauernd und

tension of the Letziwald Bridge lends it the appearance of a wild cat leaping over a precipitous gorge, thus underscoring the sheer boldness of any attempt to span such difficult terrain. The Crestawald Bridge is remarkable more for its transparency. It opens up the valley and at the same time seems to be completely at ease in the landscape in which it rests.

Two later works by Menn, the cable-stayed cantilever Ganter Bridge and Sunniberg Bridge, work according to very different principles. The concept here was derived in part from the need for a structure that would harmonize with the surrounding landscape and in part from two requirements necessitated by the structural givens: in the case of the Ganter Bridge the creep of the valley sides, which called for an extremely stiff frame, and in the case of both bridges the bent layout of the roadway that they carry. The drooped cable stays of the Ganter Bridge were anchored in concrete slabs out of physical necessity with the result that the central span of the bridge would look like an upside-down version of the Letziwald Bridge. The horizontal thermal deformation of the girder firmly connected to the abutment piers of the Sunniberg Bridge defined the shape of the supports and with it the overall concept of the bridge. While the Ganter Gorge could be confronted with an even more massive structure, lightness and transparency were the two most important criteria defining the integration of the Sunniberg Bridge in the Klosters bypass project. Both structures are tectonic feats of the first order and the proportions and design were chosen with great sensitivity on the basis of a strong concept shaped by structural considerations rather than a scientific process of incremental optimization.

The degree to which the concept of the four examples cited influenced the aesthetics of the bridge actually built is of course open to debate. Yet it was here more than anywhere that the designer's artistic license came into play, this being by no means the least of the factors that lend these bridges their unique character. The examples are also persuasive testimony to the role of architecture in bridge building and as such point up the difficulty of teaching how the two are interconnected. Only someone who has mastered the art of civil engineering, but who being endowed with the creativity of a true artist is also receptive to aesthetic issues can hope to succeed here. Which brings us full circle, for it is indeed true that, "No master ever fell from heaven." No one who has not spent years of his or her life grappling with a particular challenge or task can hope to bring forth anything exceptional.

If only for this reason, the architectural tendencies in bridge building spawned by Postmodernism and Deconstructionism cannot be taken seriously. Deconstructivist approaches, in particular, read like a complete misunderstanding of what bridge builders actually do and tend to take the form of iconic self-projections on the part of would-be bridge builders, devoid of any context. That there are still civil engineers willing to support such dubious feats is unfortunate. This is where the great schism between architecture and civil engineering is most glaringly apparent. Not only is expertise dismissed as unimportant, but the professionalism of both civil engineers and architects is undermined and their academic status devalued.

hartnäckig mit einer Aufgabe auseinandergesetzt hat, wird nicht in der Lage sein, Hervorragendes zu leisten.

Schon aus diesem Grund sind architektonische Tendenzen im Brückenbau die sich etwa an die Postmoderne oder an den Dekonstruktivismus anlehnen, nicht ernst zu nehmen. Insbesondere bei der Anwendung dekonstruktivistischer Entwurfsansätze im Brückenbau scheint eine völlige Verkennung der eigentlichen Entwurfsaufgabe vorzuliegen. Das Resultat sind ikonenhafte und kontextlose Selbstinszenierungen selbst ernannter Brückenbauer. Schade, dass sich Bauingenieure finden lassen, die entsprechende Kraftakte unterstützen. Hier tritt die Spaltung des Baumeisters besonders augenfällig in Erscheinung: Es werden nicht nur fachliche Kompetenzen als unwichtig abgetan, sondern die Berufe des Bauingenieurs und des Architekten werden ausgehöhlt und ihr akademisches Wesen wird abgewertet.

Bauwerke im Allgemeinen und Brücken im Speziellen prägen als wichtige Kulturgüter unseren Lebensraum und unsere Gesellschaft. Nachhaltigkeit und Qualität im Bauwesen können sich nicht auf kurzfristige wirtschaftliche Kriterien beschränken. Gestalterische Nachhaltigkeit muss zwingend über die Lebensdauer der Brücke formuliert werden, und dies nicht nur unter Einbeziehung von Unterhalts- und Erneuerungskosten, sondern auch unter Berücksichtigung der gestalterischen Qualität. Unter diesem Aspekt sind Brückenbau und Architektur untrennbar miteinander verbunden. Es bleibt zu wünschen, dass sich sowohl Bauingenieure als auch Architekten, die sich mit Brückenbau beschäftigen, in Zukunft wieder stärker mit den kulturellen, gesellschaftlichen und ethischen Aspekten ihres Berufes auseinandersetzen. Dies könnte einerseits die Abwärtsspirale im Ansehen dieser Berufe stoppen und andererseits die Frage nach der Bedeutung der Architektur im Brückenbau in einem ganz anderen Licht erscheinen lassen.

Buildings generally and bridges in particular are cultural assets that shape society and the world we inhabit as do scarcely any other. Sustainability and quality in building cannot be reduced to short-term economic criteria. But artistic sustainability must be conceived of as a quality that will far outlast the bridge itself; it must be about more than just maintenance and repair costs; it must attest to the quality of the design itself. In this respect, bridge building and architecture are indeed inextricably linked. It remains for us to wish that in future years, both civil engineers and those architects who become involved in bridge building will engage more profoundly with the cultural, social, and ethical aspects of what they do. This could at any rate put a stop to the steady decline in the esteem in which they are held – which in turn would encourage us to consider the role of architecture in bridge building in a completely new light.

ENTWÜRFE UND BERATUNGEN NACH 1971
DESIGNS AND CONSULTANCY AFTER 1971

Nach seiner Berufung als Professor an die ETH Zürich im Jahr 1971 übergab Christian Menn sein Büro mit sämtlichen Aufträgen an die Ingenieure Hans Rigendinger und Walter Maag. An der ETH wurde er ein engagierter Hochschullehrer, bei dem Generationen von Ingenieuren ihr Handwerk lernten. Er war nun auch als Berater, Jurymitglied und Experte gefragt. Nach seiner Emeritierung 1992 wurde Menn wieder Entwerfer und Brückenbauer: Die Spannweiten seiner Brücken wurden wesentlich grösser und vielfältiger. Nach den Bogen- und Balkenbrücken stiess er jetzt in das Gebiet der Schrägseilbrücken vor, und es kamen vermehrt Aufträge aus dem Ausland. Besonders in den USA erregte Christian Menns Gestaltungswille Aufmerksamkeit, auch wenn mit der Leonard P. Zakim Bunker Hill Memorial Bridge in Boston nur eines seiner Projekte ausgeführt wurde. Dieses markiert dafür den Höhepunkt seines Schaffens.

In der folgenden Auswahl finden sich neben weltweit bekannten Brücken wie der Ganter- und der Sunnibergbrücke einige unrealisierte Projekte, etliche in den USA und eines in den Vereinigten Arabischen Emiraten.

Wie schon im Kapitel zuvor sind auch hier die von Christian Menn verfassten Texte in zwei Abschnitte unterteilt, die jedes Projekt aus unterschiedlichen Blickwinkeln präsentieren.

After his appointment as professor at the ETH Zurich in 1971, Christian Menn handed over his engineering company complete with all work in progress to the engineers Hans Rigendinger and Walter Maag. He became a dedicated teacher at the ETH and also a much-sought-after consultant engineer and jury member. On his retirement in 1992, Menn became a designer and builder of bridges once again. By that time spans had become longer and the range of bridge types more varied than before. Having designed numerous arch and beam bridges, he now ventured into cable-stayed bridges – and began receiving more and more contracts from abroad. In the USA, especially, Menn's brilliance as a bridge designer attracted attention, even if only one of his projects there was ever built, namely the Leonard P. Zakim Bunker Hill Memorial Bridge in Boston–the high-water mark of his achievements as a bridge builder.

The selection that follows includes both world-famous structures like the Ganter Bridge and Sunniberg Bridge as well as several projects that were not pursued, many of them in the USA, one in the United Arab Emirates.

As in the previous chapter, here too the texts by Christian Menn himself fall into two sections so that each project is presented from two different angles.

GANTERBRÜCKE, RIED-BRIG
GANTER BRIDGE AT RIED-BRIG

1977–1980

Client: Valais Department of Transportation
Project in partnership with Schneller-Schmidhalter-Ritz, Brig, Bloetzer+Pfammatter, Visp and Rigendinger/Maag, Chur

[17

LOCATION
Ried-Brig
Canton of Valais
Switzerland

COORDINATES
647 200 / 127 400

TYPE
Cable-stayed bridge

LENGTH:
678 m

HEIGHT
150 m

MAIN SPAN
174 m

OPENING
1980

Der Simplonpass war bereits zur Römerzeit bekannt. Zu einem stark genutzten Alpenübergang für Säumer wurde er im 17. Jahrhundert auf Betreiben von Kaspar Jodock von Stockalper, einem adligen Kaufmann und Politiker in Brig. 1801 liess Napoleon aus strategischen Gründen den Simplon als ersten alpenquerenden Pass der Schweiz zu einer Fahrstrasse ausbauen. Im hinteren Gantertal ist die Strasse bis zur alten Napoleonbrücke stark steinschlaggefährdet. In den 1970er Jahren wurde deshalb vom Tiefbauamt des Kantons Wallis ein Projekt ausgearbeitet, das den gefährdeten Abschnitt und die lange Schleife im Gantertal mit einem S-förmigen Strassenverlauf und einer fast 700 Meter langen und 150 Meter hohen Brücke umfährt. Der steile nördliche Abhang besteht im Bereich der Brücke aus zerklüftetem, brüchigem Fels. Der südliche Abhang ist wesentlich weniger steil; der Fels liegt hier jedoch sehr tief und ist mit stark durchnässtem Moränematerial und Hangschutt überdeckt. Im Durchschnitt bewegte sich der Hang zwei bis drei Zentimeter pro Jahr talwärts.

Die Linienführung sah für die Brücke eine S-Kurve mit einem geraden Mittelstück von 174 Metern Länge vor. Der Übergang von der Kurve zur Geraden befindet sich genau über der letztmöglichen Fundationsstelle im Fels unmittelbar neben dem Saltinabach. Als Tragsystem wurde deshalb im Hinblick auf die grosse Spannweite und Höhe in der Brückenmitte ein steifes Schrägkabelkonzept mit niedrigen Pylonen und in Flügelmauern einbetonierten Kabeln gewählt. Die 678 Meter lange Brücke weist acht Felder mit Spannweiten von 35 – 50 – 127 – 174 – 127 – 80 – 50 – 35 Metern auf.

The Simplon Pass was known as far back as the Roman age. In the 17th century, it was intensively promoted by Kaspar Jodock von Stockalper, a nobleman, businessman, and politician from Brig, in a busy crossing of the Alps for trade in goods carried by pack animals. Recognizing the strategic potential of this pass, Napoleon had the Simplon developed in 1801 into a road suitable for wheeled vehicles. This road, still in use, is subject to falling rock throughout the rear portion of the Ganter valley up to the old Napoleon Bridge. In the 1970s, the Public Works Department of the Canton of Wallis developed a plan to divert the long loop through the Ganter valley and this dangerous stretch of road with an S-shaped highway and a 700 m long, 150 m high bridge. Near the bridge, the steep north slope consists of brittle, fractured rock. Although the south slope is much less steep, the rock at this location is much deeper and is overlain with saturated moraine and scree. The slope displaces downward at an average of two to three centimeters per year.

The bridge is aligned on an S-curve with a 174 m long tangent portion in the middle. The transition from the curve to the tangent is located exactly at the last possible location for a foundation on rock before the Saltina Brook. Given the long span and height of the bridge at its midpoint, the bridge was designed as a stiff cable-stayed system with low towers above the deck and the stays cast into solid concrete walls. The 678 m long bridge has eight spans distributed as follows: 3 m, 50 m, 127 m, 174 m. 127 m, 80 m, 50 m, and 35 m.

[17 GANTERBRÜCKE, RIED-BRIG

Auf der orografisch rechten, nördlichen Talseite sind die Stützen in der erforderlichen Tiefe in den Fels eingebunden. Gegenüber, am südlichen Abhang, wurden offene Schächte erstellt, wobei das Gewicht des Aushubs etwa dem Auflagerdruck der jeweiligen Stütze entspricht. Von den Schächten aus wird der Hang zusätzlich zur Oberflächendrainage entwässert. Alle Stützen sind auf Lager gestellt, damit die Stützenfüsse der Kriechbewegung des Hanges entsprechend nachgestellt werden können. Mit der intensiven Entwässerung konnte der Hang jedoch nach der anfänglichen Drainage-Nachsetzung weitgehend konsolidiert und stabilisiert werden.

Der Fahrbahnträger weist einen rechteckigen Kastenquerschnitt ohne Konsolen auf. Die Trägerabspannungen mit vorgespannten Betonscheiben wirken massiv, sind aber in der schroffen Gebirgslandschaft vertretbar. Aus technischer Sicht sollten mit dem gewählten konstruktiven Konzept ein steifes Tragsystem sowie ein guter Schutz der Spannkabel gegen Ermüdung und Korrosion erreicht werden.

In den im Grundriss gekrümmten Randfeldern erzeugen die Längsspannungen in den Dreiecksscheiben Umlenkkräfte, die als Drehmomente in den oberen Kastenecken auf den Träger wirken und dort integrierte Torsionsmomente ergeben, die von den Hauptstützen übernommen werden. Der obere Rand der Dreieckscheiben war ursprünglich aus ästhetischen Gründen entsprechend der geschwungenen Linienführung der Strasse als leicht ausgerundet vorgesehen. Leider wurden aber bei der Ganterbrücke nicht alle Details einwandfrei durchgestaltet. So wurde in den Brückenträger ein nutzloses Enteisungssystem mit einer Salzlösung eingebaut; das empfindliche System korrodierte bald und verursachte schwere Schäden im Trägerkasten und an den Stützen.

[17 GANTER BRIDGE AT RIED-BRIG

On the north side of the valley, the piers are founded on rock at the required depth. On the south side, in contrast, open shafts were constructed so that the weight of the material excavated for a given shaft was approximately equal to the reaction from the pier at that location. The slope surrounding the shafts was also drained. The piers were founded on bearings to enable the base of the piers to be displaced to compensate for the creep displacements of the slope. As a result of the intensive drainage of the slope and the settlement thus produced, however, the slope was effectively consolidated and stabilized which eliminated the need to displace the base of the piers.

The girder consists of a rectangular box cross-section without deck slab cantilevers. Although the concrete walls containing the prestressed stay cables appear massive, they make sense visually in their rugged mountain setting. From a technical perspective, this massive detail produces a stiff structural system as well as good protection of the cables against fatigue and corrosion.

In the side spans, which are curved in plan, the longitudinal stresses in the triangular walls produce deviation forces which induce torque in the upper corners of the box girder. These forces in turn produce torsional moments in the girder, which are reacted at the main piers. The upper edges of the triangular walls were originally lightly rounded for aesthetic reasons, to correspond to the curved alignment of the highway. Unfortunately, not all of the details on the Ganter Bridge were perfectly worked out. For example, a useless de-icing system using a salt solution was provided in the girder. The sensitive system corroded soon after it was installed and caused severe damage to the box girder and the piers.

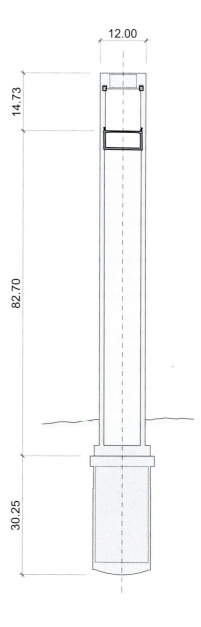

[17 GANTERBRÜCKE, RIED-BRIG / GANTER BRIDGE AT RIED-BRIG

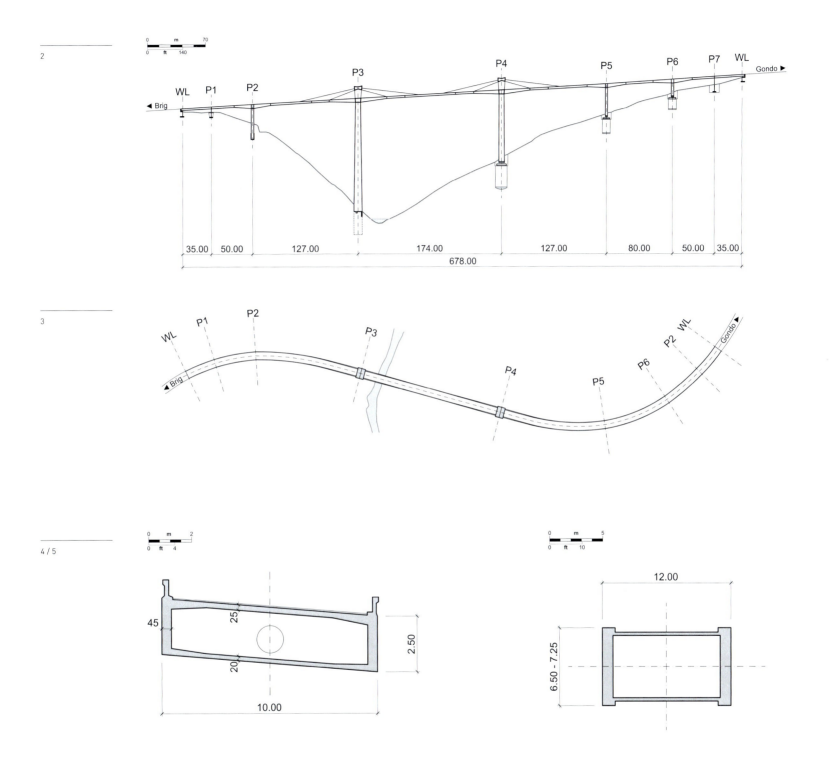

1 Querschnitt Ansicht P4 / Cross-sectional view P4
2 Längsschnitt / Longitudinal section
3 Grundriss / Plan
4 Querschnitt / Cross section
5 Bogenquerschnitt / Arch cross section

VIADOTTO DELLA BIASCHINA, GIORNICO
VIADOTTO DELLA BIASCHINA AT GIORNICO

1979–1983

Client: Ticino Department of Transportation
Project in partnership with Guzzi AG, Locarno/Zurich

[18

LOCATION
Giornico
Canton of Ticino
Switzerland

COORDINATES
709 100 / 142 200

TYPE
Beam bridge /
Cantilever construction

LENGTH
660 m

HEIGHT
110 m

MAIN SPAN
160 m

OPENING
1983

In der unteren Leventina fällt eine enge, über 100 Meter hohe Geländestufe in die Talebene von Bodio/Biasca ab. Die Stammlinie der Gotthardbahn überwindet die Geländestufe mit zwei Kehrtunneln. Die Gotthard-Autobahn A2, die hier in Fahrtrichtung Süd zwei Fahrspuren und in Fahrtrichtung Nord drei Fahrspuren aufweist, erreicht die Geländestufe im Norden über zwei getrennte, relativ weit auseinander liegende Tunnel. Die Bergspur wird auf einer 660 Meter langen Brücke geführt, die Talspur-Brücke misst 580 Meter. Beide Zwillingsbrücken wurden im Freivorbau erstellt und überqueren das Tal in einer Höhe von 100 Metern. Im Süden folgt ein 950 Meter langer Hangviadukt, der die A2 in gleichmässigem Gefälle in die Talebene führt.

Bei einem konstanten, möglichst schmalen Mittelstreifen wäre eine Bogenbrücke mit nur einem Bogen für beide Fahrrichtungen verlockend, ästhetisch besser und technisch interessant gewesen. Aber bei getrennten, in Längsrichtung versetzten Brücken wäre der Kostenaufwand wesentlich grösser als der mögliche ästhetische Vorteil gewesen.

As one descends the lower Leventina Valley from Bodio to Biasca, the elevation decreases by over 100 m. The main line of the Gotthard railway accommodates this steep drop by means of two spiral tunnels. The Gotthard Freeway A2, which has two southbound lanes and three northbound lanes, approaches the drop from the north through two relatively widely spaced tunnels. The northbound lanes are carried by a 660 m long bridge. The southbound lanes are carried by a 580 m long bridge. The twin bridges were built in cantilever construction and cross the valley at a height of 100 m. To the south, there is a 950 m viaduct following the contours of the side of the valley, which carries the A2 to the valley floor at a uniform gradient.

If the bridge had had a narrow, constant width median, an arch bridge with a single arch for both directions of traffic would have been aesthetically enticing and technically interesting. For bridges that must be separate and offset longitudinally, however, the cost of such a solution would have been significantly greater than the aesthetic benefits.

[18] VIADOTTO DELLA BIASCHINA AT GIORNICO

The main span length is 160 m for both bridges. At the middle of each bridge, the piers are about 100 m tall. In addition to the usual problems of cantilever construction, such as the module for anchoring the traveler, the module for arranging tendons and mild reinforcement, calculation of girder camber during construction (in this case, a maximum of 266 mm for a 66 m cantilever), and the procedures for placing concrete, wind loading played a critical role, especially during construction.

The wind speed was first measured at two different elevations at the bridge site over a period of a year and a half. These values were compared with long-term observations from neighbouring weather stations at Lugano, Piotta, and Lodrino. Using the exposure coefficient (which accounts for elevation above ground) from the Swiss standard SIA 160, the design value of wind speed for a five-second gust speed at the height of the girder was determined to be 47 m/s for a assumed return period of 50 years. During construction, i.e., for a return period of five years, the design value of wind speed was 42 m/s, which corresponded to a wind pressure of 1.1 kN/m2. The imposing twin bridges can be seen by passengers on the Gotthard Railway from several angles and elevations as the train passes through its spiral tunnels. Aesthetics were therefore an important consideration during design. The columns are elegant, but somewhat heavy looking. More slender columns would, however, have required more precise wind measurements and wind tunnel testing. The appearance of the bridge could have been improved to some extent through piers of greater visual slenderness but thicker walls, and through better details of the connection between girder and piers. Altogether, though, the bridge concept, setting, and costs are in an acceptable balance.

[18   VIADOTTO DELLA BIASCHINA, GIORNICO / VIADOTTO DELLA BIASCHINA AT GIORNICO

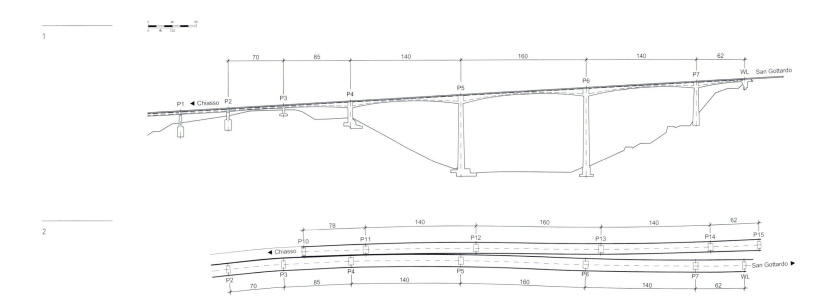

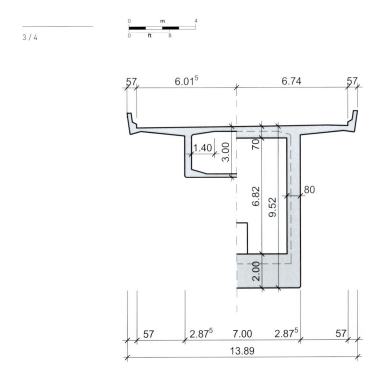

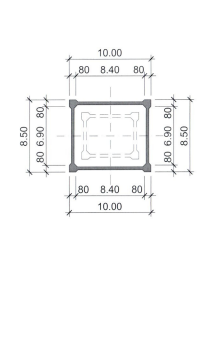

1 Längsschnitt / Longitudinal section
2 Grundriss / Plan
3 Querschnitt / Cross section
4 Pfeilerquerschnitt / Column cross section

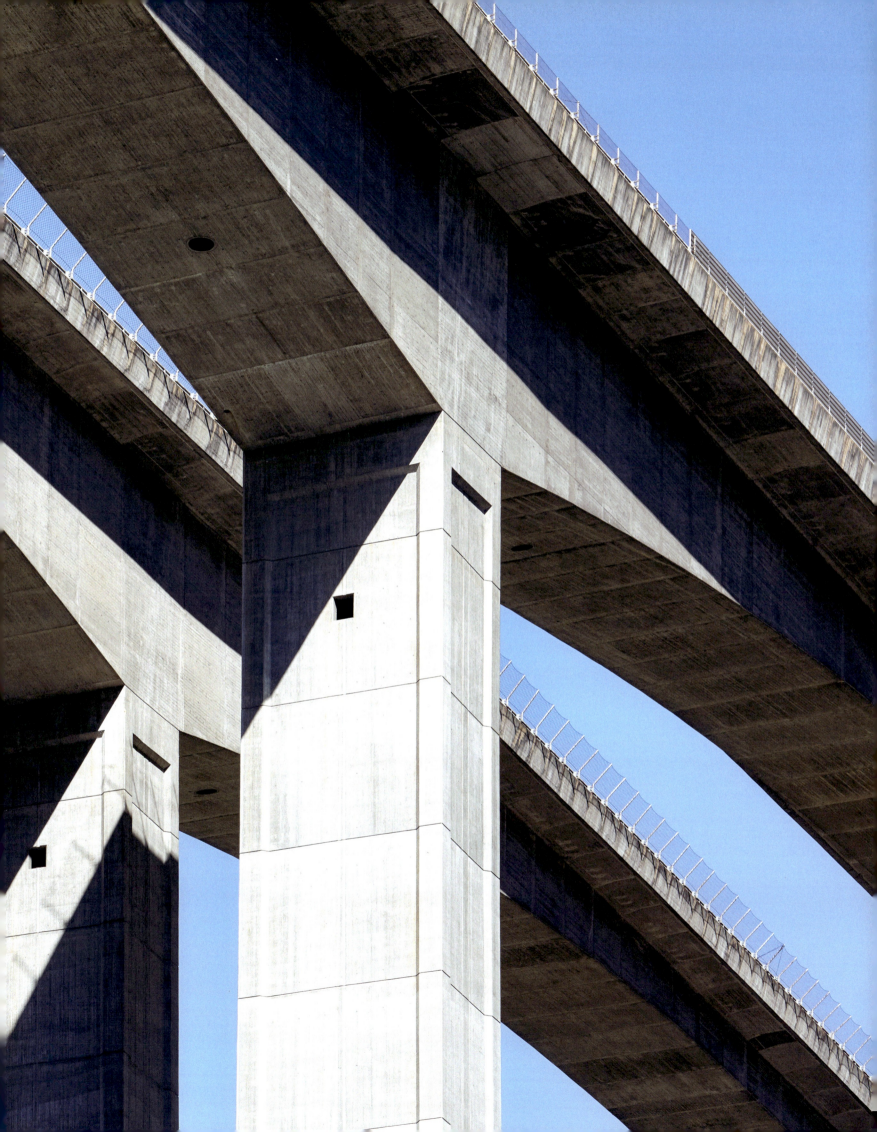

PONT DE CHANDOLINE, SION
CHANDOLINE BRIDGE AT SION

1987–1989

Client: Valais Department of Transportation
Project in partnership with KBM de Kalbermatten Burri Missbauer,
Sion und Rigendinger/Maag, Chur

[19

LOCATION
Sion
Canton of Valais
Switzerland

COORDINATES
594 300 / 119 200

TYPE
Cable-stayed bridge

LENGTH
284 m

MAIN SPAN
140 m

OPENING
1989

Zwischen den Anschlüssen Sion-Ost und Sion-West überquert die Autobahn A9 mit dem 284 Meter langen Pont de Chandoline in geringer Höhe und sehr spitzem Winkel die Rhone. Die Brücke ist im Grundriss leicht gekrümmt. Da die Autobahn östlich der Brücke aus einem Tagebautunnel aufsteigt, ist der Lichtraum zwischen dem mittleren Wasserspiegel und der wenig über der Dammkrone liegenden Unterseite des Brückenträgers nur etwa 5 Meter hoch. Das verhältnismässig kleine Lichtraumprofil hatte zur Folge, dass die Anzahl der Pfeiler im Fluss trotz der beträchtlichen Versetzung längs der Rhone auf zwei beschränkt wurde. Pfeiler im Damm waren aus flussbautechnischen Gründen nicht zulässig. Weiter wurde vorgeschrieben, dass die Sohlen der Pfeilerschächte 25 Meter unter der Sohle der Rhone liegen müssen. Für den Fall einer Dammerosion war diese Vorgabe zusammen mit den auf der Dammkrone liegenden Widerlagerfundamenten kaum zu vereinbaren. Bei diesen Rahmenbedingungen eignete sich eine dreifeldrige (72–140–72 Meter), insgesamt 284 Meter lange Schrägkabelbrücke mit zwei Zentralpylonen am besten. Zu beachten war allerdings noch die zulässige Pylonhöhe von 31 Metern wegen des nahe gelegenen Flugplatzes.

Between the Sion-East and Sion-West interchanges, the 284 m long Chandoline Bridge enables the A9 freeway to cross the Rhone. This is a low-level crossing at a sharp skew angle, with a slight curve in plan. Since the freeway emerges from a cut and cover tunnel close to the east end of the bridge, the underside of the bridge is only slightly above the crest of the existing levee and only 5 m above the average water level of the Rhone. Because of the small clearance envelope, and in spite of the significant shift along the river due to the skew angle, the number of piers in the river was limited to two. Piers in the river banks were not allowed for hydraulic reasons. Specifications required that the bottom of the shaft foundations were to be located 25 m below the bed of the Rhone. (This requirement, which implied massive scouring of the river bed and banks, was totally inconsistent with the location of abutment foundations on the crown of the levees, which would presumably be likewise severely affected by such a scour event.) Given these constraints, the most suitable solution was a cable-stayed bridge with two central towers and three spans of 72 m, 140 m, and 72 m, for a total length of 284 m. It was necessary to limit the height of the towers to 31 m due to the proximity of an airport.

[19 PONT DE CHANDOLINE, SION]

Die extrem tiefen Fundationen der beiden Pylonpfeiler erfolgten in kreisförmigen, spundwandgeschützten Senkkästen mit einem Durchmesser von 12,5 Metern. Die Pfeiler haben ebenfalls einen kreisförmigen Querschnitt mit einem Durchmesser von 6 Metern und am Kopf weisen sie ein kleines Kapitell für die Platzierung der Betongelenke auf, die für eine nominelle Last von 80 000 kN bemessen sind.

Der insgesamt 27 Meter breite Querschnitt des 2,5 Meter hohen Brückenträgers besteht aus einem 6 Meter breiten Kasten in der Brückenachse, beidseitigen, ebenfalls 6 Meter breiten, mit fachwerkartigen Streben gestützten Auskragungen und schliesslich 4,5 Meter breiten Kragplatten der Fahrbahn. Die Schrägkabel sind unten im zentralen Trägerkasten verankert und oben – entsprechend einem klassischen konstruktiven Konzept – so, dass ein Kabel aus dem Mittelfeld beidseits mit zwei kleineren Kabeln aus dem Randfeld überlappt. Die Anordnung hatte einen entscheidenden Einfluss auf die Breite der Pylone, die mit bei den Widerlagern verankerten Einzelkabeln in Querrichtung stabilisiert werden. Die Eigenlast erzeugt mit den Schrägkabeln an den Pylonen Ablenkkräfte in Querrichtung; die dadurch erzeugten Querbiegemomente werden von den Stabilisierungskabeln reduziert. Im Brückenträger entsteht wegen der kleinen Biegemomente nur eine sehr kleine Torsion. Einseitige Verkehrslast bewirkt dagegen ein Drehmoment und aufsummiert relativ grosse Torsionsmomente, die bei den Widerlagern und den Pylonpfeilern aufgenommen werden. Bei diesem Lastfall werden jedoch die Stabilisierungskabel der Pylone nicht beansprucht.

Der Pont de Chandoline vermittelte wertvolle Erfahrungen bezüglich Gestaltung, die mehr als zehn Jahre später bei Planung und Bau der Leonard P. Zakim Bunker Hill Memorial Bridge in Boston (vgl. Seite 246 ff.) von grösstem Nutzen waren.

Bei einer exponierten Brücke müssen unbedingt ein genügend grosses Modell des Gesamtbauwerks, Modelle wichtiger Details sowie Computer-Visualisierungen mit dem Umfeld erstellt werden. Die Pfeiler unter dem Fahrbahnträger und der darüber stehende Pylon sollten die gleiche Querschnittscharakteristik aufweisen. Zwillingskabel sollten bei fächer- und halbfächerförmiger Kabelanordnung vermieden werden, da in der Schrägansicht verwirrende Kabelüberschneidungen auftreten. Überlappungsverankerungen am Pylon erfordern viel Platz und sind meistens konstruktiv viel aufwändiger als direkte Stahlverbindungen zwischen den Verankerungen. Seitliche Abspannungen der Pylone mit einzelnen Kabeln stören das Erscheinungsbild.

[19 CHANDOLINE BRIDGE AT SION]

The extremely deep foundations of the two tower piers were circular shafts with a diameter of 12.5 m, built within cofferdams. The piers have a 6 m diameter circular cross-section. The tops of the piers are flared to form capitals to accommodate concrete hinges which provide the connection to the girder. These hinges are dimensioned for a nominal load of 80 000 kN.

The 27 m wide cross-section of the 2.5 m deep girder consists of: (1) A central 6 m wide box, (2) on either side of the box, a 6 m deck slab supported on inclined struts, and (3) at the outer edges, 4.5 m wide cantilever slabs. The lower ends of the stays are anchored inside the box. At their upper ends, the stays are anchored in the tower in a commonly used symmetrical arrangement, by which a given single stay originating from the main span is anchored between a pair of matching stays originating from the side span. This arrangement determined the width of the tower. The dead load of the curved girder produces transverse deviation forces in the tower, since the stays do not form a single vertical plane. The transverse bending moments in the tower thus produced were reduced through the provision of individual stabilizing cables extending from the tower to the edges of the deck at the abutments. The girder carries very little dead load torsion was a result of the relatively small bending moments due to this load. On the other hand, the live load applied to one side of the girder creates torque and relatively large torsional moments, which are reacted at the abutments and the tower piers. This load case produces no stresses in the stabilizing cables.

The Chandoline Bridge provided valuable experience in the design of major cable-stayed bridges, which proved very useful ten years later in the design and construction of the Leonard P. Zakim Bunker Hill Memorial Bridge in Boston.

The primary lessons learned are as follows: For visually exposed bridges, a sufficiently large model of the entire structure, models of important details, and computer visualizations of the bridge and its surroundings must absolutely be created and used. The piers below the girder and the tower above should have the same cross-section characteristics. Twin stays should be avoided in fan and half-fan arrangements, since they lead to confusing visual impressions in foreshortened views of the bridge due to the intersections of stays. Overlapping anchorages of stays at the tower require considerable room. The associated details are more expensive than direct steel connections between anchors. Individual stays used to stabilize the tower disturb the appearance of the bridge.

[19 PONT DE CHANDOLINE, SION / CHANDOLINE BRIDGE AT SION

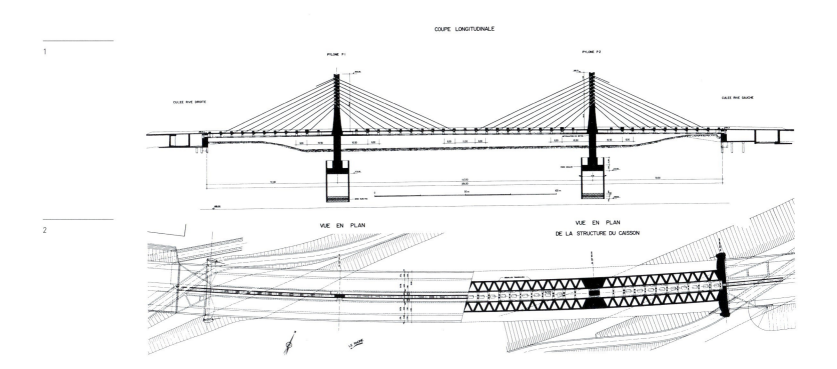

1 Längsschnitt / Longitudinal section
2 Grundriss / Plan
3 Querschnitt / Cross section

LEONARD P. ZAKIM BUNKER HILL MEMORIAL BRIDGE, BOSTON
LEONARD P. ZAKIM BUNKER HILL MEMORIAL BRIDGE IN BOSTON

1998 – 2002

[20

LOCATION
Boston, MA, United States

TYPE
Cable-stayed brigde

LENGTH
395 m

MAIN SPAN
227 m

OPENING
2002

Client: Massachusetts Department of Transportation
Project in partnership with Bechtel / Parsons Brinckerhoff, Boston,
HNTB Corporation, Boston and Wallace Floyd Associates,
Architects, Boston

Die Interstate Autobahn I-95, die entlang der amerikanischen Ostküste von Miami über Washington, New York und Boston an die kanadische Grenze führt, umfährt Boston im Westen in einem grossen Bogen. Im Osten führte eine stark überlastete Verbindung mit unzähligen Anschlüssen durch das auf einer alten Aufschüttung liegende Stadtzentrum. In den 1980er Jahren erarbeitete das Massachusetts Department of Transportation (MassDOT) ein ehrgeiziges, Central Artery Tunnel genanntes Projekt: Die Stadtautobahn sollte auf einer Länge von etwa 4 Kilometern mitsamt dem Flughafen-Anschluss als Interstate I-93 in Tunnel unter dem Grundwasserspiegel verlegt werden. Nördlich des Geschäftszentrums taucht die Autobahn auf und muss über eine zehnspurige Brücke über den Charles River geführt werden. Die Lage der Brücke war einerseits fixiert durch die Gleisanlagen der North Station und andererseits durch die benachbarten Schleusen, die den durch die Gezeiten schwankenden Wasserstand in den westlichen Flussbecken ausgleichen. Ausserdem erforderten unvermeidliche Bootsmanöver im Bereich der Brücke eine stützenfreie Überquerung des Flusses.

Am 15. Februar 1991 wurde ich zu einem Vortrag über Brückenbau an die Harvard University in Cambridge bei Boston eingeladen. Nach dem Vortrag wurde ich vom Inhaber des Bostoner Architekturbüros Wallace Floyd Associates (WFA) angefragt, ob ich als technischer Berater am Projekt mitwirken möchte. Die Beratung konzentrierte sich immer mehr auf die Überquerung des Charles River.

Der Entwurf der Brücke folgte neben der erforderlichen Spannweite noch vielen anderen Randbedingungen: Die noch bestehende Fachwerkbrücke durfte bis zur Eröffnung der neuen Brücke nicht abgebrochen werden; bei der Fundation der Brücke musste der Verlauf der U-Bahn berücksichtigt werden; unter der Brücke war ein Lichtraumprofil für die Schifffahrt vorgeschrieben; südlich der Brücke musste die Höhenlage der Tunneleinfahrt eingehalten werden; die maximale Steigung auf der Brücke war ebenfalls vorgeschrieben. Und nicht zuletzt sollte an dieser exponierten Lage grosses Gewicht auf die Ästhetik der Brücke gelegt werden.

Nach vielen, zum Teil fragwürdigen Entwurfsvarianten der Planungsfirmen und langen Diskussionen überzeugte schliesslich mein mit einem Modell präsentierter Entwurf die Politiker, das MassDOT sowie die einflussreiche Bostoner Bürgerrechts-Vereinigung von Architekten, Juristen und Wirtschaftsvertretern.

Interstate Highway I-95, which follows the U.S. east coast from Miami to the Canadian border, bypasses Boston to the west in a large loop. Freeway traffic passing through the city center follows Interstate 93, a freeway built to a large extent on fill, and incorporating a large number of interchanges. In the 1980s, the capacity of the I-93 freeway no longer satisfied current traffic demands. The Massachusetts Department of Transportation (MassDOT) therefore developed an ambitious project, called the Central Artery/Tunnel, which would relocate I-93 into a 4 km long tunnel under the water table together with a new link to the airport. North of Boston's commercial center, the freeway would emerge and cross the Charles River with new a ten-lane bridge. The location of the bridge was fixed between existing railway tracks coming from North Station to one side, and to the other side by existing locks which maintain the water level in the basin to the west. Navigational requirements on the Charles River dictated a crossing without piers in the water.

On February 15, 1991, I was invited to Harvard University to give a lecture about bridge building. After the lecture, I was asked by partners of the Boston architecture firm Wallace Floyd Associates to work with them on the Central Artery/Tunnel project as a technical advisor. My contribution focused on the crossing of the Charles River.

The design of the bridge followed from the required clear span length, as well as many other constraints: The existing steel truss bridge could not be demolished until the new bridge was put into service, the existing subway alignment needed to be considered in the arrangement of foundations, vertical clearance for navigation needed to be provided under the bridge, the elevation of the entrance to the tunnel south of the bridge had to be maintained, and the roadway gradient could not exceed specified maximum values. Last but not least, the visual impact of this highly exposed bridge was regarded as extremely important.

After long discussions of a large number of alternative designs developed by the consultant team, many of which were of questionable value, I presented my design with the help of a scale model. This design quickly convinced the politicians, MassDOT, and an influential Boston citizens' group composed of architects, lawyers, and business representatives.

[20 LEONARD P. ZAKIM BUNKER HILL MEMORIAL BRIDGE, BOSTON

Der Entwurf der 400 Meter langen, zehnspurigen Brücke, die sich nach Norden als Hochstrasse fortsetzt, sah erstmals in Amerika ein hybrides, asymmetrisches Schrägkabeltragwerk vor. Die 84 Meter langen Randfelder wurden als Gegengewichte in Beton und das 227 Meter lange Hauptfeld in Stahl-Beton-Verbund hergestellt. Die Y-Pylone stehen symmetrisch über der Fahrbahn der achtspurigen I-93 und die zweispurige Auffahrtsrampe wurde seitlich der Pylone angeordnet. Mit diesem Grundkonzept liessen sich gleichzeitig statisch-konstruktive, wirtschaftliche und ästhetische Vorteile erzielen. Die Spannweite und die Beanspruchung der Querträger der Fahrbahn wurden markant reduziert und damit die enorme Breite der Brücke visuell vermindert. Es ergaben sich sehr schöne Verhältnisse zwischen Höhe und Breite des Pylons sowie zwischen dessen Breite und der Hauptspannweite.

Ein paar kleine, nicht durchweg wünschenswerte gestalterische Änderungen hatten keinen nennenswerten Einfluss auf das Erscheinungsbild der Brücke, das hauptsächlich von den bestechenden Proportionen und der sowohl originellen wie auch erforderlichen Anordnung der Schrägkabel geprägt ist. Der Gouverneur von Massachusetts und der Bürgermeister von Boston bezeichneten die Brücke als «great new landmark for the city», der Vorsteher der Architekturschule am Massachusetts Institute of Technology nannte sie «an instant icon» und die zuvor skeptischen Bürger Bostons waren von der neuen Brücke fast ausnahmslos begeistert.

[20 LEONARD P. ZAKIM BUNKER HILL MEMORIAL BRIDGE IN BOSTON

The bridge is a 400 m long, ten lane structure which connects to an elevated highway at its north end. It is the first example in America of a hybrid, asymmetrical cable-stayed structure. The 84 m long side spans were designed as counterweights in concrete, whereas the 227 m long main span was designed as a lighter steel/concrete composite system. The inverted Y towers stand symmetrically over the roadway of the eight lane I-93. A two-lane off ramp, located to one side of the tower, is also carried by the structure. This fundamental concept enabled the structural, economic, and aesthetic goals to be achieved. The span lengths and the forces in the transverse girders of the deck were significantly reduced. The visual impact of the enormous width of the bridge was significantly reduced. The concept incorporated visually elegant relations between the height and width of the towers, and between the width of the towers and the main span length.

A few small, undesirable changes were made to the original design. These, however, had no significant effect on the appearance of the bridge, which is defined primarily by the brilliant proportions and the original arrangement of the stays developed in response to the functional requirements. The Governor of Massachusetts and the Mayor of Boston called the bridge a "great new landmark for the city". The Dean of the School of Architecture at MIT called it "an instant icon", and the previously skeptical citizens of Boston were almost unanimously enthusiastic about their new bridge.

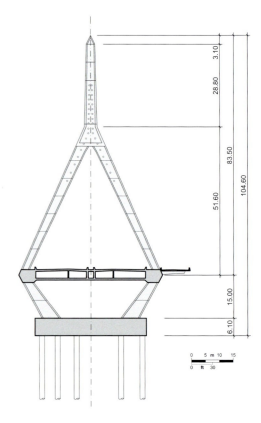

1 Pfeiler P2 / Column P2
2 Längsschnitt / Longitudinal section
3 Grundriss / Plan
4 Querschnitt / Cross section

[20 LEONARD P. ZAKIM BUNKER HILL MEMORIAL BRIDGE, BOSTON / LEONARD P. ZAKIM BUNKER HILL MEMORIAL BRIDGE IN BOSTON

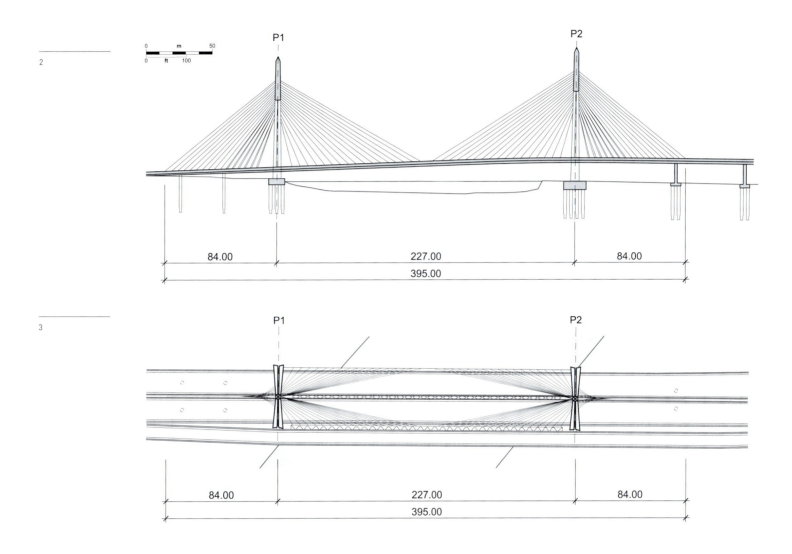

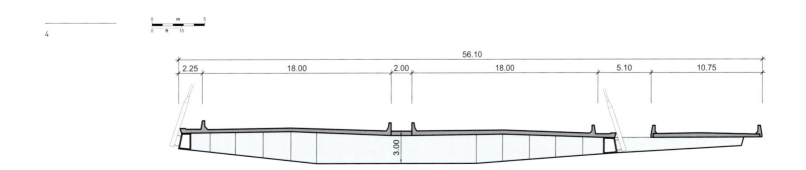

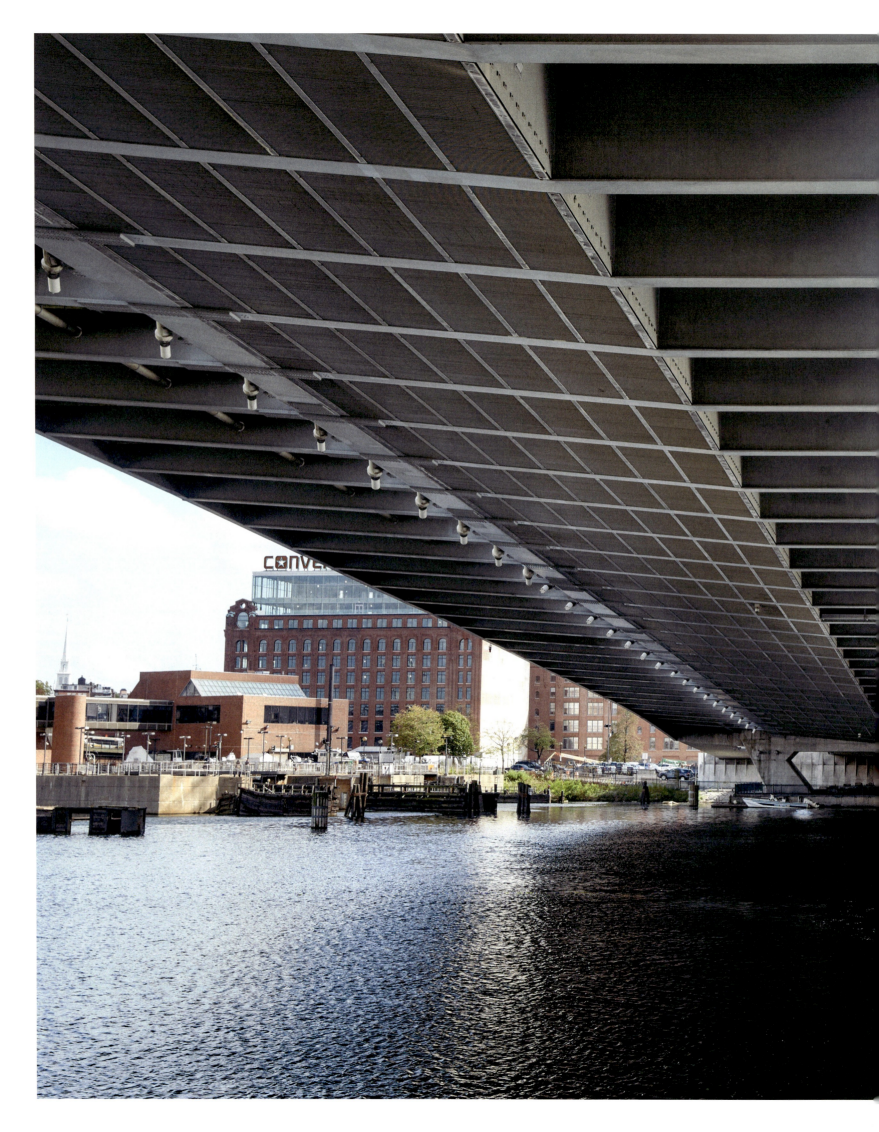

SUNNIBERGBRÜCKE, KLOSTERS
SUNNIBERG BRIDGE, KLOSTERS

1996–1998

Client: Graubünden Department of Transportation
Project in partnership with Bänziger+Köppel+Brändli+Partner, Chur
Andrea Deplazes, Architekt, Chur

[21

LOCATION
Klosters-Serneus
Canton of Graubünden
Switzerland

COORDINATES
784 300 / 195 400

TYPE
Cable-stayed bridge

LENGTH
526 m

HEIGHT
77 m

RADIUS
500 m

MAIN SPAN
140 m

OPENING
1998

Die sechs Kilometer lange Umfahrung der Ortschaften Küblis, Saas und Klosters war der schwierigste Abschnitt beim Ausbau der Prättigauerstrasse H28 von Landquart nach Davos. Die Variantenstudien dauerten rund 25 Jahre und führten von der wirtschaftlichsten, dem Talfluss folgenden Lösung bis zum definitiven, vor allem mit Rücksicht auf den Landschaftsschutz entwickelten Bauprojekt. Die Strasse führt bei Küblis und Saas zum Teil durch Tunnel den nördlichen Talhang entlang, wechselt unterhalb von Klosters mit einer Hochbrücke auf die andere Talseite und dort in den 4,2 Kilometer langen Gotschnatunnel der Umfahrung Klosters. Die relativ langen Tunnel verteuerten die ursprüngliche Variante um etwa vierzig Prozent.

Die neue Brücke sollte sich optimal in die mit grossem finanziellem Aufwand erhaltene Landschaft einfügen. Die in einem Studienauftrag vorgelegten Projekte waren zwar gut, vermochten jedoch als die Landschaft bereichernde Wahrzeichen nicht zu überzeugen. Schliesslich wurde ein von mir vorgeschlagenes Konzept der Bündner Regierung zur Ausführung empfohlen. Anstatt einer konventionellen Balkenbrücke, die bei der einen Überquerung des Tals wie ein Riegel gewirkt hätte, sollte eine mehrfeldrige Schrägkabelbrücke mit plattenförmigem Trägerquerschnitt und niedrigen Pylonen über der Fahrbahn den Durchblick möglichst wenig beeinträchtigen.

The 6 km long bypass of the towns of Küblis, Saas, and Klosters was the most difficult section of a project undertaken to improve the Prättigauerstrasse (Highway H28) between the towns Landquart and Davos. Studies of alternative solutions, which lasted about 25 years, initially considered the most economical alignment which followed the valley of the Landquart River for its entire length. Due to concerns for preservation of the natural landscape, however, the alignment that was finally chosen proceeds from Küblis to Saas along the north side of the Landquart valley, partly through tunnels. It crosses to the south side of the valley below Klosters by means of a high level bridge and then enters the 4.2 km long Gotschna Tunnel to bypass Klosters. This tunnel increased project costs relative to previously studied options by about forty percent.

The new bridge thus needed to fit ideally into the natural setting that had been preserved at great financial cost. Although the designs that had been developed through previous technical studies were good, they were nevertheless unable to enhance the landscape in a convincing way. In the end, a recommendation was made to the cantonal government of Graubünden to build a bridge based on a design concept proposed by me. Instead of a conventional girder bridge, which would have created the visual impression of a heavy bar spanning the valley, the multiple span cable-stayed bridge with slender girder and relatively short towers above the deck succeeded in minimizing the visual impact of the structure on the landscape.

[21] SUNNIBERGBRÜCKE, KLOSTERS / SUNNIBERG BRIDGE AT KLOSTERS

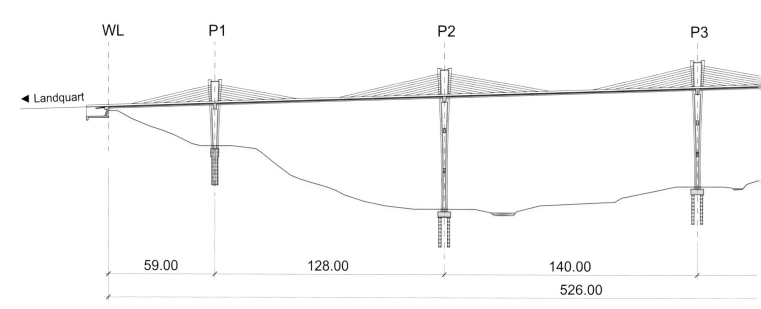

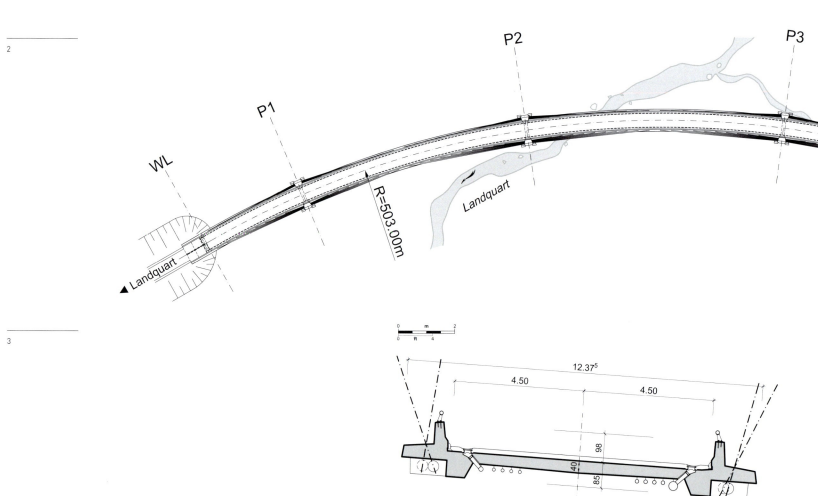

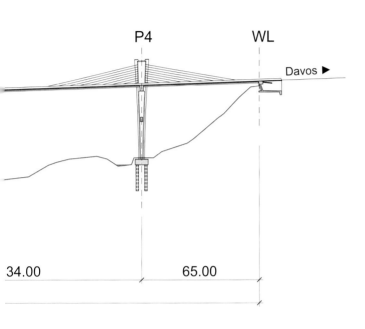

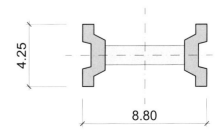

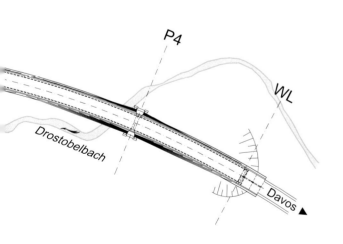

1 Längsschnitt / Longitudinal section
2 Grundriss / Plan
3 Querschnitt / Cross section
4 Pfeiler P2 / Querschnitt / Column P2 / Cross section
5 Pfeiler Querschnitt / Column / Cross section

[21 SUNNIBERGBRÜCKE, KLOSTERS

Die 526 Meter lange, 60 Meter hohe und in einem Radius von 500 Metern gekrümmte Brücke weist fünf verschiedene Spannweiten auf; die Hauptspannweite beträgt 140 Meter. Die Wahl der Spannweiten ergab sich aus der Topografie, dem Flussverlauf und dem erwünschten, schlanken Trägerquerschnitt. Im Unterschied dazu wurde die Höhe der Pylone subjektiv bestimmt; sie ist aus ästhetischen Gründen niedrig, erfordert aber entsprechend stärkere Schrägkabel. Im Übrigen erfolgte die Gestaltung des Tragwerks ausschliesslich aus konstruktiven Überlegungen im Hinblick auf ein Tragsystem, das einen effizienten Kraftverlauf visualisiert. Die Querschnitte des Fahrbahnträgers, der Stützen und Pylone weisen im Prinzip den gleichen, einheitlichen Charakter eines flachen Plattenbalkens auf.

Die Sunnibergbrücke ist die erste lange, fugenlose Spannbeton-Brücke der Schweiz. Längenänderungen des Trägers infolge Temperaturdifferenzen werden durch Krümmungsänderungen der Brücke in der Horizontalebene kompensiert. Damit entfallen am Brückenende sämtliche Lager und Bewegungsfugen. Die Stützenköpfe sind in Längsrichtung unverschieblich; daraus ergab sich nicht nur die sich nach unten verjüngende, elegante Stützenform, sondern auch eine hohe Erdbebensicherheit.

Die Fundation besteht bei den Widerlagern und der ersten Stütze auf der nördlichen Talseite aus Betonkästen, alle andern Stützen sind in ein Pfahl-Bankett eingespannt, das auf 16 Meter langen Pfahlgruppen ruht.

Der Träger wurde im Freivorbauverfahren hergestellt: In zwei Phasen wurden auf einem kleinen Gerüst sechs Meter breite Etappen betoniert – entsprechend dem Verankerungsabstand der Kabel. Nach der Erhärtung des Betons konnte der Abschnitt des Trägers mit einem neuen Kabel an den Pylon zurückgebunden werden. Bei den Pylonen sind die Schrägkabel an einem einbetonierten, horizontal und vertikal verbundenen Stahlgrill verankert.

Im frei stehenden Zustand waren die dem Wind ausgesetzten T-Systemteile der Brücke äusserst empfindlich, da der Fuss der zweistieligen Stützen eine extrem kleine Torsionssteifigkeit aufweist. Sie wurden zwar für die Windbelastung bemessen; ihre Verformung musste aber ständig und ganz genau kontrolliert werden. Mit gekreuzten Niederhaltekabeln am Fahrbahnträger, etwa 20 Meter vom Pylon entfernt, wurde zudem die Torsionssteifigkeit des T-Systems erhöht.

Der Bau der Brücke stellte höchste Anforderungen an alle Beteiligten. Wegen der Krümmung im Grundriss, der Steigung der Fahrbahn und des Quergefälles waren die Justierung des Vorbauwagens sowie die Schalung der Kabelverankerungen auf der im Bauzustand sehr weichen Brücke besonders anspruchsvoll.

Im Bauprogramm der gesamten Anlage der H28 wurde die Sunnibergbrücke vorgezogen, weil fast der ganze Gesteinsausbruch aus dem Gotschnatunnel – insgesamt etwa 700 000 Tonnen (ohne Fahrzeuge) – über die Brücke transportiert und auf der nördlichen Talseite deponiert werden musste.

Nach einigen Vorbereitungsarbeiten im Spätherbst 1995 begannen im Frühjahr 1996 die eigentlichen Bauarbeiten, die im Herbst 1998 abgeschlossen wurden. Die Einweihung und Eröffnung von Brücke und Tunnel erfolgte am 9. Dezember 2005 mit einem von der Gemeinde Klosters organisierten Volksfest in Anwesenheit von Bundesrat Moritz Leuenberger, Baudirektor Stefan Engler und Finanzdirektorin Eveline Widmer-Schlumpf als Repräsentanten des Kantons Graubünden sowie von Prinz Charles, dem Thronfolger der englischen Krone, als Ehrengast.

[21] SUNNIBERG BRIDGE AT KLOSTERS

The bridge has a total length of 526m, height above the valley of 60 m, and follows a curve in plan of 500 m radius. It consists of five spans of various lengths, the longest of which is 140 m. The arrangement of span lengths was based on considerations of topography, the course of the river below, and the desired slender girder cross-section. The height of the towers above the deck, on the other hand, was chosen on a somewhat subjective basis. Based on aesthetic considerations, it was made to be relatively short. This required stronger stays. Apart from this, the design of the structure proceeded from exclusively technical considerations, with the goal of creating a structural system that gave visual expression to an efficient flow of forces. The cross-sections of the girder, the columns, and the towers generally exhibit the same, unified character of a relatively thin T-section.

The Sunniberg Bridge is the first long jointless prestressed concrete bridge in Switzerland. Changes in the lengths of the girder due to temperature shifts are accommodated by a change in curvature of the bridge. This enabled bearings and expansion joints to be eliminated at the ends of the bridge. The absence of bearings at the abutments effectively prevented longitudinal displacement at the tops of the piers, thus enabling the piers to be given an elegant taper from top to bottom, and enhancing the ability of the overall structural system to withstand seismic action. The foundations of the abutments and the first pier on the north side of the valley are hollow concrete shafts. All other piers are founded on pilecaps supported by a group of 16 m long drilled piles.

The girder was built in cantilever construction. Segment length was six meters, corresponding to the the spacing of stay anchorages along the girder. Each segment were constructed in two phases. After concrete in a given segment had gained sufficient strength, it was tied back to the tower with a pair of stays. At the towers, the stays are anchored in a steel grid that is connected horizontally and vertically, and cast into the concrete.

Before closure of the girder, the free-standing structures consisting of pier, tower, and double cantilevers for the girder were extremely sensitive to wind load, since the torsional stiffness at the foot of the twin-leg piers was extremely small. Although these components were dimensioned to provide adequate capacity to resist wind load, their deformations had to be continually and precisely monitored. Temporary hold-down cables arranged in the shape of an X and anchored to the girder at about 20 m from the tower were provided to increase the torsional stiffness of the system.

The construction of the bridge placed the highest demands on all who contributed to the project. Due to the curvature in plan, the gradient of the roadway in profile, and the cross-slope, the adjustment of the travelers and the forming of the stay anchorages was especially challenging given that the structure was very flexible during construction. The Sunniberg Bridge needed to be completed early in the overall schedule of the Highway H28 project, since almost all of the rock excavated from the Gotschna Tunnel (approximately 700 000 tonnes in all) had to be transported over the bridge and deposited on the north side of the valley.

Following preparations in the late fall of 1995, actual construction began in early 1996 and was completed in the fall of 1998. The official opening ceremony for both bridge and tunnel took place on December 9, 2005 with a public festival organized by the town of Klosters. The event was attended by Federal Councillor Moritz Leuenberger, Director of Construction Stefan Engler and Director of Finance Eveline Widmer-Schlumpf as representatives of the Canton of Graubünden, as well as a the honorary guest Prince Charles, heir to the English throne.

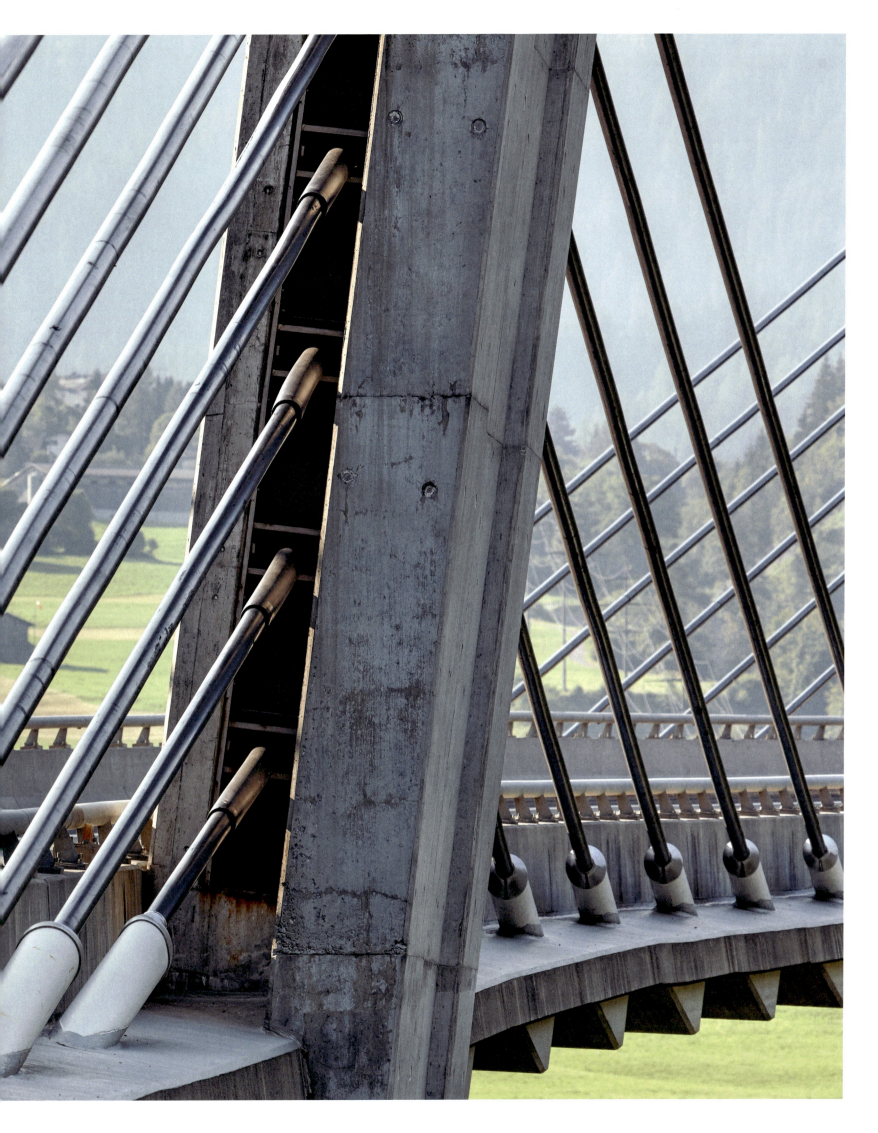

AL SHOWAH ISLAND BRIDGES, ABU DHABI
AL SHOWAH ISLAND BRIDGES, ABU DHABI

2007

Client: Abu Dhabi Department of Transportation
Design: Christian Menn Partners AG, Chur

[22   [23

Abu Dhabi, die Hauptstadt der Vereinigten Arabischen Emirate, plante Anfang der Nullerjahre auf einer der Stadt vorgelagerten Insel ein neues Zentrum. Die Insel wurde mit Aufschüttungen etwas erweitert. Sie liegt in einer Entfernung von 200 bis 400 Metern vor einer Bucht der Stadt und ist etwa 2,5 Kilometer lang und 600 Meter breit. Auf der Insel sollen die wichtigsten Gebäude für Wirtschaft, Bildung und Gesundheit errichtet werden. Die Erschliessungspläne für den Verkehr wurden von einer grossen amerikanischen Ingenieurfirma ausgearbeitet, die ihrerseits Christian Menn Partners beauftragte, zwei so genannte «signature bridges», also einprägsame, markante Brücken, zu projektieren, die vom Festland ins Zentrum der Insel führen sollten. An den Enden der Insel waren einfache Brücken mit kleinen Spannweiten aus vorfabrizierten Elementen vorgesehen. Die beiden grossen Brücken, die vorläufig als Al Showah-Brücke 3 und 4 bezeichnet werden, sind 468,5 beziehungsweise 707 Meter lang und 38,1 beziehungsweise 43,6 Meter breit. Im Grundriss sind beide Brücken leicht gekrümmt (R = 900 respektive 1050 Meter).

Seit der Auftragserteilung 2007 fanden bei der Bauherrschaft und deren Vertretung immer wieder Wechsel statt. Es wurde auch kurzfristig ein Wettbewerb mit international namhaften Architekturbüros ausgeschrieben; trotzdem blieb das vorliegende ursprüngliche Projekt siegreich. Mit grossem Aufwand wurde es schliesslich bekannten Bauunternehmungen zur Offertstellung unterbreitet, wobei verschiedene Unternehmungen von weltbekannten Teams von Brücken-Ingenieuren und Architekten Varianten ausarbeiten liessen; allerdings ohne Erfolg. Für Brücke 3 wurde unser Projekt zur Ausführung in Auftrag gegeben und begonnen. Mitte 2013 wurde der Auftrag storniert – eine amerikanische Firma erhielt den Auftrag, statt «signature bridges» billige, triviale, vorfabrizierte Tragwerke mit kleinen Spannweiten auszuführen.

At the beginning of the new millennium, Abu Dhabi, the capital of the United Arab Emirates, planned a new city center on an offshore island, where the most important buildings for finance, education, and health were to be built. The existing island was expanded using fill, resulting in an area 2.5 km long and 600 m wide, and separated from the mainland by 200 to 400 m. The plans for traffic access were prepared by a large American engineering firm, which gave Christian Menn Partners the assignment to design two so-called "signature bridges": impressive, prominent bridges that would carry traffic from the mainland to the central portion of the island. At the ends of the island, simple bridges with short spans constructed of prefabricated components would be built. The two large bridges, which were given the preliminary names Al Showah Bridges 3 and 4, are 468.5 m and 707 m long, and 38.1 m and 43.6 m wide respectively. In plan, both bridges are lightly curved (radius 900 m and 1050 m respectively).

Since this assignment was awarded in 2007, there has been much change among the owner's staff and representatives. A design competition involving famous international architecture firms was held at short notice, but the original design was maintained. At great expense, leading contracting companies were asked to submit design/building proposals, with the participation of world-famous bridge engineers and architects who submitted design alternatives, but without success. For Bridge 3, the decision was made to proceed to construction according to our design. In mid-2013, however, the contract was canceled. An American firm received a contract to build cheap, trivial, prefabricated structures instead of signature bridges.

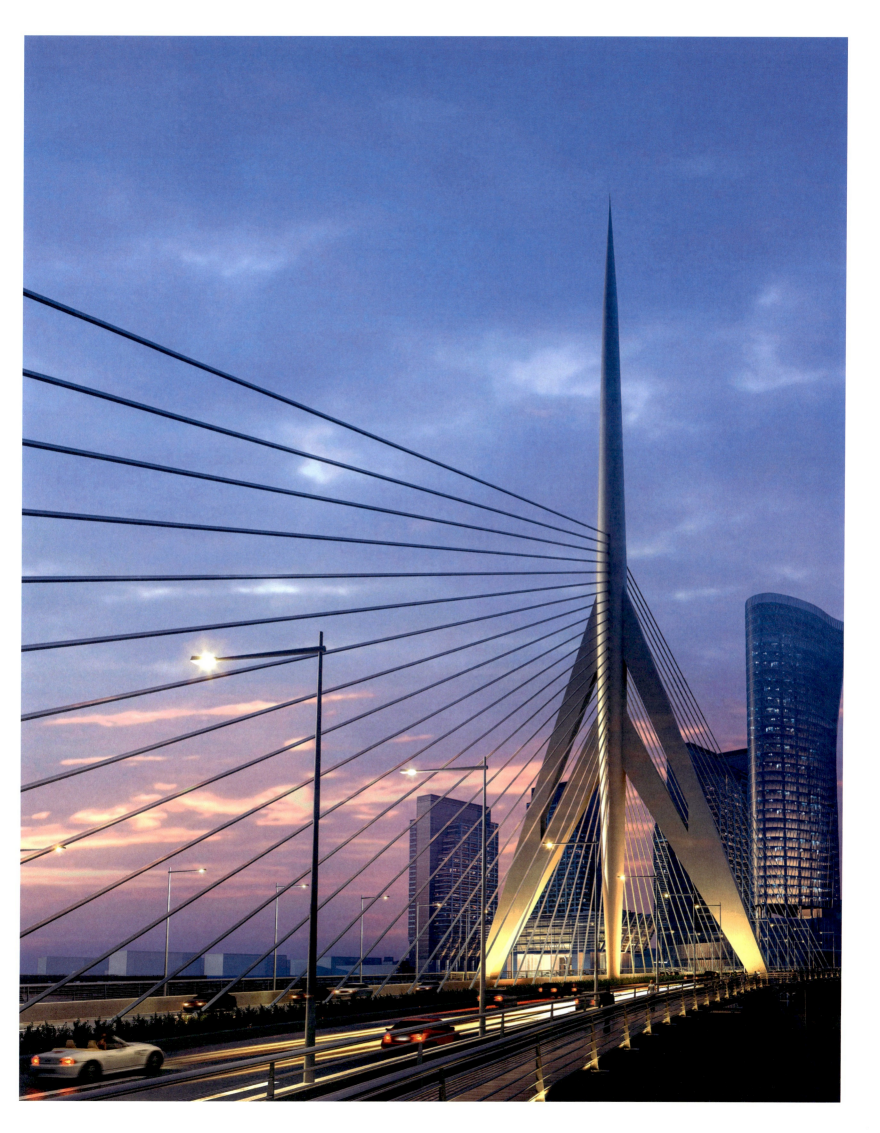

[22 AL SHOWAH-BRÜCKE 3, ABU DHABI]

Brücke 3 ist eine Schrägkabelbrücke mit zwei Spannweiten von je 165 Metern sowie Randspannweiten von 30 + 40 beziehungsweise 40 + 28,5 Metern und einem 117 Meter hohen Zentralpylon im Mittelstreifen. Der Pylon hat die Form einer Spindel, damit die Breite des Mittelstreifens auf das erforderliche Minimum reduziert werden kann. Die Schrägkabel sind im Mittelstreifen verankert und bilden nur eine einzige windschiefe Kabelfläche. Bei Eigenlast verhält sich der Brückenträger wie ein Balken, der bei jeder Kabelverankerung gestützt ist. Die relativ kleinen positiven und negativen Biegemomente erzeugen in der oberen und unteren Kastenplatte des Trägers entsprechend kleine Normalkräfte, deren Ablenkkräfte in Querrichtung praktisch keine Verdrehung (Drehmomente) und somit auch keine Torsion erzeugen. Auch bei Verkehrslast in nur einem Feld – der ungünstigsten Laststellung – treten nur kleine Dreh- und Torsionsmomente auf.

Die einseitige Verkehrslast auf dem breiten Trägerquerschnitt erzeugt jedoch sehr grosse Drehmomente, die integriert entsprechend grosse Torsionsmomente zur Folge haben. Die Umwandlung der Drehmomente als Folge vertikal wirkender Verkehrslast in Umlauftorsion kann bei dieser Breite der Brücke nur mit zahlreichen biegesteifen Querträgern bewerkstelligt werden.

Am Pylon entstehen aus dem Knick der Kabelkräfte im Grundriss grosse seitliche Ablenkkräfte, die nur mit seitlichen Scheiben am Pylon aufgenommen werden können. Der Biegewiderstand des Pylons ermöglicht aber Öffnungen in den Pylonscheiben. Die 10 Meter hohe und 50 Meter lange Pfeilerwand unter dem Pylon und dem Fahrbahnträger wird deshalb auch mit Öffnungen aufgelöst, sodass eine konsistente, elegante, transparente und wirtschaftliche Form für Pfeiler und Pylon entsteht.

[22 AL SHOWAH ISLAND BRIDGE 3 IN ABU DHABI]

Bridge 3 is a cable-stayed bridge with two spans of 165 m and side spans of 30 m and 40 to one side, and 40 m and 28.5 m on the other. There is a 117 m tall central tower located in the median. The tower has the shape of a spindle, so that the width of the median can be reduced to the required minimum. The stays are anchored in the median and form a single plane. Under dead load, the girder behaves as a beam supported at the cable anchorages. The relatively small positive and negative moments produce correspondingly small axial forces in the top and bottom slabs of the girder, which produce practically no torque and thus only negligible torsion. Live load applied to only one span, the most severe arrangement of load, likewise produces only small torques and torsional moments.

One-sided live load on the wide girder cross-section does, however, produce large torques which integrate into large torsional moments. The transformation of the torques due to vertical load into a closed shear flow can be managed, however, with a large number of stiff diaphragms.

Large transverse deviation forces are produced in the tower due to the angle break in the cable forces. These can be resisted only by walls located to the sides of the tower. The bending capacity of the tower makes it possible, however, to provide openings in these walls. The 10 m high and 50 m long pier wall under the tower and the girder is thus also provided with openings, to produce a consistent, elegant, transparent, and economical shape for both pier and tower.

[23 AL SHOWAH-BRÜCKE 4, ABU DHABI]

Im Gegensatz zur eleganten, modernen Schrägkabelbrücke 3 ist Brücke 4 ein triumphales, überhöhtes Bogentragwerk. Die Zufahrten zum Bogenabschnitt sind zwar nur konventionelle Trägerviadukte, doch wie schon beim Gateway Arch in St. Louis dominiert der Bogen das gesamte Umfeld. Bei einer Brückenlänge von 707 Metern und einer Fahrbahnbreite für Motorfahrzeuge und Schnellbahn von 41,1 Metern weist der Bogen eine Spannweite von nur 120 Metern auf und wirkt dadurch wie ein Solitär. Konstruktiv interessant ist die aus der leicht gekrümmten Linienführung und den System-Steifigkeiten resultierende Tragwerksgestaltung. Der Bogen muss im Grundriss tangential aus der gekrümmten Linienführung des Brückenträgers herauswachsen; der schlanke Bogen, der fast nur Achsialkräfte und kaum nennenswerte Biegung und Torsion aufnehmen kann, muss durch den Fahrbahnträger ausgesteift werden. Es handelt sich somit um einen erweiterten Stabbogen, bei dem der Träger neben der Biegung zusätzlich die Torsion aufnimmt. Deshalb befindet sich der Bogen im Grundriss immer über der Trägerachse und ist leicht auf die Kurvenaussenseite geneigt. Die Hänger, die die Last des Trägers auf den Bogen abgeben, werden auch bei gleichmässig verteiltem Gewicht unterschiedlich belastet, sodass auf den Träger das volle Drehmoment des Systems wirkt. Der Brückenträger, der vom Bogen die Biegung infolge Verkehrslast übernimmt, muss auf einer Seite – in der Nähe der Durchdringung von Bogen und Träger – ein Gelenk aufweisen, damit er nicht als Zugband wirkt. Der Stabbogen, der nicht nur die Biegung, sondern auch die Torsion an den Versteifungsträger abgibt, ist eine Neuentwicklung und als solche technisch originell.

[23 AL SHOWAH ISLAND BRIDGE 4 IN ABU DHABI]

In contrast to the modern cable-stayed Bridge 3, Bridge 4 is a triumphal arch structure extending above the roadway. The approaches to the arch section are conventional girder spans, which permits the arch to dominate the entire field of vision, as with the Gateway Arch in St. Louis. The entire length of the bridge is 707 m and its width is 41.1 m, consisting of traffic lanes and rapid transit. The arch span is 120 m and is visually distinct from the remainder of the bridge. The choice of the structural system is a consequence of the lightly curved alignment and the distribution of system stiffness to the structural elements. At its springing lines, the arch must be tangent to the girder in plan. The slender arch, which has practically no capacity to resist bending or torsion, must be stiffened by the girder. The system provided is essentially an extended deck-stiffened arch, in that the girder resists not only system bending but also system torsion. The arch in plan is always located above the axis of the girder and is gently inclined towards the centre of the curve. The suspenders, which transfer load from the girder to the arch, are loaded unequally by uniform load, so that the entire system torque is resisted by the girder. The girder, which resists bending due to live load, must have a hinge near the intersection of arch and girder to prevent it from working as a tie. The deck-stiffened arch, in which not only bending but also torsion is resisted by the girder, is a new, technically original development.

BRÜCKE ÜBER DEN GRIMSELSEE, GUTTANNEN
BRIDGE OVER LAKE GRIMSEL AT GUTTANNEN

2005

Client: Kraftwerke Oberhasli KWO, Innertkirchen
Project in partnership with Bänziger/Brändli, Chur,
Martin Deuring, Winterthur and Walt+Galmarini, Zurich

[24

Die Grimsel ist eine Hochgebirgsregion im zentralen Alpenmassiv. Auf der Berner Seite steigt die Strasse auf den Grimselpass auf einer Distanz von nur etwa 15 Kilometern 1550 Meter an. Etwa 150 Höhenmeter unterhalb der Passhöhe biegt das Tal scharf nach Westen ab in ein 5 Kilometer langes, relativ flaches Vorland, das sich bis zu den Gletschern der höchsten Berner Alpengipfel erstreckt. In diesen ausserordentlich günstigen Verhältnissen bezüglich hoch gelegenem Stauraum und grossem Gefälle wurde 1925 eines der ersten grossen Schweizer Kraftwerke mit einem Stausee von 100 Millionen Kubikmetern Inhalt gebaut. Inzwischen wurden in der erweiterten Region acht Kraftwerke mit 1125 Megawatt Leistung und 2350 Millionen Kilowattstunden Spitzenenergie erstellt. Jüngstes Projekt der Kraftwerkgesellschaft KWO ist die Erhöhung der beiden 1925 erbauten Staumauern um 22 Meter, damit der ganze Zufluss für Winterenergie genutzt werden kann.

Zur Zeit führt die Passstrasse am östlichen Ufer des Stausees entlang. Neu soll sie der erhöhten Mauer entlang auf ein höheres Niveau beim Grimsel-Hospiz hinaufführen. Mit einer 352 Meter langen Brücke soll die Strasse dann den Stausee maximal 60 Meter über dem Seegrund und 4 Meter über dem Stauziel überqueren, um auf der gegenüberliegenden Seite wieder an die bestehende Strasse anzuschliessen.

The Grimsel is a high mountain region in the central Alps. On the Bern side, the highway climbs 1550 m towards the Grimsel Pass over a distance of about 15 km. About 150 m in elevation below the pass summit, the valley bends sharply to the west and into a 5 km long, relatively flat foreland, which extends to the glaciers of the highest peak in the Bernese Alps. In 1925, taking advantage of the extremely favorable conditions regarding high elevation, capacity for storage, and large head, one of Switzerland's first large power stations was constructed with a storage capacity of 100 million cubic meters. Since then, eight power stations were built with a combined capacity of 1125 megawatts and 2350 million kilowatt hours peak energy. The most recent project of the KWO corporation seeks to increase the height of the dams built in 1925 by 22 meters, to use the entire influx to satisfy winter energy demand.

The pass highway currently runs along the eastern shore of the lake. It will need to be relocated along the raised crest of the dam upwards from the Grimsel Hospice. A 352 m long bridge will be built to enable the highway to cross the lake at 60 m above the lake bed and 4 m above the maximum water elevation. From there, the highway will connect with the existing road.

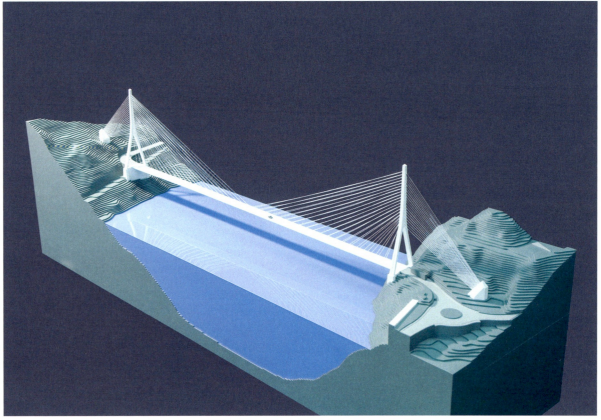

[24 BRÜCKE ÜBER DEN GRIMSELSEEE, GUTTANNEN / BRIDGE OVER LAKE GRIMSEL AT GUTTANNEN

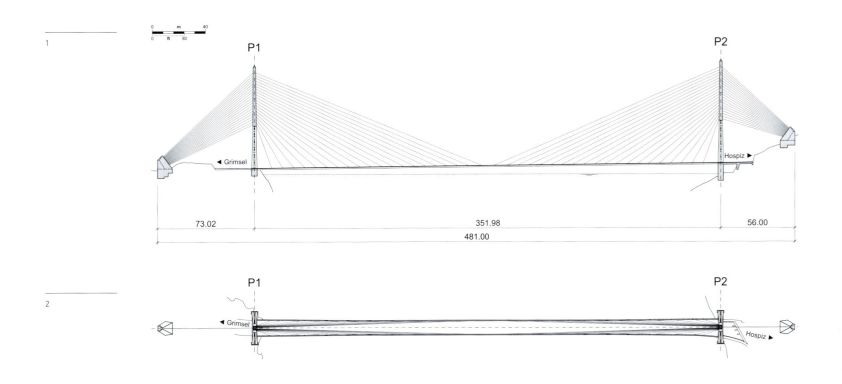

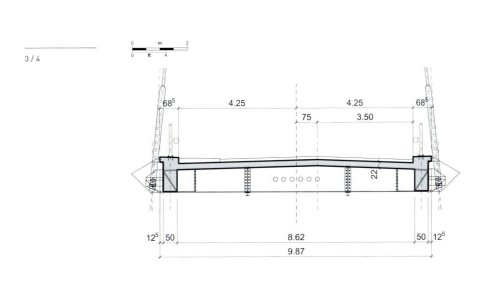

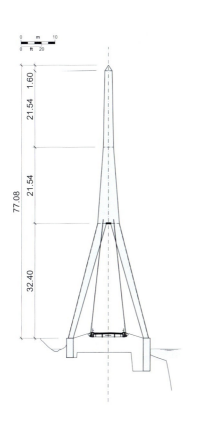

1 Längsschnitt / Longitudinal section
2 Grundriss / Plan
4 Querschnitt / Cross section
3 Ansicht Pfeiler 1 / View of Column 1

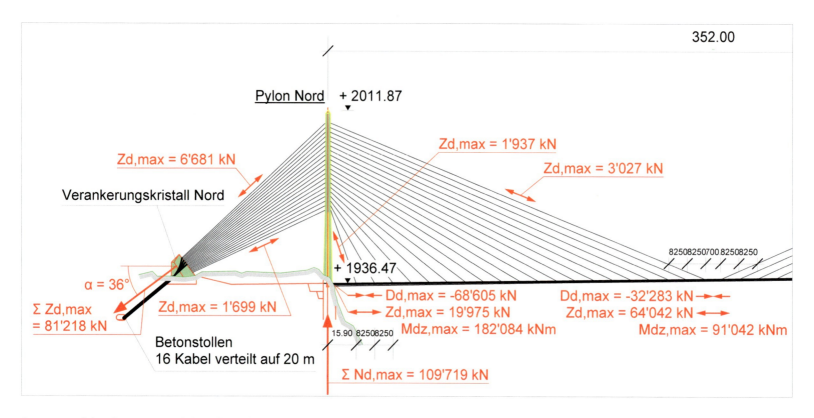

Grenzwerte einiger Bemessungsschnittkräfte im Tragwerk
am Pylon Nord (D = Druck, Z = Zug)
Maximum design forces in the structural system at the north tower
(D = compression, Z = tension)

[24 BRÜCKE ÜBER DEN GRIMSELSEE, GUTTANNEN

Als Tragsysteme kamen Balkenbrücken mit Spannweiten von 60 bis 80 Metern, Schrägkabelbrücken oder Hängebrücken in Frage. Gewählt wurde ein Schrägkabelsystem, da bei Balkenbrücken gefährlicher Eisdruck auf die hohen Stützen zu befürchten war und Hängebrücken – obwohl am elegantesten – vor allem wegen der Verankerungen auf der Südseite im hangparallel geschichteten Fels zu hohe Kosten verursacht hätten.

Die weiterentwickelte Schrägkabelbrücke ist 352 Meter weit gespannt und 11,9 Meter breit. Im Hinblick auf die klimatischen Verhältnisse und die damit verbundene kurze zur Verfügung stehende Bauzeit ist ein Stahl-Verbundträger mit vorfabrizierten Betonplatten vorgesehen. Die Stahlträger bestehen aus zwei Hutträgern, die durch Querträger miteinander verbunden sind. Die 76 Meter hohen Pylone sind an den Brückenenden fest im Fels verankert. Der Kabelabstand am Träger beträgt 8,25 Meter – der Stahlkonstruktion und der Länge der Betonplatten entsprechend. Die Rückhaltekabel sind in sorgfältig gestalteten Betonblöcken verankert, die ihrerseits in Anker-Stollen zurückgespannt werden.

Die Brücke weist mehrere aussergewöhnliche Besonderheiten auf: die Tragwerksausbildung in Brückenmitte, das Tragwerksverhalten bei Temperaturveränderungen und Kabelvereisungen.

Die Brücke verläuft ohne Fuge von Pylon zu Pylon. Ein funktionstüchtiges Gelenk in der Mitte hätte vor allem in horizontaler Richtung zu grosse Verformungen bewirkt. Bei tiefen Temperaturen wird deshalb der Zug in den Schrägkabeln vergrössert und der Druck im Fahrbahnträger vermindert. Im Beton sorgen zulässige Risse für die Kompensation der Verkürzung als Folge tiefer Temperaturen. Bei den vorgegebenen Tiefsttemperaturen (aus örtlichen Messungen bei einer Wiederkehrperiode von 200 Jahren für ±45°C) ist der Zug im Träger auch am Brückenende immer noch grösser als der Druck, der bei Eigen- und Nutzlast von den Schrägkabeln auf die Widerlager übertragen wird. Das bedeutet, dass der Brückenträger im Fels verankert werden muss und dass aus dem Schrägkabelsystem ein Hängebrücken-System wird. Bei den gewählten Abmessungen ist die Verankerungskraft allerdings viel kleiner als bei einer Hängebrücke.

Das dynamische Verhalten des Tragwerks und der Kabel, wurde bei Verkehr, Wind, Erdbeben etc. bezüglich Verformungen und Ermüdung untersucht. Es wird unterschieden zwischen Tragwerk und Schrägkabeln. Im Hinblick auf Wind ist die Querschnittsausbildung des Brückenträgers besonders wichtig: Mit Windnasen am Trägerrand, aber auch mit Flaps kann die kritische Windgeschwindigkeit erheblich gesteigert werden. Die Untersuchung erfolgte mit komplexen Berechnungen und Versuchen im Windtunnel. Der Vergleich der kritischen Windgeschwindigkeit bei den beiden Methoden war befriedigend bis gut.

Bei der Untersuchung der Kabelschwingungen spielte die Kabelvereisung eine wichtige Rolle, da sie sämtliche Kabelparameter stark ändert. Es ist notwendig, Dämpfungskabel und Dämpfer an den Kabelverankerungen vorzusehen.

Mit Unterstützung von Meteorologen sowie Beobachtungen an vorhandenen seeüberquerenden Kabeln und Installationen vor Ort und auf der Passhöhe wurde das Risiko von Kabelvereisungen untersucht. Es darf angenommen werden, dass es nur dann gross ist, wenn unterkühlte, hohe

Feuchtigkeit in der Luft bei laminarer Strömung auf die Kabel trifft. Im schroffen Bergtal ist die Windströmung jedoch turbulent und unterkühlte Feuchtigkeit kondensiert bereits an den Talflanken, bevor sie die Brückenkabel erreicht. Trotzdem wurde den statischen Berechnungen eine Vergrösserung des Kabelradius von 10 Zentimetern infolge Schnee und Eis zugrunde gelegt.

Umweltverbände haben Einspruch erhoben gegen die geplante Erhöhung der Staumauer um 22 Meter, die eine Vergrösserung des Stauvolumens von 80 Prozent bewirkt. Begründet wurde die Einsprache mit der Überflutung eines kleinen Hochmoors und einiger Arven am Südhang im hintersten Teil des Stausees. Das Berner Parlament hat diese Einsprache jedoch abgelehnt; nun müssten die Gerichte entscheiden. Das Brücken-Projekt ist allerdings so weit fortgeschritten, dass mit den Bauarbeiten umgehend begonnen werden könnte.

[24 BRIDGE OVER LAKE GRIMSEL AT GUTTANNEN

Structural systems considered for this crossing included girder bridges with spans of 60 to 80 m, cable-stayed bridges, and suspension bridges. A cable-stayed system was chosen due to the dangers associated with ice pressure applied to the tops of tall piers in the water. Suspension bridges, although the most elegant solution, would have been expensive due to the need to build an anchorage on the south side in rock layered parallel to the slope.

The outcome of the design process was a cable-stayed bridge with a span of 352 m and a width of 11.9 m. Due to prevailing weather conditions which dictate a short construction season, a steel-concrete composite system with precast concrete slabs was chosen. The steel structure consists of two main edge girders that are connected by floorbeams. The 76 m tall towers are anchored solidly into the rock at the ends of the bridge. The cables are spaced at 8.25 m, corresponding to the length of the steel segments and concrete slabs. The backstays are anchored into carefully designed concrete blocks, which are tied back into anchorage tunnels.

The bridge has the following unique characteristics: Structural arrangement at midspan; structural behaviour due to change in temperature; measures to deal with icing of stays.

The bridge has no joints between towers. A functional hinge at midspan would have permitted large deformations in the girder, which would have increased the tension in the stays and reduced the compression in the girder. Instead, the shortening of the girder due to a drop in temperature was accommodated by allowing the concrete in the deck to crack. Based on measurements at the site, the design range of temperature extended from +45 to −45 degrees C for a return period of 200 years. Tension in the girder due to the minimum design temperature is greater than compression due to dead load and live load, even at the girder ends. This implies that the bridge girder must be anchored into rock at its ends and the inclined cable system must be capable of carrying the load as a suspension bridge. The anchorage force will, however, be much smaller than that of a comparable suspension bridge.

The dynamic behavior of the entire structure and the stay cables has been investigated under traffic load, snow, wind, earthquakes etc. and has been analyzed in view of displacements and fatigue. Structure and cables have been investigated separately.

With regard to wind, the shaping of the cross section is very important. Through wind noses along the edge of the deck and wind flaps the critical wind speed can be increased considerably. The investigations have been made with complex calculations and wind tunnel tests. The congruence of results for both methods was quite satisfying.

For the determination of cable vibration, the icing-up of the cables played a very important role, because the formation of ice on the cables changes all wind parameters. Damping cables as well as dampers at the anchors must be provided.

The risk of ice accretion on the stay cables was investigated with the support of meteorologists who made observations of existing cables crossing lakes and existing facilities at the site and at the pass summit. These studies showed that a significant risk occurs only when a laminar flow of supercooled, highly humid air comes into contact with the cables. In this rugged mountain valley, however, the wind flow is generally turbulent and supercooled humidity tends to condensate the valley flanks, i.e. before it would contact the bridge cables. In spite of this positive conclusion, design calculations considered ice accretion equivalent to a 10 cm increase in the radius of a given stay.

Environmental groups mounted pressure against the planned 22 m increase in height of the dam, which would have increased the storage volume by 80 percent. Opposition was based on the flooding of a small marshland and a few Swiss stone pines on the south slope of the farthest part of the lake. The Bernese parliament rejected this protest, so now the courts must decide. The bridge design has now progressed so far that construction could begin immediately.

HOOVER DAM BYPASS BRIDGE
HOOVER DAM BYPASS BRIDGE

2001

Client: Arizona and Nevada Departments of Transportation
Project in partnership with Parsons Transportation Group Inc., Washington

[25

Der stark frequentierte U.S. Highway 93 überquerte etwa 40 Kilometer östlich von Las Vegas auf der Grenze zwischen Nevada und Arizona den Colorado River auf dem Hoover Dam. Die 1935 fertiggestellte, 220 Meter hohe Bogenstaumauer fand damals in der Bautechnik grosse Beachtung und wurde ein beliebtes Ausflugsziel für Touristen. Der aufgestaute See, die Mauer und die Schlucht des Colorado River sind landschaftlich faszinierende Elemente. Für die vielen Besucher wurden in der Nähe der rechtsseitigen Mauerkrone verschiedene Parkierungsdecks und Restaurants erstellt. Der Verkehr auf dem Highway über den Damm wurde dadurch allerdings empfindlich beeinträchtigt. Die Departements of Transportation (DOT) der Bundesstaaten Nevada und Arizona beschlossen deshalb mit dem Ausbau des Highway 93 eine Umfahrung des kritischen Abschnitts mit einer Brücke, die die Schlucht etwa 300 Meter flussabwärts vom Damm in einer Höhe von 280 Metern überquert.

Eine grosse amerikanische Ingenieurfirma, die bereits ein paar Vorstudien beim Nevada DOT eingereicht hatte, erteilte mir 2001 den Auftrag, einen Entwurf für eine Betonbogenbrücke auszuarbeiten.

Die bestehende Strasse umfährt auf der rechten Seite, etwa zwei Kilometer vor dem Erreichen des Hoover Dam einen Felskopf, führt dann zu einer Haarnadelkurve hinunter und nach etwa 300 Metern zur Mauerkrone. Die neue Linienführung zwcigt bereits vor dem erwähnten Felskopf ab und quert etwa 30 Meter über der Haarnadelkurve die Schlucht.

For many years, the busy US Highway 93 crossed the state line dividing Nevada and Arizona about 40 km east of Las Vegas at the Hoover Dam on the Colorado River. The 220 m high arch dam, completed in 1935, was of great technical significance and was a favourite tourist attraction. The lake behind the dam, the dam itself, and the Colorado River canyon are fascinating elements in the visual landscape. To serve the large numbers of visitors coming to the Hoover Dam, parking areas and restaurants were provided near the top of the dam on the right side. As a result, traffic on the highway over the dam was affected. The Departments of Transportation (DOT) of the states of Nevada and Arizona thus decided to bypass this critical section with a bridge over the canyon located about 300 m downstream of the dam at a height of 280 m.

A large American engineering firm, which had already prepared preliminary studies for the Nevada DOT, gave me the assignment to prepare a design for a concrete arch bridge.

On the right side, the existing highway travels around a promontory located about two km from the dam, drops down into a hairpin curve, and after about 300 m reaches the top of the dam. The new alignment deviates immediately before the promontory and crosses the canyon about 30m above the hairpin curve.

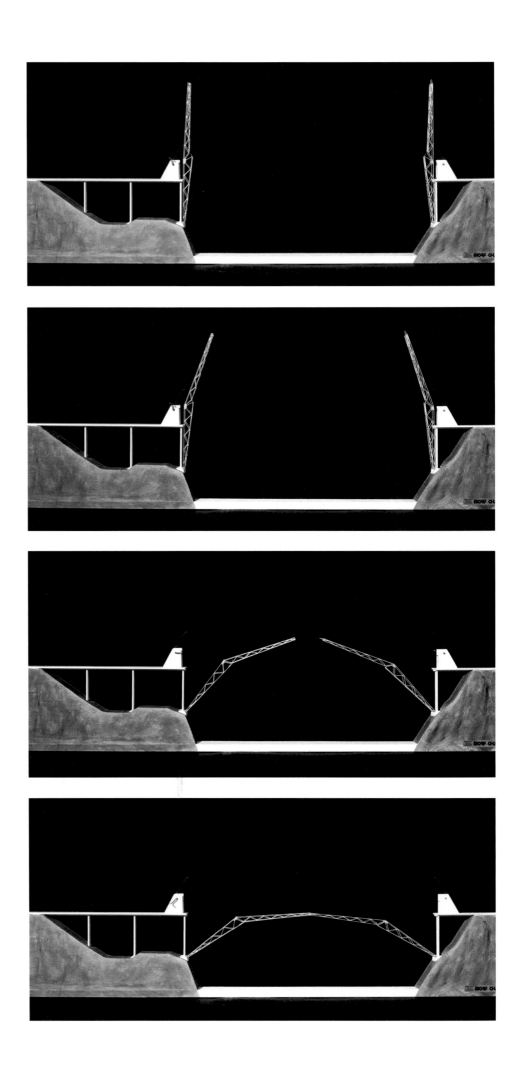

Der von mir vorgeschlagene Entwurf sah eine kleine Verschiebung dieser Linienführung vor, sodass der Bogenkämpfer unmittelbar neben der Haarnadelkurve zu liegen käme. Das vorgeschlagene Tragsystem bestand im Prinzip aus einem originellen Dreigelenkbogen. Die Brücke hätte mit dem Hoover Dam eine Einheit gebildet. Der Bogenkämpfer auf der rechten Seite wäre von den Parkierungsdecks aus leicht erreichbar gewesen; eine Rolltreppe hätte zum Kasten der Scheitelpartie hinaufgeführt und dort wäre ein Museum über den Brückenbau eingerichtet worden. Das Einschwenken der 175 Meter hohen Fachwerktürme wäre eine besonders spektakuläre Attraktion gewesen. Im Bogenscheitel war zudem ein Ausstieg auf einen Fussgängersteg entlang der Brücke vorgesehen, der eine faszinierende Aussicht geboten hätte. Leider konnte dieser Entwurf dem beurteilenden Gremium nicht vorgestellt werden.

[25   HOOVER DAM BYPASS BRIDGE

Der über 300 Meter weit gespannte Dreigelenkbogen sollte mit einem neuartigen Bauvorgang hergestellt werden: Zunächst wären die Zufahrtsabschnitte bis zu den Kämpferstützen konventionell gebaut worden und mit einem Kran über den Kämpferstützen hätte man die 175 Meter hohen Fachwerktürme mit einem Gelenk auf halber Höhe montiert. Diese Fachwerke wären dann mit einer relativ leichten Rückverankerung in ihre definitive Lage abgedreht und miteinander zum Bogenlehrgerüst verbunden worden.

Vom U-förmigen Bogenquerschnitt wäre sodann in geeigneten Abschnitten und in reduzierter Dicke die Bogenplatte mit dem ummantelten Untergurt des Fachwerks als Bewehrung hergestellt worden, und im nächsten Schritt hätten sich problemlos die Querschnittsstege und die restliche Plattendicke betonieren lassen. Das der Melan-Bauweise entsprechende Tragwerk hätte noch eine Verstärkung mit einigen Spannkabeln in den Stegen erfordert.

Gebaut wurde schliesslich eine konventionelle Bogenbrücke im Freivorbau mit einem gewaltigen Aufwand an Rückverankerungskabeln. Mein Gegenentwurf wäre originell, modern und vor allem viel wirtschaftlicher gewesen.

My design incorporated a small shift in this alignment, so that the arch foundations could be immediately beside the hairpin curve. The proposed structural system incorporated an original concept for a three-hinged arch. The bridge would have formed a unit with the Hoover Dam. The arch foundations on the right side would have been easily accessible from the parking areas. An escalator would have brought visitors up into the box and the arch crown, where a museum about the construction of the bridge would have been established. The tilting into position of the 175 m tall truss towers would have been a particularly spectacular attraction. In the crown of the arch, an exit onto a pedestrian bridge running along the bridge would have been provided, which would have offered a fascinating view. Unfortunately, this concept could not be presented to the committee charged with evaluating the designs.

[25   HOOVER DAM BYPASS BRIDGE

An innovative construction method would have been used to build the three-hinged arch, which would span in excess of 300 m. First, the approaches would be built using conventional methods up to the piers above the springing lines. Then, using a crane, 175 m tall truss towers would be erected, each with a hinge at mid-height. These trusses would then be lowered to their final location using relatively small backstay cables and connected together to form the falsework for the arch.

The bottom slab of the U-shaped arch cross section would then be cast in reduced thickness, incorporating the lower chord of the truss as reinforcement. In the next step, concrete for the webs and the remainder of the bottom slab could have been cast without problem. The structure, based on the Melan method of reinforced concrete construction, would then be strengthened using posttensioning tendons in the webs.

In the end, a conventional arch bridge was built. The cantilever construction of this structure required a large quantity of expensive backstay cables. My counter proposal would have been original, modern, and, above all, far more economical.

Bauvorgang: 175 Meter hohe Fachwerktürme werden geneigt und zu einem Bogenlehrgerüst verbunden.
Construction stages: 175 meter high falsework towers are inclined and connected to form the centering of the arch.

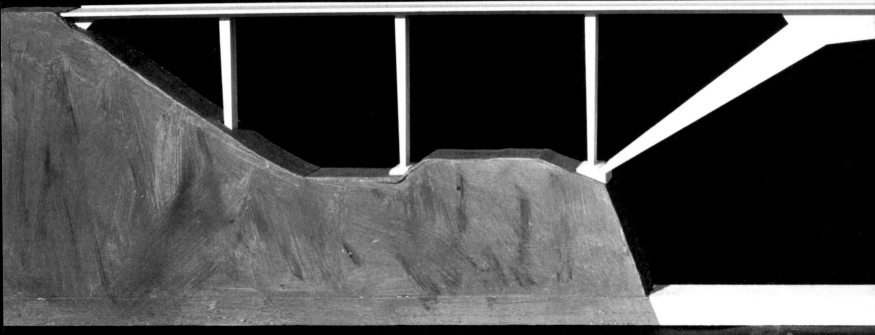

PEACE BRIDGE, BUFFALO
PEACE BRIDGE AT BUFFALO

PROJEKTZEITRAUM 2001–2014
PROJECT PERIOD 2001–2014

Client: The Buffalo and Fort Erie Public Bridge Authority
Design Studies in partnership with Figg Engineering Group, Tallahassee
Project in partnership with Parsons Transportation Group Inc., Washington

[26

Buffalo, the second largest city in the American state of New York, is located at the east end of Lake Erie, a few kilometers upstream from Niagara Falls. The city has had several economic ups and downs throughout its history. Around 1800, Buffalo had 1500 inhabitants. The trade in bulk goods from the areas surrounding the lake, which were transported by ship to Buffalo, enabled the city to grow rapidly in the nineteenth century. In 1900, the population of Buffalo was 250 000.

To serve the growing motor vehicle traffic across the international boundary, the imposing Peace Bridge was built between Buffalo and the Canadian city of Fort Erie in 1927. Construction in 1957 of the St. Lawrence Seaway on the Canadian side isolated Buffalo from navigation. In that year, the population of Buffalo was 580 000. Currently, the population of Buffalo has decreased to 260 000. The transportation of goods is now maintained only by the bridge and the customs facility.

The bridge is currently no longer sufficient for heavy transport. It must be frequently repaired and strengthened. In the late 1990s, the Public Bridge Authority therefore chose to develop designs for a new bridge. After extensive discussions, it was decided to construct a new bridge beside the existing structure, which would be maintained for local traffic. Two contradictory requirements made the task more difficult. Buffalo wanted a prestigious, imposing bridge as an icon of the recovery of the city. The Canadian province of Ontario wanted a simple, economical bridge. In addition, the US wanted their customs plaza, which required considerable space, to be located on the Canadian side and to be linked to the Canadian plaza.

[27 REUSS-BRÜCKE, WASSEN

Die unmittelbar unter dem Dorf Wassen gelegene Reussbrücke der Autobahn A2 ist eine konventionelle, vorgespannte Balkenbrücke. Sie besteht aus zwei getrennten Tragwerken mit Längen von 232 Metern und fünf Spannweiten für die Talspur sowie 192 Metern und vier Spannweiten für die Bergspur. Die Reuss wird in einer Höhe von etwa 30 Metern überquert; bei den südlichen Widerlagern führen die beiden Brücken auch über die auf einer hohen Stützmauer gelegene Kantonsstrasse.

Im August 1987 entwickelte sich im Gotthardgebiet eine ungewöhnliche Wetterlage. Von Süden her drang sehr feuchte Luft über den Alpenkamm nach Norden vor, wo sie auf Kaltluft stiess und extrem starke Niederschläge verursachte, wie sie sonst nur in der Südschweiz vorkommen. Im Urserental wurden nach ergiebigen Niederschlägen in den vorhergehenden Tagen in den 24 Stunden vom 24. auf den 25. August 150 Liter Regen pro Quadratmeter gemessen. Das Hochwasser der Reuss richtete im ganzen Kanton Uri gewaltige Schäden an. Bahnen und Strassen waren unpassierbar.

Im oberen Reusstal führte das Hochwasser im Flussbett eine Pendelbewegung aus und erodierte damit die seitlichen Ufer. Bei Wassen wurde auf einer Länge von rund 200 Metern der Damm unter den Gleisen der Gotthardbahn weggespült und bei der Reussbrücke wurde bei der Talspur der Autobahn ein 25 Meter vom Flusslauf entferntes Stützenfundament unterspült, sodass sich Stütze und Träger etwa 90 Zentimeter senkten. Im Träger bildete sich in der unteren Kastenplatte ein Riss von etwa 8 Zentimetern Breite. Am bedrohlichsten war aber die freigelegte Stützmauer der Kantonsstrasse. Beim Absturz der Mauer wären bei beiden Brücken die unmittelbar neben und unter der Mauer fundierten Stützen weggeschlagen worden. Deshalb wurde unverzüglich die Lücke unter der Stützmauer mit 15 000 Kubikmetern Steinblöcken geschlossen, um die Stützmauer und die Brückenstützen zu sichern.

Nach kurzen Diskussionen wurde sodann im Einvernehmen mit dem Baudirektor des Kantons Uri und dem Direktor des Bundesamtes für Strassen beschlossen, die eingesunkene Talspur-Brücke so weit wie möglich wieder hochzupressen. Diese Arbeit war bezüglich Planung und Ausführung sehr anspruchsvoll. Sie wurde Schritt für Schritt mit zulässigen Toleranzen für Bewegungen und Pressenkräfte genau überwacht und gelang schliesslich auch zur vollen Zufriedenheit aller Beteiligten.

[27 BRIDGE OVER THE REUSS AT WASSEN

The bridge carrying the A2 freeway over the Reuss, located immediately below the village of Wassen, is a conventional prestressed concrete girder bridge. It consists of two separate structures: a 232 m long five span structure for the northbound lanes and a 192 m long four span structure for the southbound lanes. The Reuss is crossed at a height of about 30 m. At the south abutments, both bridges cross a cantonal road which is supported by a tall retaining wall.

In August of 1987, unusual weather conditions developed in the Gotthard region. Very humid air from the south was driven northward over the Alps, where it collided with cold air from the north. This produced heavy rain north of the Alps, which normally would occur only in the southern parts of Switzerland. In the Urseren valley, after significant rainfall in previous days, 150 litres of rain per square meter was measured in the 24 hour period from August 24 to 25. Flooding of the Reuss River thus caused major damage throughout the Canton of Uri. Highways and railways were impassable.

In the upper Reuss valley, the floodwaters caused a pendulum movement in the river bed which eroded the river banks. At Wassen, the embankment under the tracks of the Gotthard railway were scoured away over a length of 200 m. At the northbound structure of the A2 Bridge over the Reuss, soil under a pier foundation 25 m away from the Reuss channel was scoured away, causing a 90 cm settlement of the girder. This downward displacement produced an 8 cm wide crack in the bottom slab of the box girder. The greatest threat came from the exposed retaining wall of the cantonal road. If this wall were to collapse, the piers of both bridges that were founded immediately beside and under the wall would have been destroyed. The holes under the retaining wall were therefore immediately filled with 15 000 cubic meters of boulders, to secure the wall and the bridge piers.

After some brief discussions, the director of construction of the Canton of Uri and the Director of the Federal Department of Highways agreed to raise, to the extent possible, the sunken northbound structure back to its original position. This work was very challenging from the perspective of both design and construction. It was precisely monitored step by step with allowable tolerances for displacements and jacking forces. The work was completed with great success to the full satisfaction of all parties concerned.

VISIONEN / VISIONS
BRÜCKEN MIT SPANNWEITEN VON 3000 METERN
BRIDGES WITH SPANS IN EXCESS OF 3000 METERS

[28

Brücken mit extrem grossen Spannweiten sind in der Regel zollpflichtig. Die Festsetzung des Brückenzolls ist abhängig von den Kosten der Brücke, vom jeweiligen Verwendungszweck des Zolls und von der Anzahl der Nutzer und diese wiederum von der Höhe des Zolls. Die Ermittlung des Zolls ist jedenfalls mit viel mehr Unsicherheiten verbunden als die Planung und Erstellung des Bauwerks selbst.

Extrem weit gespannte Brücken lassen sich nur als Kabelbrücken, das heisst als Hängebrücken oder Schrägkabelbrücken erstellen. Hängebrücken sind trotz des längeren Kraftweges den Schrägkabelbrücken überlegen, da letztere im Mittelbereich der Spannweite relativ flache und entsprechend starke Kabel erfordern und im Bereich der Pylone sehr grosse Druckkräfte im Träger aufweisen.

Bei den Kosten der Brücke spielen nicht nur die üblichen Aufwendungen für Erstellung, Betrieb, Unterhalt und Abbruch sowie die vorgesehene Nutzungsdauer eine Rolle, sondern auch die Bauzeit bis zur Inbetriebnahme des Bauwerks. Die Brücke muss deshalb so projektiert werden, dass an mehreren Stellen gleichzeitig gebaut werden kann.

Deshalb bestehen bei vielen Brücken – so etwa bei Bogenbrücken – Zufahrts- und Bogenbereich aus verschiedenen Tragsystemen. Aus demselben Grund ist es bei einer extrem weit gespannten Hängebrücke vorteilhaft, dieser im Pylonbereich ein Schrägkabelsystem zu überlagern. In diesem Fall können die Arbeiten im Prinzip bei beiden Brückenwiderlagern und beiden Pylonen gleichzeitig begonnen werden; zusätzlich kann eine beachtliche Länge des Trägers parallel zum Spinnen der Hängekabel hergestellt werden.

SCHWINGUNGEN
Bei Hängebrücken spielen die Schwingungen eine wichtige Rolle. Es geht dabei einerseits um die Einwirkung der Wirbelablösung am Brückenträger und andererseits um die Auswirkung beziehungsweise das Verhalten des Brückenträgers infolge der Wirbelablösung. Einwirkung und Auswirkung beeinflussen sich gegenseitig. Die Einwirkung ist im Wesentlichen abhängig von der Querschnittsform, insbesondere den Querschnittsrändern. In Bezug auf die Auswirkung ist vor allem das Flattern – eine Kombination von Biege- und Torsionsschwingung – ein gefährliches Phänomen. Es entsteht, wenn am Tragsystem die Frequenz der Biegeschwingung gleich gross oder um ein Mehrfaches grösser ist als diejenige der Torsionsschwingung. Die Berechnung der kritischen Windgeschwindigkeit bei Flattern ist sehr komplex; sie muss bei grösseren Brücken immer mithilfe von Windkanalversuchen ermittelt werden. Beim Entwurf von Brücken mit extremer Spannweite wird meistens ein Verkehrsprofil mit drei Fahrbahnen in beiden Richtungen für Motorfahrzeuge, einer Doppelspur für die Eisenbahn zwischen den Autospuren und Gehwegen am Querschnittsrand angenommen. Die gesamte Trägerbreite beträgt somit etwa 50 bis 60 Meter.

KABELSYSTEME
Für Brückendeck und Kabelsystem gibt es grundsätzlich drei verschiedene konzeptionelle Varianten: Variante 1 sieht nur zwei Kabelstränge vor, die am Trägerrand verankert sind. Die drei Längsträger für die Motorfahrzeug-Spuren und die Bahn geben ihre Last bei einem gewaltigen Querträger ab, der seine Last über die Hänger an die Hauptkabelstränge überträgt.

Variante 2 weist drei Hauptkabelstränge auf: zwei am Querschnittsrand und den dritten in der Mitte zwischen den beiden Bahngleisen. Der Querträger muss bei dieser Variante nicht höher sein als die Längsträger.

Variante 3 hat vier Hauptkabelstränge; zwei an den Querschnittsrändern und zwei beidseits des Gleislängsträgers.

Es sind schon Tragsysteme mit sechs Haupttragkabeln vorgeschlagen worden, mit je einem Hauptkabelstrang an den Rändern der drei Längsträger.

VERSCHIEBUNGEN
Hängebrücken mit orthotropem Stahlquerschnitt (Platten-Aussteifungen in einer Richtung) können insbesondere bei Eisenbahnbrücken ohne Dilatationsfugen ausgeführt werden. Der Brückenträger wird bei den Endwiderlagern beziehungsweise den Verankerungsblöcken der Haupthängekabel verankert. Bei konstantem Querschnitt treten nur Spannungen in Längsrichtung der Brücke auf und der Träger weist infolge von Temperaturänderungen keine Verschiebungen auf – wie verschweisste Schienen. Bei variablem Querschnitt – wenn etwa der Querschnitt, infolge eines überlagerten Schrägkabelsystems verstärkt wird – entstehen infolge Tempe-

raturänderungen kleinere Dehnungen und dementsprechend auch kleine Trägerverschiebungen.

Bei grossen Trägerauskragungen im Bauzustand muss die seitliche Trägerverschiebung mit temporären Türmen (im Wasser) oder verankerten Schiffen vermindert werden. Bei grosser Höhe der Fahrbahn über Grund oder Wasser lässt sich eine höhere Seitensteifigkeit mit Schrägkabeln, die an seitlichen Auslegern der Pylone befestigt sind, ebenfalls erreichen.

Hängebrücken mit extrem grossen Spannweiten weisen zahlreiche konstruktive Parameter auf. Das optimale Tragsystem erfordert die Überprüfung eines umfangreichen Katalogs von Konzepten.

Bridges with extremely long spans are normally operated as toll bridges. The tolls are usually determined as a function of the construction cost of the bridge, the intended use of toll revenue, and the number of users, which in turn depends on the cost of the toll. In all cases, setting the level of bridge tolls is a far more risky undertaking than the design and construction of the structure itself.

Extremely long span bridges must be designed as cable-supported structures, i.e., as suspension bridges or cable-stayed bridges. In spite of their longer load path, suspension bridges are superior to cable-stayed bridges, since the latter require relatively flat and hence large cables near midspan, and exhibit large compressive forces in the girder near the towers.

In addition to the cost of construction, operation and maintenance over the anticipated service life, and demolition, the cost of toll bridges is determined to a large extent by the duration of construction, which establishes the time at which the facility can begin to generate revenue. For extremely long span bridges, the duration of construction can be minimized by working at several locations simultaneously. Extremely long span bridges must therefore be designed to make this possible.

For this reason, several different structural systems are used for different portions of bridges, as is the case for many arch bridges, which use different systems for the approach spans and the arch proper. For the same reason, it is beneficial for extremely long span suspension bridges to combine near the towers a cable-stayed system with a hanging cable system. In such cases, erection of the girder can begin simultaneously at the abutments and at the towers. In this way, it would also be possible to erect a significant portion of the girder in parallel to the spinning of the main suspension cable.

VIBRATIONS

Vibrations play an important role in the design of suspension bridges. On the one hand, the shedding of vortices applies a dynamic load to the girder, while on the other hand, the response of the girder affects the characteristics of the shedding of vortices. Cause and effect, i.e. loading and response, are thus mutually related. The load is mainly dependent on the shape of the cross-section, especially the details at the edges of the section. The combination of bending and torsional oscillation known as flutter is generally regarded as a dangerous phenomenon. It occurs in structural systems for which the frequency of flexural vibration is equal to or a multiple of the frequency of torsional vibration. The calculation of the critical wind speed for flutter is very complex. For large bridges, it must always be determined on the basis of wind tunnel studies.

CABLE SYSTEMS

Bridges with extremely long spans will normally carry a highway cross-section with three traffic lanes in both directions, a double track for railway between the highway lanes, and footpaths along the edges. The total width of the girder is thus in the 50 to 60 m range. Bridge deck and cable systems, therefore, will generally consist of one of the three following alternative concepts:

Alternative 1 consists of only two cable groups which are anchored along the outer edges of the deck. Three main longitudinal girders are provided, one for each direction of highway traffic and one for railway. These girders transfer their load to strong transverse beams, which in turn transfer their load to suspenders and the main cables.

Alternative 2 consists of three main cable groups, two along the edges of the deck and the third in the middle between the two railway tracks. For this alternative, the transverse beams must not be deeper than the main girders.

Alternative 3 has four main cable groups, two along the edges of the deck and two either side of the longitudinal girder for the railway. Structural systems with six main cable groups have been proposed, with one cable group at each edge of the three main longitudinal girders.

DISPLACEMENTS

Suspension bridges with orthotropic steel cross-sections (plates stiffened in one direction) can be built without expansion joints, especially for railway bridges. The girder is anchored at the end abutments or the anchorages of the main cables. For a constant cross-section, only longitudinal stresses are produced and the girder exhibits no displacements due to change in temperature, in a similar manner to welded rails. For bridges with a variable cross-section, as would be the case for a girder strengthened by the addition of a cable-stay system, small strains and hence small girder displacements are produced. During construction, the lateral displacement of long girder cantilevers must be minimized through the use of temporary towers or anchored ships. For bridge decks that are aligned relatively high over land or water, a higher lateral stiffness than that produced by the girder alone is desirable. This can be achieved with inclined cables fixed to lateral masts attached to the towers.

Suspension bridges with extremely long spans have numerous design parameters. The ideal structural system requires the checking of an extensive catalog of concepts.

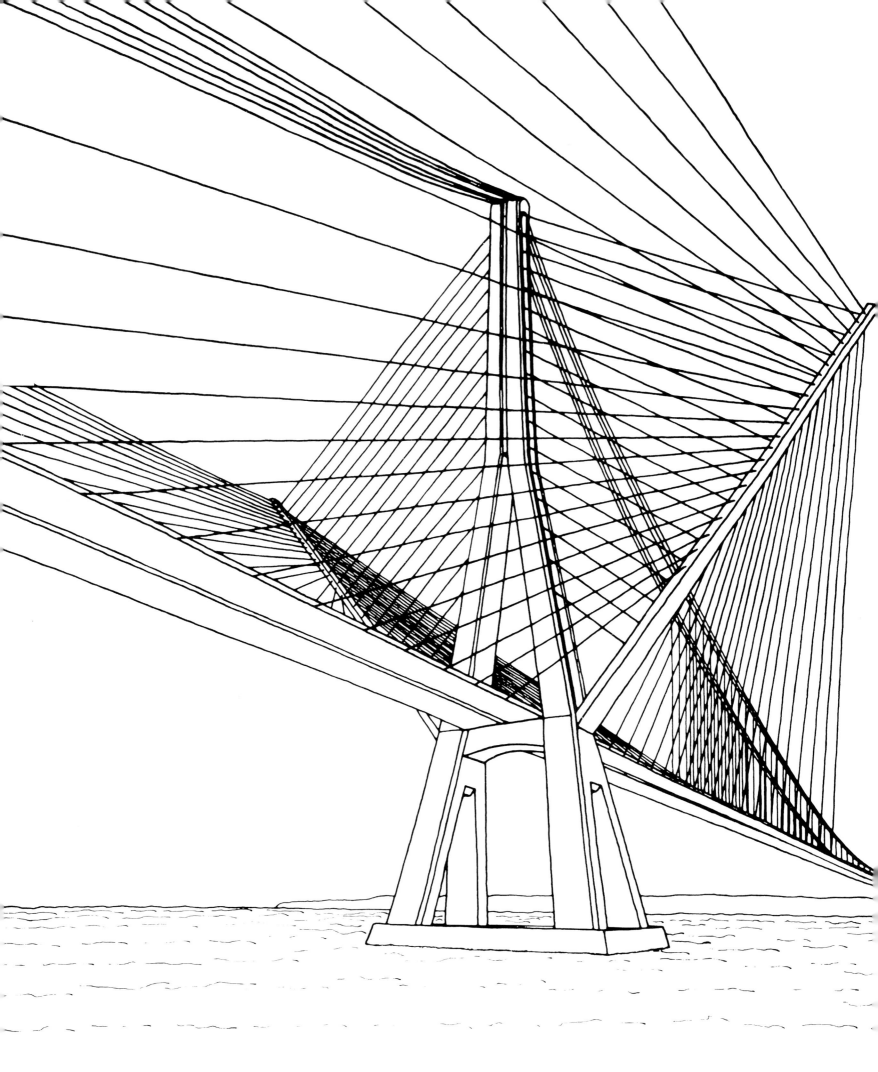

[28 BRÜCKEN MIT SPANNWEITEN VON 3000 METERN / BRIDGES WITH SPANS IN EXCESS OF 3000 METERS

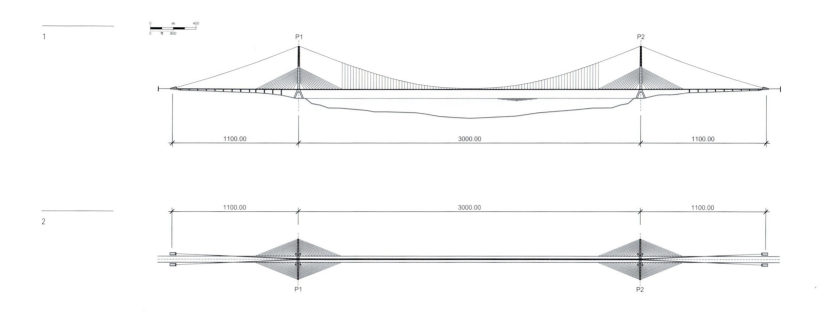

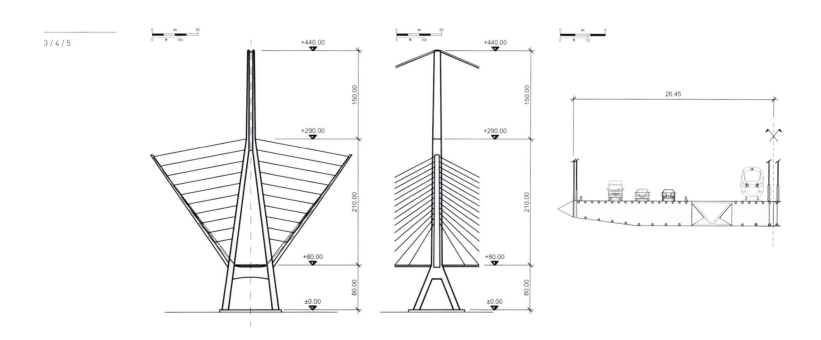

1 Längsschnitt / Longitudinal section
2 Grundriss / Plan
3 Ansicht Pylon / Transverse elevation of tower
4 Längsschnitt Pylon / Longitudinal elevation of tower
5 Querschnitt / Cross-section

Gottfried Keller, *Alte Brücke*, 1850

Schöne Brücke,
hast mich oft getragen, /
Wenn mein Herz
erwartungsvoll geschlagen.

Fair bridge,
thou hast so often borne me, /
With my heart
beating expectantly.

BRÜCKENGESCHICHTEN
BRIDGE STORIES

ISO CAMARTIN

Im Siegel der Universität Regensburg ist nicht etwa der berühmte Dom dieser Stadt zu sehen. Abgebildet wird die Steinerne Brücke, der *pons optimus,* wie man stolz das mittelalterliche Bauwerk schon im 12. Jahrhundert nannte. Es war offenbar bautechnisch die allerbeste Brücke, die damals über die Donau führte. Im Lauf der Jahrhunderte hat sie ihr Aussehen nur unwesentlich verändert: Zwei der urspünglichen Wehr- und Wachtürme sind zwar verschwunden. Aber noch immer stehen die Steinbögen stark und mächtig da, die Wassermassen der Donau trotzig spaltend, als könnte nichts sie ins Wanken bringen. Und noch immer staunt man darüber, wie damals diese Pfeilerfundamente in den reissenden Fluss gelegt werden konnten, wie man die Steinquadermauern darauf setzte, dann die 14 elegant einander folgenden Brückenbögen über die grosse Flussbreite errichtete: ein Wunderwerk nachrömischer Brückenkunst. Später wurden die Pfeilerinseln erweitert, was dazu führte, dass das fliessende Wasser durch die verengten Bögen in Bedrängnis kam und die berühmten «Donaustrudel» bildete. Der Brückenbau war derart kühn, dass man hier den Teufel unter den beteiligten Baumeistern vermutete. Und so erzählt man sich auch bei dieser Brücke allerlei Geschichten, wie es denn gelang, am Ende den Teufel zu überlisten, ohne dass arme Menschenseelen ihm als Lohn für seine Arbeit in die Hölle folgen mussten. Um Brücken blühen seit der frühesten Zeit Sagen und Legenden. Bis zum heutigen Tag geht von der Kühnheit grosser Brücken eine Faszination aus.

«Als wir jüngst in Regensburg waren, sind wir über den Strudel gefahren», haben wir als Studenten gesungen. Vor wenigen Wochen stand ich wieder einmal auf Regensburgs Steinerner Brücke, die gerade wieder saniert wird, und erinnerte mich daran, dass Brücken auch priviligierte Orte für erotische Liebesabenteuer sind, für Küsse und Umarmungen, Begegnungen und Abschiede. Davon weiss man nicht nur in Paris Geschichten zu erzählen, auch in Regensburg hat mancher Student sich nach Mitternacht auf der Brücke von seiner Liebsten getrennt und die Schöne in Richtung Katharinenspital nach Stadtamhof in die Dunkelheit entschwinden lassen – weil sie dies so wünschte und ihren neuesten Verehrer so den elterlichen Augen entziehen konnte. Liebesgeschichten, die auf oder unter Brücken spielen, gibt es zu Tausenden. Wer in Paris die Seine überquert, kann dabei gar nicht anders als an *Les amants du Pont-Neuf* denken, jene Geschichte einer verrückten Liebe zwischen einem

The official seal of the University of Regensburg shows not the city's famous cathedral, but rather its medieval stone bridge, the Steinerne Brücke hailed as *pons optimus* as long ago as the twelfth century. In those days, it seems, it was the best engineered crossing on the Danube. Its appearance has not changed much over the centuries. Two of the original fortified watchtowers have disappeared, but the arches are as strong and sturdy as ever, defiantly sundering the waters of the Danube as if nothing could shake them. That there were engineers even in medieval times who knew how to anchor piers in fast-flowing waters, how to erect walls of quarried stone on top of them, and how to span fourteen elegant arches across the full breadth of such a mighty river continues to amaze us to this day. The Stone Bridge of Regensburg is indeed a miracle of post-Roman bridge building. The enlargement of the islands on which the piers stand at a later date impeded the river's flow, giving rise to the notorious maelstrom known as the "Danube Strudel". But the bridge had always been daring–so daring, in fact, that Satan himself is rumored to have had a hand in it. Thus, as with so many other bridges, all manner of yarns were spun about how the Devil was at last outwitted without the poor souls of Regensburg being rewarded for their pains by having to follow him into Hell. Bridges have attracted all sorts of sagas and legends since time immemorial and the sheer boldness of the largest of them continues to fascinate us to this day.

As students we used to sing an old folksong about crossing the "Strudel" in Regensburg. And when I was there just a few weeks ago and took the opportunity to saunter across the Stone Bridge that is currently being restored, I was reminded that bridges are a favorite spot for amorous adventures, too–for clandestine kisses and embraces, trysts and tender farewells. Not just in Paris, but in Regensburg too, many a student would take leave of his heart's joy up on the bridge and then look on longingly as she disappeared into the darkness towards the Katharinenspital and Stadtamhof–because she herself had wanted it thus, if only to spare her new admirer her parents' scrutiny for a while. How many thousand love stories take place on or underneath bridges! No one who crosses the Seine in Paris can fail to recall *Les amants du Pont-Neuf,* the story of an amour fou between a clochard and a blind painter that in 1991 touched the hearts of moviegoers the world over. *The Bridges of Madison County* of

Clochard und einer erblindenden Malerin, die im Jahr 1991 so viele Kinogänger erschütterte. *The Bridges of Madison County* war 1995 eine etwas sentimentale, aber schauspielerisch bewegende Hollywood-Geschichte mit Meryl Streep und Clint Eastwood über einen Fotografen, der alte Brücken suchte und die grosse Liebe fand. Es scheint beinahe jede Brücke nicht nur ihre verbindende Funktion zu haben, sondern auch ihre ganz eigenen Geschichten hervorzubringen. Aufgabe der dichterischen Fantasie ist es offenbar, diese Geschichten nachzuerzählen oder sie auch neu zu erfinden, um sie der Welt bekannt zu machen.

Die Weltliteratur kennt zahlreiche Gedichte, Erzählungen und Romane, in deren Mittelpunkt Brücken stehen. In seiner Studienzeit verliebte sich der nicht mehr ganz junge Stipendiat Gottfried Keller in Heidelberg in die Professorentochter Johanna Kapp. Die 16-Jährige gab ihm jedoch zu verstehen, sie sei mit dem Philosophen Feuerbach liiert. Seinen Liebesschmerz vertraute Keller 1850 der *Alten Brücke* an, die er oft überquerte, um auf der rechten Neckarseite seine Angebetete im Haus des Philosophen Kapp zu besuchen: «Schöne Brücke, hast mich oft getragen, / Wenn mein Herz erwartungsvoll geschlagen.» Anfangs glaubt der Liebende, die stolzen Brückenbögen hätten seine Freude mitgefühlt und ihn in seiner Liebeskühnheit bestärkt. Jetzt aber, da er die Wahrheit erfahren hat und unter der Zurückweisung schwer leidet, spürt er, dass der Last seines Herzwehs «kein Joch sich fühlend biegt». Müsste er jetzt nicht anderswo, vielleicht weit oben in den Bergen, nach einem schwachen Steg Ausschau halten, «der sich meinem Kummer zitternd fügt»? Böse kann er weder der Brücke noch der Geliebten sein, und so bittet der Dichter die Brücke, die Frau «mit anderem Weh und anderen Leiden / Und im Herzen andere Seligkeiten» weiterhin leicht über die Brücke zu tragen, denn: «Ewig aber wird es nicht geschehen, / dass ein bessres Weib hinüberwallt!» – Ein anderes schönes Gedicht über eine Brücke – die Karlsbrücke in Prag – hat der Arzt und Dichter Hugo Salus geschrieben. Er vergleicht die Hast der Menschen, die während des Tages über die Brücke eilen, mit der Gelassenheit der Moldau, deren Fluten Tag und Nacht wie träumend unter der Brücke hinwegziehen. Das Gedicht lautet:

Prager Brücke
Über der alten Brücke in Prag
Hängt ein verschlafener Frühlingsmorgen.
Über die Brücke in Lust und Plag'
Hasten die Freuden und schleichen die Sorgen.

Nacht und Morgen und leuchtender Tag,
Und kein Zögern und kein Sich-Sputen.
Unter der alten Brücke in Prag
Wälzt der Strom seine träumenden Fluten…

1995 starring Meryl Streep and Clint Eastwood is a similarly moving, if slightly sentimental, story of a photographer whose search for old bridges leads him to the love of his life. It is as if almost every bridge were more than just a link between two places, as if almost every bridge had the capacity to generate stories of its own. It follows that the job of the poet or storyteller is to retell, reinvent, and embellish these tales to make them more widely known.

World literature is full of poems, short stories, and novels at the heart of which is a bridge. As a student in Heidelberg, the not so young stipendiary Gottfried Keller fell hopelessly in love with the professor's daughter Johanna Kapp. Although no more than sixteen at the time, Johanna gave him to understand that she was already promised to the philosopher Ludwig Feuerbach. Keller confided the misery of unrequited love to the Old Bridge that he had so often crossed to visit the object of his desire at the home of Professor Kapp on the other side of the River Neckar: "Fair bridge, thou hast so often borne me, / With my heart beating expectantly." Having at first persuaded himself that the "proud arches" share his joy and support him in his suit, on learning the truth–and still reeling from his beloved's rejection–he realizes that the burden in his heart is one to which "no span feelingly bends". Should he now venture into the mountains in search of some more pliant plank, "that will shake and sag under my sorrows," he wonders? Yet he resents neither the bridge nor his beloved and ends on an upbeat note by asking the bridge to continue carrying the woman of his dreams, "with other woes and other torment, / her heart with other joys content," since "Surely no eternity shall pass, / E'er there comes a better lass!"

Another beautiful poem about a bridge, in this case the Charles Bridge in Prague, was composed by the physician-poet Hugo Salus. The comparison drawn here is between the hustle and bustle on the bridge during the day and the dream-like serenity of the River Vltava by day and by night:

The Prague Bridge
Over the ancient bridge in Prague
Hangs a slumberous springtide morn.
Over the ancient bridge in Prague
Hasten the joyous, creep the careworn.

Night and morning and radiant day,
Unhurriedly, unwaveringly,
Under the ancient bridge in Prague
Rolls the great river, dreamily…

Viele schöne Gefühle und Gedanken kreisen in der Dichtung um Brücken, ihr Verbindendes und ihr Trennendes bedenkend. Denn diesseits der Brücke ist nicht jenseits, und es herrschen des Öfteren auf der einen Seite ganz andere Sitten und Lebensgesetze als auf der anderen Seite der Brücke. Wir wollen uns hier nur auf einige der berühmtesten Brücken in der Literaturgeschichte beschränken. Ich könnte auch sagen: auf meine Lieblingsbrücken, die dies nicht allein durch ihre Erbauer, sondern durch die Vorstellungskraft von Dichtern und Erzählern geworden sind.

HALLUZINATIONEN

Die literarisch bedeutendste Brücke aller Zeiten dürfte die Rialtobrücke in Venedig sein und bleiben, an der sich nach Shakespeare der Jude Shylock und der Kaufmann von Venedig auf waghalsige Geschäfte miteinander einliessen. So weit wollen wir jedoch nicht zurückgreifen. Wir setzen hier mit literarischen Zeugnissen ein, die gegen Ende des 19. Jahrhunderts Ereignisse um und auf Brücken aufgreifen. In der Sammlung *Tales of Soldiers and Civilians* des amerikanischen Journalisten und Schriftstellers Ambrose Bierce erschien 1891 erstmalig in Buchform seine Kurzgeschichte *An Occurrence at Owl Creek Bridge (Zwischenfall auf der Eulenfluss-Brücke)* – ein so faszinierender wie verstörender Bericht, wie während des amerikanischen Sezessionskrieges ein Spion der Südstaaten von einem Detachement von Unionssoldaten auf der Brücke gehängt wird. Bierce, der selbst am Krieg der unierten Nordstaaten gegen die konföderierten Südstaaten teilgenommen hatte, galt bei seinen Zeitgenossen als genialer, bitterböser Zyniker. Er war nicht nur als Journalist für seine rücksichtslose Kritik gefürchtet (sein heute berühmtestes Buch heisst *Das Wörterbuch des Teufels*), sondern mit Edgar Allan Poe wurde er auch als der Mitbegründer der Gattung der «Horrorgeschichten» berühmt. In der erwähnten Sammlung verarbeitete er zum Teil seine schaurigen Erlebnisse als Unionssoldat am Potomac River im Jahr 1861.

Die Brückengeschichte ist ein raffiniert konstruierter Bericht, wie ein Exekutionskommando der Unionstruppen die Hinrichtung des Pflanzers und Kundschafters Peyton Farquhar vorbereitet und ausführt. Zunächst sieht alles nach sachlich-mitleidloser Berichterstattung aus. Doch bald einmal spüren wir, dass der Erzähler uns in ganz andere Vorstellungswelten hineinzieht. Wir sitzen als Leser selbst im Kopf des zu Hängenden und erleben im Augenblick, da man ihm das Brett unter den Füssen wegzieht und er nur noch an dem an einem Kreuzbalken der Brücke befestigten Seil hängt, eine halluzinatorische Rettungsvision voller realistischer Details, die uns seinen Fall in den Fluss, sein Untertauchen und sein Schwimmen, die Befreiung aus der Schlinge, das Entkommen aus den Gewehrsalven, seine Gedanken an Frau und Kinder, seine Rettung aus dem Fluss, das Verbergen in einem Wald- und Wiesenfeld mitfühlen lassen. Wir sind Zeugen einer unglaublich scheinenden Befreiung, sehen mit dem Entkommen die Mücken über der Wasseroberfläche schwirren, die zuckenden Beine der Wasserspinnen, hören das Vibrieren der Libellen, streifen mit dem Mann einen Tag und eine Nacht durch die Landschaft, im Schutz der Pflanzen und der Dun-

With their connotations of connection and separation, bridges tend to evoke all sorts of fine feelings and thoughts in poets. For this side of the bridge is not the same as the other, and the customs and rules prevailing on this bank may be very different from those on the one opposite. We shall confine ourselves here to just a few of the most famous bridges in the history of literature – or rather to those bridges which, thanks to the engineers who built them and the poets and writers who have since then imagined them, have become firm favorites of mine.

HALLUCINATIONS

The most important bridge of all time in the world of literature is surely the Rialto Bridge in Venice, for it was there that Shylock and the Merchant of Venice in the play of that name agreed to the highly dubious deal on which the whole plot hinges. But we shall not go back as far as that here. Instead we shall start with works of literature from the late nineteenth century and later, all of which turn on events on or around bridges. The short story "An Occurrence at Owl Creek Bridge", first anthologized in the 1891 collection *Tales of Soldiers and Civilians* by the American writer and journalist Ambrose Bierce, is a fascinating and deeply troubling account of an incident during the American Civil War, when a Confederate spy was hanged by a detachment of Union soldiers on the bridge of the title. Bierce, who himself saw action in the war between the pro-Union northern states and the secessionist "slave states", was regarded by contemporaries as a brilliant, if sharp-tongued cynic. Not only was he feared as a journalist capable of penning searing critiques (his most famous book these days is *The Devil's Dictionary*), but he was also acclaimed as a co-initiator, alongside Edgar Allan Poe, of the genre now known as "horror fiction", The aforementioned collection shows us Bierce trying to come to terms with his experiences – some of them horrific – as a Union soldier stationed on the Potomac River in 1861.

"An Occurrence at Owl Creek Bridge" is an ingeniously structured account of how a Union execution commando prepares and carries out the execution of a gentleman planter and Confederate scout by the name of Peyton Farquhar. At first it reads like factual, utterly unsentimental reportage. But before long we realize that the narrator is drawing us into a completely different fantasy world. He even affords us readers a glimpse inside the head of the man about to be hanged, allowing us to experience with him the moment the board is pulled away, leaving him dangling from a noose tied to a crossbeam of the bridge. What follows is Farquhar's hallucinatory vision of his own rescue, which is full of realistic detail such as his fall from the bridge, his plunge into the river, his struggle to free himself from the cord still wound around him, his success at evading the volleys of gunfire aimed at him, his thoughts of his wife and children, and his eventual emergence from the river to the life of a fugitive in the forests and fields. As eyewitnesses of his miraculous escape, we share with him the sight of the gnats dancing above the river and the twitching legs of the water spiders, just as we hear with him the beating of the dragonflies' wings. We are at his side when he roams the landscape day and night, seeking the shelter of trees and

kelheit, erleben den Sternenhimmel über ihm, spüren die Schmerzen in seinem schrecklich geschwollenen Hals, stehen am Ende mit ihm am Tor seiner eigenen Farm, glauben die wehenden Kleider seiner Frau zu sehen, die ihm von der Veranda entgegenkommt, «ein Lächeln unendlichen Glücks auf den Lippen. Unvergleichliche Grazie und Würde liegt in ihrer Haltung. Wie schön sie doch ist!» Hat der Mann es geschafft, seinen Henkern zu entkommen? «Als er seine Frau gerade umfangen will, fühlt er einen betäubenden Schlag auf den Nacken. Mit einem Knall wie ein Kanonenschlag schiesst blendendweisses Licht rings um ihn auf – dann ist alles dunkel und still.»

Alles nur Wahn und Traum! Die Realität ist unerbittlich. Es war diese Flucht im Kopf des Peyton Farquhar nur der Versuch eines nicht ganz herzlosen Schriftstellers, in der Todessekunde eines hingerichteten Soldaten sich die Vision seiner Rettung auszumalen. Die nicht mehr als zehnseitige Geschichte endet mit den Worten: «Peyton Farquhar war tot. Mit gebrochenem Genick schwang sein Körper unter den Schwellen der Eulenfluss-Brücke sanft von einer Seite zur anderen.» Könnte es sein, dass sein Tod am Ende doch eine Rettung war? Wo immer ich auf Brücken stehe, durch deren Planken ich das unten fliessende Wasser sehen kann, muss ich an den braven Farmer Peyton aus den Südstaaten denken, dem der Krieg so übel mitgespielt hat.

ZUFALL ODER GOTTESPLAN?
Weit grössere Berühmtheit als die Geschichte von Bierce erlangte freilich der 1927 erschienene Roman von Thornton Wilder *The Bridge of San Luis Rey (Die Brücke von San Luis Rey)*. Im Jahr 1714 riss eine bereits von den Inkas gebaute Hängebrücke zwischen Lima und Cuzco. Fünf Menschen, die in diesem Augenblick die Brücke überquerten, stürzten in die tiefe Schlucht und in den Tod. Das Unglück ist ein historisch dokumentiertes Ereignis. Der Franziskanermönch Bruder Juniper will erkunden, ob es purem Zufall zu verdanken ist, oder ob es doch durch Lenkung göttlicher Vorsehung erklärt werden kann. Das heisst: Entsprach der Tod dieser fünf Menschen einem Gottesplan, weil für die betroffenen Menschen aus göttlichem Blickwinkel der Lebenssinn gerade in diesem Augenblick erreicht war und somit ihr Tod auch gerechtfertigt? Als sei das Unglück dieser Menschen in einem «perfekten Laboratorium Gottes» vorbereitet und durchgeführt worden? «Vielleicht ein Zufall» lautet der Titel des ersten Kapitels, «Vielleicht eine Fügung» ist das letzte überschrieben. Bruder Juniper versucht deshalb, die Lebensgeschichte der fünf Opfer zu erforschen. Die damals auch in Südamerika operierenden Geister der katholischen Inquisition finden die Aufzeichnungen des Mönchs, erklären sie für ketzerisch, machen dem Franziskanermönch den Prozess und verurteilen ihn zum Tod auf dem Scheiterhaufen. Aus dieser Geschichte, die eine theologische Frage ins Zentrum stellt, – nämlich: Gibt es für ein solches Unglück überhaupt eine religiöse Rechtfertigung? – entwickelt Thornton Wilder ein faszinierendes Kaleidoskop von Menschenschicksalen, die sich berühren und an einem bestimmten Punkt ihres Lebenswegs, wie von göttlicher oder teuflischer Hand geführt, gemeinsam auch ihr

darkness, and trying to decipher the "great golden stars." We even feel the soreness of his horribly swollen neck and stand with him at the gate of his home, like him convinced that the "flutter of female garments" must be his wife coming towards him from the veranda, "with a smile of ineffable joy, an attitude of matchless grace and dignity," leading us to sigh with him, "Ah, how beautiful she is!" So has Farquhar indeed escaped his executioners? "As he is about to clasp her he feels a stunning blow on the back of the neck; a blinding white light blazes all about him with a sound like the shock of a cannon—then all is darkness and silence."

So it was all just delirium and dream! The remorselessness of reality! Farquhar's imagined escape turns out to be no more than the attempt of a not entirely heartless writer to have a condemned soldier paint himself a vision of his own rescue in the very second of his death. The story, which is just ten pages long, ends with the bitter truth of the matter: "Peyton Farquhar was dead; his body, with a broken neck, swung gently from side to side beneath the timbers of the Owl Creek Bridge." Could it be that ultimately his death was also a kind of rescue? Whenever I happen to be standing on a bridge where the gaps between the planks afford me a glimpse of the waters gliding past below, I cannot help but think of the secessionist farmer Peyton Farquhar and the injustice dealt him by the war.

CHANCE OR PROVIDENCE?
Far more widely known than Bierce's story is Thornton Wilder's novel *The Bridge of San Luis Rey* of 1927. This is the story of an Inca rope bridge on the road from Lima to Cuzco, which in 1714 collapsed, sending five people to their deaths in the canyon below. The tragedy is a historically documented event. The book, however, centers on a Franciscan friar, Brother Juniper, who sets out to ascertain whether the accident was pure chance or brought about by divine providence. He wants to know whether the fatalities were part of God's plan–perhaps because the five people in question had fulfilled their purpose in life, at least from the point of view of the Almighty, making their death justifiable? Was the misfortune that befell them prepared and seen through to completion in "God's perfect laboratory"? The title of the first chapter, "Perhaps an Accident", is echoed in the title of the last, "Perhaps an Intention". In the course of his inquiry, Brother Juniper tries to find out more about the lives of the five victims. The Inquisition, however, which by that time had become active even in South America, finds the friar's notes and cites them as evidence for the prosecution in the ensuing trial for heresy, which predictably ends with Juniper being convicted and sentenced to burn at the stake. Out of this story, which essentially turns on a theological question–Can there ever be any religious justification for such a tragedy?–Wilder develops a fascinating kaleidoscope of five life stories that in places intersect and on one fateful day share the same end, though whether through divine intervention or the work of the Devil remains a moot point. The last words of the novel are spoken by the abbess of a convent in Lima: "There is a land of the living and a land of the dead and the bridge is love, the only survival, the only meaning."

Ende finden. Die letzten Worte des Romans, gesprochen von der Äbtissin eines Klosters in Lima, lauten: «Da ist ein Land der Lebenden und ein Land der Toten, und die Brücke zwischen ihnen ist die Liebe – das einzige Bleibende, der einzige Sinn.»

So erzählt Wilder konsequenterweise in diesem Roman die Liebesgeschichten der von der Brücke von San Luis Rey in den Tod stürzenden Figuren. Die Geschichte zunächst der Dona Maria de Montemayor, die ihre in Spanien lebende Tochter Clara abgöttisch liebt, ihr sehnsuchtsvolle Briefe schreibt, ohne von dieser Gegenliebe zu erfahren. Man kann eben begütert sein und dennoch hilflos und verblendet wie Dona Maria. In dem ihr gewidmeten Kapitel heisst es an einer Stelle: «Die Natur ist taub; Gott ist gleichgültig gegen unsere Ängste; nichts in der Menschen Macht vermag den Lauf der ewigen Gesetze zu ändern.» In Begleitung ihrer wunderbaren Betreuerin Pepita wird das Schicksal die Marquesa auf der Brücke einholen. – Es folgt die Geschichte des Bauern Estaban, der erfolglos versucht, die Liebe seines Bruders Manuel zu erringen. «Es war bloss dies, dass im Herzen des einen noch Raum war für eine sorgfältig genährte, fantasievolle Zuneigung, und im Herzen des anderen nicht.» Als er merkt, dass diese Liebe für ihn verloren ist, lässt er sich von einem Kapitän als Matrose anheuern, doch er kommt nur bis auf die Brücke. – Darauf folgt die Geschichte von Onkel Pio, einem Abenteurer und begabten Frauentröster, der sich in die Schauspielerin Camila Périchole verliebt. Es ist jene Sängerin, die wir als Mätresse des Vizekönigs von Peru aus Jacques Offenbachs komischer Oper La Périchole kennen. Freilich ist auch diese Liebe keine glückliche dauerhafte. «Was gibt es Entzückenderes auf der Welt als ein schönes Weib, das einem spanischen Meisterwerk gerecht wird?», fragt sich dieser Pio. Er muss erfahren, dass Schönheit noch keine Garantie für gegenseitige Liebe ist. «Er betrachtete die Liebe als eine Art grausame Krankheit, welche die Erwählten gegen Ende ihrer Jugendzeit durchmachen müssen und aus der sie bleich und erschüttert, jedoch vorbereitet auf das Geschäft des Lebens hervorgehen.» Onkel Pio, dem Camila nach anfänglichem Zögern ihren Sohn anvertraut, damit dieser in der Stadt zu einer guten Ausbildung gelangt, wird mit diesem Kind und den drei anderen Personen an jenem Schicksalstag von der Brücke in die Schlucht stürzen. Eine grosse Anzahl anderer Figuren erhalten in diesem Roman ihre rätselhafte Rolle und ihren Platz in der Berührung mit dem Leben der fünf Sterbenden. Ihre Bestimmung ist es freilich, vom Unglück der einreissenden Hängebrücke verschont zu bleiben. Die erwähnte Äbtissin sagt im Schlusskapitel zur Tochter der Marquesa de Montemayor, die nach dem Tod ihrer Mutter nach Peru zurückkehrt: «Wir alle, wir alle haben gefehlt. Man wünscht sich, dafür bestraft zu werden. Man ist bereit, jede Art von Busse hinzunehmen, aber wisst Ihr, meine Töchter, wenn wir lieben –, ich wage es kaum zu sagen – wenn wir lieben, scheinen unsere Verfehlungen nicht lange zu währen.» Ein grandioser Roman um eine Brücke und um Menschen, die in ihrem Leben die Liebe suchen, und sie doch nicht als dauerhaftes Lebensglück erfahren. Der Autor hat kurz nach dem Erscheinen des Buches für dieses Meisterwerk der Schicksalserkundung den Pulitzer-Preis erhalten.

The conceit on which the novel rests makes it necessary for Wilder to relate the love lives of the five people thrown off the bridge of San Luis Rey as well. First we are told the story of Dona Maria de Montemayor, who so idolizes her daughter Clara in Spain that she writes her one adoring letter after another without ever having her affections returned. So one can be well-off but at the same time pathetically deluded, like Dona Maria. The chapter devoted to her contains the following passage: "Nature is deaf. God is indifferent. Nothing in man's power can alter the course of law." When fate finally catches up with the Marquesa on the bridge, her loyal companion Pepita also plunges to her death. Next comes the story of Estaban the farmer, who tries in vain to love his brother Manuel. "It was merely that in the heart of one of them there was left room for an elaborate, imaginative attachment and in the heart of the other there was not." Realizing that his love is doomed, Esteban allows himself to be recruited by a sea captain looking for sailors to sail around the world with him, but before he gets that far, he first has to cross the bridge. Next comes the story of Uncle Pio, an adventurer and talented womanizer, who falls in love with the actress and singer Camila Périchole–familiar to opera-lovers as the mistress of the Viceroy of Peru in Jacques Offenbach's eponymous comic opera. That this love, too, is anything but happy or long-lasting goes almost without saying. "What was there in the world more lovely than a beautiful woman doing justice to a Spanish masterpiece?" Pio asks himself. But he, too, soon has to learn that beauty is no guarantee of reciprocated love. "He regarded love as a sort of cruel malady through which the elect are required to pass in their late youth and from which they emerge, pale and wrung, but ready for the business of living." Uncle Pio, to whom Camila, after some initial hesitation, has entrusted her son Jaime in the firm belief that her admirer will at least give him a good education, will also fall to his death on that fateful day–as will the little boy with him. Many of the other figures owe their place in the novel to the role they play in the lives of the five doomed protagonists. Yet their destiny is not to be cast into the canyon by the collapsing rope bridge. For as the aforementioned abbess remarks to the daughter of the Marquesa de Montemayor, who in the final chapter has returned to Peru following her mother's death: "All, all of us have failed. One wishes to be punished. One is willing to assume all kinds of penance, but do you know, my daughter, that in love–I scarcely dare say it–but in love our very mistakes don't seem to be able to last long?" *The Bridge of San Luis Rey* is a great novel about a bridge and about the fate of those who spend their whole lives searching for love but never really find it–or at least not as a permanent condition. A year after its publication in 1927, Wilder was awarded the Pulitzer Prize for this masterpiece of moral inquiry.

BRIDGE OVER THE TIDE OF HISTORY

The Yugoslav author Ivo Andrić was awarded the Nobel Prize in Literature largely in recognition of his novel *The Bridge on the Drina,* first published in Serbo-Croatian in 1945 and later in translation (the English edition came out in 1959). Perhaps the most encyclopedic account of a single bridge ever written, it tells both of the building

BRÜCKE ÜBER DEN STROM DER GESCHICHTE

Den Literaturnobelpreis erhielt der serbokroatische Autor Ivo Andrić insbesondere für seinen 1945 erschienenen Roman *Die Brücke über die Drina* (in deutscher Sprache erstmals 1953 erschienen). Es handelt sich wohl um die eindrücklichste Chronik, die je über eine einzelne Brücke geschrieben wurde: über die Umstände ihrer Errichtung durch den Grosswesir Mehmed Pascha Sokoli im 16. Jahrhundert, über Menschen, die in den folgenden Jahrhunderten an und auf der Brücke lebten, die Bauern und Arbeiter, Soldaten und Offiziere, Händler und Zigeuner, die an der Brücke über die Drina in Višegrad einander näher kamen, Moslems aus dem ottomanischen Reich und aus Bosnien, serbische Christen und Juden aus dem späteren Bosnien und der Herzegowina. Das Buch endet mit der Sprengung der Brücke durch Angehörige der österreichischen Armee zu Beginn des Ersten Weltkriegs, im Augenblick also, als der Fluss Drina zur Frontlinie zwischen den verfeindeten Armeen wird. Wir erleben also Menschen an dieser Brücke über vier Jahrhunderte – Figuren, die aus dem Strom der Geschichte aufsteigen und wieder verschwinden, meisterhaft vorgeführt von einem Erzähler, der sich als ein objektiver Chronist versteht und uns die grössten Grausamkeiten und die schönsten Hilfeleistungen, zu denen Menschen fähig sind, getreu und detailreich schildert, ohne Partei zu ergreifen und ohne über Recht oder Unrecht, Güte oder Bosheit zu Gericht sitzen zu wollen. Die Hauptfigur des Buches ist die Brücke, an der Menschen sich treffen, sich ergänzend oder einander bekämpfend finden und sich im Laufe der Zeit auch wiederum verlieren. Vom Autor Andrić stammen die Worte: «Alles im Leben ist eine Brücke – ein Wort, ein Lächeln, das wir dem anderen schenken. Ich wäre glücklich, könnte ich durch meine Arbeit ein Brückenbauer zwischen Ost und West sein.»

Der entführte Bosnier Mehmed, der beim Sultan in Konstantinopel Karriere macht, will mit dem Bau der Brücke der Verbindung zwischen dem islamischen Orient und dem christlichen Abendland Beständigkeit verschaffen. Das Bauwerk an der Grenze soll «eine Brücke zwischen zwei sich bekriegenden Welten» werden. Die Balkankriege unserer Zeit – der Jugoslawien-Krieg von 1991 und der Kosovo-Krieg von 1998 – haben erneut gezeigt, wie wenig aus historischer Betrachtung der Wunsch dieses Grosswesirs Mehmed Pascha Sokoli in Erfüllung gegangen ist. Die wiederaufgebaute Brücke über die Drina, die seit 2011 zum Weltkulturerbe gehört, ist nach wie vor ein Mahnmal für die schwer zu erringende Versöhnung zwischen christlichen Serben und moslemischen Bosniaken. Andrićs Roman ist die bestmögliche Lektüre, um Schlüsselmomente dieses Konflikts historisch zu begreifen. Es gab Zeiten eines friedlichen Zusammenlebens, aber zu häufig führten ferne machtpolitische Entscheidungen dazu, dass die innerhalb der Stadt Višegrad herrschende Eintracht Schaden nahm. Der Krieg in angrenzenden Ländern führte zu Konflikten und Radikalisierungen der Gruppen in der Kleinstadt. Das Leben in Višegrad und auf beiden Seiten der Brücke ist der getreueste Spiegel dessen, wie Konflikte zwischen Nationen, Kulturen und Religionen ein friedliches Leben verhindern und zerstören. Einzelne Figuren ragen aus dieser Chronik

of the bridge over the River Drina in Višegrad under Grand Vezir Mehmed Pasha Sokolovici in the sixteenth century and of the many vicissitudes in the lives of the people who lived with it and even on it in the centuries that followed. The vast cast of characters includes the peasants and laborers, soldiers and officers, merchants and gypsies who met and interacted there, whether they were Moslems from Bosnia and the Ottoman Empire, Serbian Christians, or Jews from Bosnia-Hercegovina. The book ends with the dynamiting of the bridge by the Austrian Army in the early days of the World War I when the River Drina became the front line between two hostile armies. The novel thus covers a timespan of four centuries, in the course of which all sorts of figures emerge from the tide of history only to be swept away again. It is a tale masterfully told by an objective narrator who relates, factually and in detail, both the worst atrocities and the finest acts of kindness and courage of which humans are capable, without partiality and without passing judgment over right and wrong, good and evil. The book's chief protagonist is the bridge where people meet–sometimes as friends, sometimes as foes–and in the course of time lose each other again. Andrić himself had the following to say about his central motif: "Everything in life is a bridge–a word, a smile, which we give others as a gift. I would be happy if, through my work, I could be a bridge builder between East and West."

Mehmed, who as a boy is abducted and taken to Constantinople, where he enjoys a meteoric career in the service of the sultan, wants his bridge over the Drina to become a permanent link between the Islamic East and Christian West. Situated on the border, it was to be a bridge "between the two warring sides". The Yugoslav Wars of our own era that began in 1991 and ended with the Kosovo War of 1998/99 are but a recent reminder of how reality, viewed from the historical perspective, has failed to live up to the vision of Grand Vezir Mehmed Pasha Sokolovici. The rebuilt bridge over the Drina, which has been a World Heritage Site since 2011, remains a monument to the hard-won reconciliation between the Christian Serbs and Moslem Bosniacs of Višegrad. Reading Andrić's novel is an ideal way of understanding the historical weight of all the key factors in this conflict. While there were indeed times when the different ethnic groups lived together in peace and harmony, the spirit of tolerance prevailing in the town of Višegrad was all too often undermined by political decisions made in far-away places or by war in neighboring countries, which inevitably led to friction and the radicalization of certain groups within the town. Andrić's description of life in Višegrad on both sides of the bridge is a poignant reflection on how unresolved conflicts between peoples of different ethnicity, culture, and religion can thwart and even wreck any chance of peaceful coexistence.

The novel is teeming with characters, a few of whom snap into focus whether as unforgettable paragons of integrity, courage, and industriousness or as examples of corruption, cruelty, schadenfreude, and hatred; wretchedness, dire poverty, and broken spirits abound. Andrić's Višegrad, in other words, is populated by characters who do indeed engage our sympathies, whether because of

heraus und werden durch die Schilderungen des Autors zu unvergesslichen Gestalten der Rechtschaffenheit, des Mutes und des Arbeitswillens, aber auch der Korruption, der Grausamkeit, der Schadenfreude und des Hasses, der Not und der Armut, ja sogar des zerstörten Geistes. Kurzum, dieses Višegrad ist voll von Mitleid auslösenden Menschen und Schicksalen. Ich werde hier nicht eine Prozession ergreifender Figuren wie Tosun Effendi, Meister Antonio, des gepfählten Bauern und Saboteurs Radisaw oder der gehörlosen und geisteskranken Wöchnerin Ilinka veranstalten, sondern nur beifügen: Man muss dieses Buch lesen, um zu begreifen, wie eine Brücke zur stummen Zeugin guter Tage, aber auch heilloser Epochen im Leben unterschiedlichster Menschen werden kann. Wir hören, wie Ängste und Gerüchte Menschen verunsichern und zu unsinnigen Taten treiben. Wie Besonnenheit und Unvernunft zwischen den Religionen und ihren Vertretern eine gut verteilte Sache sind, und wir erleben, wie Menschen in Zeiten der Not – etwa bei Hochwasser – zusammenhalten und in ungewohnter Weise sich finden und schätzen. Andrić ist alles andere als ein schönfärberischer Autor, er geht der herrschenden Grausamkeit nicht aus dem Weg. Auch über die Register der Komik und der Ironie verfügt er. Etwa wenn er aufzeigt, dass die erpresserische Steuerpolitik der jeweils herrschenden Fraktion weder unter den Osmanen noch im habsburgischen Vielvölkerstaat human und einsichtsvoll war. Aber immer wieder gibt es herrlich komische Episoden, so wenn Andrić die Wirtin Lottika und ihr «Hotel zur Brücke» schildert, in dem das ganze Gelichter der Stadt «und anderes überall zu findendes Ungeziefer» einkehren. Der Autor hat 1945 noch zwei weitere Romane publiziert, die man zusammen mit dem Roman über die Brücke von Višegrad als seine «bosnische Trilogie» bezeichnen (*Wesire und Konsuln,* deutsch 1961, sowie *Das Fräulein,* deutsch 1945.) Wenn es nach Lev Tolstoi je einen Autor gab, dessen Werke in gleicher Weise Geschichtskunde wie kollektive und individuelle Seelenerforschung sind: hier haben wir ihn. Darum müsste *Die Brücke über die Drina* zum obligatorischen Schulstoff aller Länder und Kontinente gehören.

EHRGEIZ UND HELDENTUM

Ein eigentlicher Kriegsroman, zentriert um den Bau einer Eisenbahnbrücke, erschien im Jahr 1952. Der Autor hiess Pierre Boulle und er starb 1994 84-jährig in Paris. Er verarbeitete in seinem Buch *Le Pont de la Rivière Kwai (Die Brücke am Kwai)* seine Erlebnisse während des Zweiten Weltkriegs, als die Japaner eine Gruppe alliierter Kriegsgefangener zwangen, für die sogenannte «Todeseisenbahn» zwischen Thailand und Burma (dem heutigen Myanmar) eine Brücke zu bauen. Historisches Faktum ist, dass an die 94 000 asiatische Zwangsarbeiter und etwa 14 000 alliierte Kriegsgefangene beim Bau dieser Bahnlinie den Tod gefunden haben. Das Buch wurde berühmt dank seiner Verfilmung durch David Lean im Jahr 1957. Alec Guinness spielt den stolzen britischen Oberstleutnant Nicholson, der sich zunächst internationalen Konventionen gemäss dagegen wehrte, als Offizier von den Burma besetzt haltenden Japanern zur Zwangsarbeit verpflichtet zu werden. Schliesslich wird sein Ehrgeiz, den Japanern zu zeigen, dass die Brücke über den Kwai unter

who they are or because of the fate that befalls them. Instead of reeling off a list of the most affecting of them—which would have to include figures like Tosun Effendi, Mastro Antonio, the impaled peasants, Radisav the saboteur, or the deaf and mentally unstable Ilinka in childbed—I would like to say only this: that to understand how a bridge can silently bear witness not only to the halcyon days but also the grimmest periods in the lives of all sorts of people, you need only read this book. Here, you will learn how anxiety and rumors can so frighten people that they are driven to acts of mindless violence; how considerateness and irrationality are to be found in equal measure in all religions and in all those who espouse them; and how people can pull together and count on each other in times of need after all, as when the town is hit by severe flooding. Andrić is certainly not one to romanticize; nor does he skate over the all too ubiquitous cruelty; but comedy and irony are also well within his compass, as when he reveals how people were taxed beyond endurance no matter who held the reins of power, the Ottomans or the Habsburgs. And there are some wonderfully comic episodes, too, such as Andrić's description of the landlady Lotte, whose "Hotel at the Bridge" is frequented by all the leading lights of the town "and other such vermin as are found everywhere". In 1945, the author published two more novels, *Vezirs and Consuls* and *The Woman from Sarajevo,* which together with the one about the bridge of Višegrad make up his "Bosnian Trilogy". If there was ever an author apart from Leo Tolstoy, whose works embrace the vast sweep of history while at the same time probing the human heart, then surely it must be Andrić. *The Bridge on the Drina* should therefore be required reading for schoolchildren in all countries and on all continents.

AMBITION AND HEROISM

The year 1952 saw the publication of a war novel centered on the building of a railway bridge. *Le Pont de la Rivière Kwai (The Bridge over the River Kwai)* is based on the wartime experiences of the author Pierre Boulle, who died in Paris aged eighty-four in 1994. Boulle was among the many thousands of Allied POWs who during World War II were forced by the Japanese to work on the Burma-Siam Railway, the "Death Railway" whose construction cost some 94,000 Asian forced laborers and around 14,000 Allied POWs their lives. The book was made famous by David Lean's movie of the same name, released in 1957, with Alec Guinness in the role of the haughty British Lieutenant-Colonel Nicholson who at first adamantly refuses to work for the Japanese occupier, citing international conventions that exempt officers from hard labor. What causes Nicholson to relent is his determination to prove to the Japanese that the bridge will be both better and built faster under his command. Ambition, it seems, is a more powerful driving force than principle. So eager is Nicholson to persuade his Japanese counterpart, Colonel Saito, of his battalion's superiority that he is even ready to aid and abet the enemy doing so. For the British officer, the bridge becomes a symbol of resistance, a material manifestation of the will to live. Unlike the book, the movie ends with the Allied POWs dynamiting the wooden bridge they have just built. In fact, both the wooden bridge and

seinem Kommando besser und in kürzerer Zeit gebaut werden kann, mächtiger als sein Offiziersstolz. Dem japanischen Oberst Saito will Nicholson die Überlegenheit seines Bataillions beweisen, auch wenn er den Feinden damit Vorteile verschafft. Die Brücke wird für ihn zum Symbol des Widerstandes, zum Ausdruck des Lebenswillens. Im Film wird am Schluss – anders als im Buch – die Holzbrücke von den Alliierten gesprengt. Historisch wurden in der Tat die Holzbrücke wie die später gebaute Eisenbrücke im Jahr 1945 durch Bomben aus Flugzeugen der Alliierten zerstört. Bereits im Juni des gleichen Jahres musste der Verkehr auf der Verbindungsstrecke zwischen Thailand und Burma eingestellt werden. Die Japaner standen kurz vor der Kapitulation.

Das Merkwürdige am Buch und am Film ist die Tatsache, dass es sich eindeutig um Antikriegsliteratur handelt, allerdings um eine solche, die auch eine seltsame Faszination für die Perversionen des Krieges und der Kampfhandlungen zwischen verfeindeten Gruppen ausstrahlt. Zu Buch und Film gab es viele Kontroversen über die Frage, ob die Darstellung der vorgefallenen Ereignisse nicht auch eine Glorifizierung von Kriegsheldentum sei. Die Lektüre dieses Augenzeugenberichtes ist nur jenen zu empfehlen, die sich dem «konstruktiven Delirium» des Krieges stellen wollen. Einiges fliesst hier ununterscheidbar ineinander: Nationalstolz einerseits, persönlicher Ehrgeiz bis zu wahnhaftem Enthusiasmus für eigene Leistungen andererseits. Im Schlusskapitel des Buches berichtet ein Augenzeuge seinem Vorgesetzten, wie es sich in seiner Wahrnehmung mit dem Oberstleutnant Nicholson verhält, der am Schluss zusammen mit anderen «Helden» der Geschichte auf tragische Weise umkommt: «Dieses alte Rindvieh mit den strahlenden Augen hatte wahrscheinlich ein ganzes Leben davon geträumt, einen dauerhaften Bau auszuführen. Da er keine Stadt und keine Kathedrale zur Verfügung hatte, hat er sich auf die Brücke verlegt. Und die sollte er nun zerstören lassen?» Man braucht gute Nerven, um dieses Buch durchzustehen. Doch ein erschütterndes Dokument über menschliche Schicksale beim Bau einer Brücke in widrigen Zeiten sind Buch und Film halt doch! Auch hier haben wir einen doppelten Blick auf die Realität: Historisch Vorgefallenes interessiert uns genauso wie menschliche Charakterstudien. Die Brücke am Kwai wurde nach ihrer Zerstörung im Jahr 1946 von einer japanischen Firma wieder aufgebaut. Im Jahr 1971 hat man sie restauriert. Sie ist bis heute als Eisenbahnbrücke in Betrieb. Man kann sie besuchen!

ROSENSTOCK UND ROSMARIN

Am Ende dieses kleinen Exkurses über bedeutende Brücken in der Literatur noch einige wenige Worte über einen meiner Lieblingsromane. Das Buch erschien 1953 mit dem Titel *Nachts unter der steinernen Brücke*. Es hat eine lange Entstehungsgeschichte. Leo Perutz, in Prag geboren, in Wien aufgewachsen, begann im Jahr 1924 daran zu arbeiten, vollendete den Roman jedoch erst 1951 in Tel Aviv, sechs Jahre vor seinem Tod. So berühmt und beliebt Perutz als Schriftsteller in der Zwischenkriegszeit auch war, seit seiner Flucht im Jahr 1938 nach Palästina ins Exil wurde es still um ihn. Er hatte zu kämpfen, dass Verleger sich noch um seine Bücher kümmerten, ob-

the iron bridge built to replace it were destroyed by Allied aerial bombing in 1945; and with the Japanese on the verge of capitulation, services on the Burma-Siam line were discontinued in June of the same year.

What is strange about both book and film is the fact that while there can be no doubting their antiwar credentials, both rely heavily on a curious fascination with the perversions of war and armed conflict between two hostile forces. Both also sparked controversy over whether their depiction of the events in Siam might not also be interpreted as a glorification of heroism on the battlefield. The book is therefore recommended only to those willing to face the "constructive delirium" of war head on. Several things are conflated in these pages: national pride on the one hand and personal ambition verging on near-manic conceit on the other. In the final chapter of the book, an eyewitness reports to his superior on Nicholson, whose life ultimately ends tragically, like that of the story's other "heroes": "That old brute with his blue eyes had probably spent his whole life dreaming of constructing something which would last. In the absence of a town or a cathedral, he plumped for this bridge. You couldn't really expect him to let it be destroyed." Reading this book from start to finish calls for strong nerves, for like the movie, it is a shattering account of what bridge building in times of adversity can mean. Here, too, we are afforded two perspectives on reality, and the historical facts of the matter are just as much of interest to us as are the human character studies. After its destruction in 1946, the bridge over the River Kwai was rebuilt – by a Japanese contractor. It was restored in 1971 and is still in use as a railway bridge today. It has even become a tourist attraction.

ROSE TREE AND ROSEMARY

This brief exploration of the great bridges of world literature would not be complete without a few words about one of my favorite novels. First published in German as *Nachts unter der steinernen Brücke* in 1953, nearly forty years would pass before it was translated into English as *By Night under the Stone Bridge*. The novel has a long backstory. The author, Leo Perutz, was born in Prague and grew up in Vienna, where he became an actuary and began work on his novel in 1924. By the time he finished it in 1951, just six years before his death, he was living in Tel Aviv. As famous and popular as Perutz was as a writer during the interwar years, there was little talk of him after he went into exile in Palestine in 1938. Despite writing wonderful books, Perutz had to fight to find publishers willing to take him on, even in his mature years. Not that there was any shortage of critical acclaim; it was just that ordinary readers seemed not to want to know anything about this delightfully eccentric thinker and storyteller. When he died at the age of seventy-five in Bad Ischl in 1957, only in literary circles was the gravity of his loss really felt.

True, Perutz does not make it easy for his readers. His plots are often convoluted and require readers to interpret clues and put two and two together. Thus his novel about the Charles Bridge in Prague presents the reader with a challenging puzzle that has to be pieced together out of fourteen different narratives and an epi-

wohl der ehemalige Versicherungsmathematiker und Literat auch in seiner späten Zeit wunderbare Bücher schrieb. Die Kritiker lobten ihn zwar, doch das lesende Publikum schien von diesem wundersam kauzigen Denker und Erzähler nichts wissen zu wollen. Als er 1957 75-jährig in Bad Ischl starb, wusste man nur in literarisch eingeweihten Kreisen, was für ein bedeutender Autor nicht mehr unter uns weilte.

Zugegeben: Perutz erzählt nicht einfach und gradlinig. Seine Geschichten sind oft verwickelt und fordern vom Leser den Willen zu eigener Kombination und Deutung. So ist auch der Roman um die Prager Karlsbrücke ein herausforderndes Zusammensetzspiel, bestehend aus 14 verschiedenen Erzählungen und einem Epilog. Die Rahmenhandlung versetzt uns in die Zeit der Zerstörung der Prager Judenstadt zurück, also in die Jahre 1893–1913, die man euphemistisch auch als «Sanierung der Josefsstadt» bezeichnete. Die 14 Geschichten greifen jedoch Ereignisse im sagenumwobenen Prag Kaiser Rudolfs II. auf, also gegen Ende des 16. und zu Beginn des 17. Jahrhunderts. Die grossen Figuren, die im Buch auftauchen, sind neben Kaiser Rudolf der jüdische Geschäftsmann Mordechai Meisl und seine unwiderstehlich schöne Frau Esther, der Kabbalist Rabbi Löw, dessen Grab Touristen bis heute noch auf dem jüdischen Friedhof in Prag besuchen, der Hofastronom Johannes Kepler und der Heerführer im Dreissigjährigen Krieg Wallenstein. Zahlreiche Nebenfiguren bereichern diese Geschichten, Adlige und Bauern, Gutsherren und Kammerdiener, Maler und Alchemisten, Offiziere und Jurastudenten. Auch Musikanten wie Koppel-Bär und Jäckele-Narr beleben die Szenerie, wir begegnen Bettlern und Diebesbanden, zwielichtigen Gestalten zuhauf, die durch die engen Gassen der Prager Altstadt und der Judenstadt ziehen. Ein wichtiger Protagonist dieses Buches ist der Tod: in Prag ist die Pest ausgebrochen, Kinder und Erwachsene sterben in Massen dahin. Wen wundert's also, dass auch Magie, Zauberkunst und alchemistische Rezepte erprobt werden, um dem allgemeinen Sterben die Stirn zu bieten. Perutz greift tief ins Sagen- und Legendengeflecht des rudolfinischen Prag. Religiöse Überzeugungen sind ebenso taugliche Überlebensstrategien wie okkulte Praktiken und magische Experimente. Wer also die Faszination dieser Epoche vor und während des Dreissigjährigen Krieges in der Stadt Prag erspüren will, muss unbedingt dieses Buch lesen.

Eine der Erzählungen trägt den Titel des Buches. Es ist die Geschichte um die Liebe zwischen Kaiser Rudolf und der schönen Esther, der Ehefrau des Mordechai Meisl. Der Kaiser hat eine Frau entdeckt, die schönste, die er sich vorstellen kann, und verlangt nun – unter Androhung von Verfolgung und Vertreibung der Juden aus der Stadt – von Rabbi Löw, dass dieser ihm die Frau auf die Burg bringe. Rabbi Löw weiss, dass es sich um Meisls Gattin handelt. Um seine Getreuen zu schützen, vollzieht der Rabbi eine magische Handlung. Er pflanzt unter der steinernen Brücke einen Rosenstock für Rudolf und einen Rosmarinstrauch für die schöne Esther. Von diesem Augenblick an vereinigen sich die beiden Liebenden Nacht für Nacht, wenn auch nur im Traum. In *Nachts unter der steinernen Brücke* lesen wir, wie Kaiser Rudolf von Esther träumt, wie diese im

logue. The main plot takes us back to the time of the demolition of Prague's Jewish Quarter in the years 1893–1913, euphemistically referred to as the "redevelopment of Josefov". The fourteen stories in *By Night under the Stone Bridge,* however, relate to events that took place much earlier, during the reign of the near-legendary Emperor Rudolf II in the late sixteenth and early seventeenth century. The cast of characters includes the Jewish merchant Mordechai Meisl and his irresistibly beautiful wife Esther as well as historical figures like the Emperor himself, the Kabbalist Rabbi Loew, whose grave in the Jewish Cemetery still attracts visitors to this day, the court astronomer Johannes Kepler, and Albrecht von Wallenstein, the most famous general of the Thirty Years' War. Alongside these, there is a whole host of minor roles including nobles and peasants, landowners and valets, painters and alchemists, officers and law students. Musicians like Koppel-the-Bear and Jäckele-the-Fool liven up many a scene and we encounter beggars and bands of thieves as well as many more of the shady characters who prowl the streets and alleys of the Old Town and the Jewish Quarter by night. One of the most important protagonists is Death, for Prague is also in the grip of the "great pestilence" and children and adults are dying like flies. Little wonder, then, that people are resorting to magic and sorcery, mixing all manner of alchemical concoctions in a vain attempt to ward off Death. Perutz digs deep into Rudolfian Prague's dense web of yarns, taking us back to a time when religious convictions were no less a legitimate survival strategy than were occult practices and experimentation with magic. Anyone interested in knowing more about Prague during that fascinating time immediately before and during the Thirty Years' War should be sure to read this book.

The story to which the book owes its name tells of the love that flowered between Emperor Rudolf and Esther, the beautiful wife of Mordechai Meisl. After catching sight of this natural beauty – the fairest woman imaginable, but as yet unidentified – the Emperor summons Rabbi Loew and orders him to bring her to him at the castle, threatening to expel him personally and drive out all the Jews should he fail to comply. Rabbi Loew knows that it is Meisl's wife the Emperor is lusting for. To protect his flock, therefore, he performs a magic trick. He plants a rose tree for Rudolf and a rosemary bush for Esther underneath the stone bridge. From this moment on, the two lovers are united, night after night, even if only in their dreams. We read how Esther becomes trusting and affectionate towards the Emperor, but always takes her leave of him and hastens away before he wakes up again and realizes he has been dreaming. Awaking next to her husband Meisl at more or less the same time, Esther whispers to herself "… the same dream night after night. A lovely dream, but praised be the Lord, only a dream!" When the Angel Asael scolds the Rabbi for meddling in God's plans, informing him that the punishment for this will be the death of large numbers of children from the plague, the Rabbi tears up the rosemary bush underneath the bridge and throws it in the River Vltava. That night, Esther dies of the plague, which then disappears from the city leaving everyone else unscathed.

Traum ihm nah und zutraulich ist, doch auch wie sie vor dem Erwachen immer Abschied von ihm nimmt und fort will. Der Kaiser erwacht und erkennt, dass Esthers Liebe nur sein Traum ist. Zur gleichen Zeit erwacht Esther neben ihrem Mann Meisl: «Und immer, Nacht für Nacht, der gleiche Traum! Ein schöner Traum, aber, gelobt sei der Schöpfer, doch nur ein Traum!» Als der Engel Asael erscheint und dem Rabbi kundtut, mit seiner Magie greife er in die Pläne Gottes ein und die Strafe dafür sei das Kindersterben durch die Pest, reisst der Rabbi den Rosmarinstrauch unter der steinernen Brücke wieder aus dem Boden und wirft ihn in die Moldau. Noch in dieser Nacht stirbt die schöne Esther. Die Pest verschwindet aus der Stadt.

Dies ist nur eine der Geschichten, die wir aus Perutz' Roman erfahren. Nachts unter der steinernen Brücke von Prag geschahen damals aber noch viele andere Dinge, bei denen wir nie genau wissen, wer die Hand im Spiel hat: Die Mächte des Himmels, die Geister der Hölle, die der Verstorbenen, vielleicht auch die von Rabbi Löw, der mit seiner Magie die Welt so einzurichten vermochte, dass die Menschen unter der Schwere von Gottes Geboten einigermassen überleben konnten. Die Brücke, die Prager Burg und die Judenstadt sind die Hauptorte, die den Lesern dieses Romans zu Bewusstsein bringen, dass unser Verstand zu beschränkt und zu befangen ist, um alles zu begreifen, was unterm Sternenhimmel vor sich geht.

Vielleicht sind ja Brücken nicht nur ein Ausdruck davon, wie die Menschen natürliche Kräfte, iridische Materie, Wasser und Winde zu bändigen und zu eigenem Nutzen zu verwenden vermögen. Vielleicht sind Brücken auch jene Orte, an denen das Unheimliche und die Rätsel der Natur am ausgeprägtesten Unterkunft und Bleibstatt finden. Wir dürfen die Schönheit, die Kühnheit und alle Erleichterungen der Welt bestaunen, die Brücken uns verschaffen. Nicht vergessen sollten wir aber auch die Tatsache, dass die Natur an jedem Ort der Welt im Verlauf der Zeiten und der Jahrhunderte auch die festesten Brücken in Schutt und Staub zu verwandeln vermag. Darum sind womöglich jene Brücken in unserem Leben die wichtigsten, die neben der Bewunderung immer auch einen leichten Schauder in uns bewirken.

This is just one of the many stories to be found in Perutz's novel. Numerous other inexplicable things happen in *By Night under the Stone Bridge,* and we can never really say who had a hand in them – whether it was heavenly powers, demons, the ghosts of the departed, or perhaps spirits summoned by Rabbi Loew, who had no qualms about using magic to make the world bearable for those living under the yoke of God's commandments. Much of the action plays out on or under the bridge, at Prague Castle, or in the Jewish Quarter, and in all of these places we readers are made to realize that our intellects are simply too limited and too prejudiced by what we already know to grasp all that can and does happen under the starry canopy of the sky.

Perhaps bridges are more than just an expression of how we humans have learned to harness natural forces, earthly matter, water and wind, and turn these to our advantage; perhaps they are also the places where nature's many mysteries and all things supernatural find an enduring abode. We may marvel at the beauty, the boldness, and the sheer convenience of bridges as much as we wish, but we should never forget that over the centuries, nature can and indeed will reclaim them all, reducing even the sturdiest structures to rubble and dust. Possibly the most meaningful bridges in our lives, therefore, are those that besides evoking a sense of wonder also send a slight shiver down our spine.

BIOGRAFIE
BIOGRAPHY

CHRISTIAN MENN
*1927 in Meiringen BE, Bürger von Zillis GR und Chur (Ehrenbürger).

Nach der Matura am Gymnasium der Kantonsschule in Chur studierte Christian Menn an der ETH in Zürich Bauingenieurwesen und erwarb 1950 das Diplom. Anschliessend war er – zwischen dem Militärdienst – in einem Ingenieurbüro in Chur und einer Bauunternehmung in Bern tätig. Dann kehrte er als Assistent von Prof. Dr. Pierre Lardy an die ETH zurück und promovierte 1956 zum Dr. sc. techn. Hierauf arbeitete er ein Jahr lang in einer Unternehmung in Paris, wo er u. a. mit der Ausarbeitung von Pier Luigi Nervis Entwürfen für das UNESCO-Gebäude zu tun hatte. Nach seiner Rückkehr in die Schweiz eröffnete er 1957 mit Brückenprojekten für die Kraftwerke Hinterrhein ein eigenes Büro in Chur. Im Auftrag des Tiefbauamtes Graubünden erhielt er Gelegenheit, zahlreiche Brücken in Graubünden zu projektieren, war aber oft auch in anderen Kantonen tätig. 1970 gewann Menn zusammen mit dem Ingenieurbüro Emch und Berger in Bern den Wettbewerb für die 1100 Meter lange Felsenaubrücke in Bern, die zentrale Brücke im Schweizer Autobahnnetz.

1971 wurde Menn zum ordentlichen Professor für Baustatik und Konstruktion in der Abteilung für Bauingenieurwesen der ETH Zürich gewählt, wo er bis zu seiner Emeritierung 1992 Lehre und Forschung im konstruktiven Ingenieurbau betreute. Daneben war er Präsident der Kommission SIA 162 für Betonbauten sowie Experte, Berater oder Entwerfer für die meisten grösseren Brücken in der Schweiz. Bekannt sind u. a. die Ganterbrücke am Simplon, der Lehnenviadukt Beckenried oder der Viadotto della Biaschina in der Leventina. Christian Menn hielt im In- und Ausland unzählige Vorträge, so auch an der Harvard University in Boston, wo er in das 15 Mrd. Dollar teure Central Artery/Tunnel-Projekt involviert wurde und die Zakim Bunker Hill Bridge entwarf, die bereits kurz nach der Eröffnung zu einem erstrangigen Wahrzeichen der intellektuellen Metropole an der Ostküste wurde. Nach seiner Emeritierung befasste sich Menn weiter mit Brückenprojekten, z. B. mit der international viel beachteten und preisgekrönten Sunnibergbrücke bei Klosters.

Ehrungen (Auswahl):
– Kulturpreis des Kantons Graubünden
– Freyssinet Gold Medal of the Fédération International de la Précontrainte
– Carl-Friederich-Gauß-Medaille der Braunschweigischen Wissenschaftlichen Gesellschaft, Deutschland
– Grand Award of the American Council of Engineering Companies
– Bridge Design Award of the New York City Bridge Engineering Association
– Ehrendoktor der Universität Stuttgart
– Ehrendoktor der ETH Lausanne
– Proclamation of the Massachusetts Governor Argeo P. Celluci: November 3th, 2000 to be Christian Menn Day in Massachusetts

CHRISTIAN MENN
born 1927 in Meiringen, Canton of Bern, citizen of Zillis and honorary citizen of Chur, Canton of Graubünden

After attending high school in Chur, Christian Menn enrolled at the Swiss Federal Institute of Technology (ETH Zurich) to study civil engineering. After graduating with a diploma in 1950, he worked as an engineer—between periods of military service—for a firm in Chur and a building contractor in Bern. He then returned to the ETH as Assistant to Prof. Dr. Pierre Lardy, and was awarded a doctorate (Dr. sc. techn.) in 1956. During a year spent at a firm of engineers in Paris, he was able to work on details of Pier Luigi Nervis's plans for the UNESCO building, among other projects. On returning to Switzerland in 1957, he became head of his own engineering company in Chur and began work on various bridge projects for the Kraftwerke Hinterrhein. A contract with the Cantonal Department of Civil Engineering gave him an opportunity to plan numerous bridges in the Canton of Graubünden, although he was active in other cantons, too. Menn and the engineering firm Emch und Berger in Bern. In 1970, won the competition for the 1100-m long Felsenau Bridge in Bern, the keystone of Switzerland's highway network.

A year later, Menn was appointed Professor of Structural Engineering in the Department of Civil Engineering at the ETH Zurich, where he remained right up to his retirement in 1992. At the same time, he chaired the SIA 162 Commission for Concrete Structures, and as an expert, consultant, and designer was henceforth involved in most major bridge projects in Switzerland. His Ganter Bridge on the Simplon, the Lehnen Viaduct in Beckenried, and the Viadotto della Biaschina in the Leventina are among his best known achievements. He has also given innumerable lectures both in Switzerland and abroad, including at Harvard University in Boston, where he had a hand in the 15-billion-dollar Central Artery/Tunnel project as well as designing the Zakim Bunker Hill Memorial Bridge, which shortly after it opened became a landmark of the first order for the East Coast's intellectual center. After retiring, Menn remained actively involved in numerous projects, many of them for prize-winning bridges that have won international acclaim, such as the Sunniberg Bridge near Klosters.

Honors (selected):
- Culture Prize of the Canton of Graubünden
- Freyssinet Gold Medal of the Fédération International de la Précontrainte
- CarlFriederich Gauss Medal of the Braunschweigische Wissenschaftliche Gesellschaft, Germany
- Grand Award of the American Council of Engineering Companies
- Bridge Design Award of the New York City Bridge Engineering Association
- Honorary Doctor of the University of Stuttgart
- Honorary Doctor of the ETH Lausanne
- Governor Argeo P. Celluci declared November 3rd, 2000 to be Christian Menn Day in Massachusetts.

WERKVERZEICHNIS
LIST OF WORKS

LEGENDE / KEY

A	Balkenbrücke / Beam bridge
B	Freivorbaubrücke / Cantilever bridge
C	Bogenbrücke / Arch bridge
D	Rahmenbrücke / Frame bridge
E	Plattenbrücke / Plate bridge
F	Schrägseilbrücke / Cable-stayed bridge
G	Verbundbrücke / Composite bridge
Pr	Preisrichter / Jurors
PV	Projektverfasser / Project author
PV*	Projektverfasser in Arbeitsgemeinschaft / Project author group
E	Entwurf / Design
E*	Entwurf in Arbeitsgemeinschaft / Design group
Ex	Experte / Prüfingenieur / Expert / Test engineer
iV	Projekt in Vorbereitung / Project in preparation
*	Brücke wurde abgebrochen / Bridge not completed

WERKVERZEICHNIS PROJEKTVERFASSER

ORT	BRÜCKENNAME	TYP	HAUPT-SPANNWEITE	BAUJAHR	BEITRAG
Sufers	Crestawaldbrücke (Projekt 01)	C	71,5	1958	PV
Avers	Averserrheinbrücke Cröt (Projekt 02)	C	66,0	1959	PV
Avers	Averserrheinbrücke Letziwald (Projekt 03)	C	66,5	1959	PV
Avers	Bächen Brücke II	A	33,5	1959	PV
Avers	Brücke Underplatta I	A	31,5	1959	PV
Flims	Stennabrücke	A	58,0	1959–60	PV
Sufers / Splügen	Wyssbachbrücke	A	27,0	1959–72	PV
Avers	Brücke Underplatta II	C	39,6	1960	PV
Vicosoprano	Vallone del Largo	A	40,0	1960	PV
Maienfeld	SBB-Überführung	E	22,9	1960–62	PV
Sils i. D.	Cugnielertobelbrücke I	A	27,0	1961	PV
Splügen	Grünebrücke (Projekt 04)	C	49,8	1961	PV
Fläsch	Kanalbrücke Trippolis	D	36,0	*1961	PV
Fläsch / Bad Ragaz	Rheinbrücke Bad Ragaz I (Projekt 05)	A	82,0	1961–62	PV *
Buseno / Castaneda	Ponte ad Arco sulla Calancasca	C	88,0	1962	PV
Domat/Ems	Überführung A13 Felsberg	A	20,1	*1962	PV
Grono	Ponte Pianec sopra	A	26,0	1962	PV
Sils i. D.	Cugnielertobelbrücke II	A	23,0	1962	PV
Uors / Surcasti	Valserrheinbrücke (Projekt 12)	C	86,0	1962	PV
Igis / Malans	Landquartbrücke Felsenbach	D	62,4	1962–63	PV
Domat/Ems	Überführung Anschluss Vial	E	27,4	1962–63	PV
Domat/Ems	Überführung der RhB Reichenau	A	27,6	1963	PV
Grono	Ponte Tiieda II	A	22,4	1963	PV
Grono	Ponte Val del Infern	A	36,8	1963	PV
Hinterrhein	Hinterrheinbrücke Bernhardintunnel	A	27,0	1963	PV
Ilanz	Rheinbrücke	A / E	50,0	1963	PV
Roveredo	Ponte Moesa Norantola	A	33,0	1963	PV
Sils i. D.	Caselertobelbrücke	A	36,0	1963	PV
Splügen	Hinterrheinbrücke Splügen-West	A	40,0	1963	PV
Tamins	Rheinbrücke (Projekt 06)	C	100,0	1963	PV
Vicosoprano	Albignabrücke	D	45,0	1963	PV
Chur	Plessurbrücke I	A	23,0	1963–64	PV
Grono	Ponte Tiieda I	A	28,0	1964	PV
Mesocco	Isolabrücke (Projekt 10)	C	49,5	1964	PV
Mesocco	Ponte Fracch	A	32,0	1964	PV
Scuol	Innbrücke Pradella	A	23,8	1964	PV
Splügen	Hinterrheinbrücke Splügen-Ost	A	32,0	1964	PV
Splügen	Untere Häusernbachbrücke	E	20,0	1964	PV
Mesocco	Ponte Isola	C	49,5	1964–65	PV
Wil	Viadukt Mühle Rickenbach (Projekt 14)	A	57,0	1964–65	PV
Mesocco	Ponte Zoccola	A	30,0	1964–66	PV
Scuol	Clozzatobelbrücke	C	42,7	1965	PV
Zillis	Kirchlitobelbrücke	A	35,5	1965	PV
Mesocco	Ponte Val di Can	A	31,0	1965–66	PV

WERKVERZEICHNIS PROJEKTVERFASSER

ORT	BRÜCKENNAME	TYP	HAUPT-SPANNWEITE	BAUJAHR	BEITRAG
Zürich	Hardturm-Viadukt SBB	A	38,0	1965–68	PV*
Andeer	Roflabrücke	A	60,0	1966	PV
Mesocco	Ponte Beis	A	40,0	1966	PV
Mesocco	Ponte Maloda sopra	A	40,0	1966	PV
Andeer	Averserrheinbrücke A13	D	21,0	1966–67	PV
Mesocco	Ponte Maloda sotto	A	30,0	1966–67	PV
Mesocco	Naninbrücke (Projekt 07)	C	112,0	1966–67	PV
Mesocco	Ponte Quadinei	A	40,0	1966–67	PV
Zillis	Viamalabrücke (Projekt 09)	C	96,0	1966–67	PV
Mesocco	Ponte Anzone	A	27,0	1967	PV
Mesocco	Ponte Leso	A	26,0	1967	PV
Mesocco	Cascellabrücke (Projekt 07)	C	96,0	1967–68	PV
Vevey / St-Légier	Pont sur la Veveyse	A / G	129,0	1967–69	PV*
Würenlos	Limmatbrücke (Projekt 15)	A	60,0	1967–70	PV
Grono	Ponte Calancasca	A	36,5	1968	PV
Dietikon	Limmatbrücke A1	A	66,5	1968	PV*
Mesocco	Salvaneibrücke (Projekt 08)	A	60,0	1968–69	PV
Buchs	SBB-Überführung (Projekt 13)	A	32,0	1968–69	PV
Stein	Unterführung Kantonsstrasse	A	34,0	1969–71	PV
Mesocco	Ponte Valascia	A	50,0	1970–71	PV
Soazza	Ponte Dres	A	55,0	1971	PV
Wiesen	Mühletobelbrücke	A	36,0	1971	PV
Wiesen	Sägentobelbrücke	A	21,0	1971	PV
Fläsch / Bad Ragaz	Rheinbrücke Bad Ragaz II	A	81,3	1971–72	PV
Soazza / Mesocco	Pregordabrücke (Projekt 11)	A	40,0	1971–73	PV
Wassen	Reussbrücke Wassen (Projekt 27)	A	64,0	1972	PV
Bern	Felsenaubrücke (Projekt 16)	A / B	144,0	1972–74	PV*
Valangin	Viaduc sur la Sorge	A / G	43,5	1972–75	PV*
Soazza	Ponte Verbi	D	22,0	1973	PV
Davos	Landwasserbrücke	A	40,0	1974	PV
Wassen	Reussbrücke Wattingen	A / B	70,0	1975–78	PV
Ried-Brig	Ganterbrücke (Projekt 17)	B / F	174,0	1977–80	E* / Ex
Chiggiogna / Giornico	Viadotto della Biaschina (Projekt 18)	A / B	160,0	1979–83	E* / Ex
Sion	Pont de Chandoline (Projekt 19)	B / F	140,0	1987–89	E* / Ex
Klosters-Serneus	Sunnibergbrücke (Projekt 21)	B / F	140,0	1996–98	E*
Boston (USA)	Leonard P. Zakim Bunker Hill Memorial Bridge (Projekt 20)	F	227,0	1998–2002	E*
Las Vegas (USA)	Hoover Dam Bypass Bridge (Projekt 25)	B	352,0	2001	E*
Alexandria (USA)	Woodrow Wilson Bridge	F	100,0	2004	E*
Guttannen	Brücke über den Grimselsee (Projekt 24)	F	352,0	2005–	E*
Abu Dhabi (UAE)	Al Showah Island Bridges (Projekte 22/23)	F	165,0/120,0	2007	E*
Buffalo (USA)	Peace Bridge (Projekt 26)	F	260,0	2001–14	E*

WERKVERZEICHNIS EXPERTE

BRÜCKENNAME	TYP	HAUPT-SPANNWEITE	BAUJAHR	BEITRAG
Achereggbrücke Stansstad	A	50,0	1961–64	Pr/Ex
Reusstalbrücke Mülligen	A/G	84,5	1966–69	Pr
Traversabrücke Sufers	A	63,0	1967–68	Pr
Lützelmurgviadukt Aawangen	A/G	48,0	1967–68	Ex
Viaduc de la plaine du Rhône, Villeneuve	A	29,8	1968–70	Pr/Ex
Limmatbrücke Neuenhof	A	80,0	1968–71	Pr
Bünztalbrücke Othmarsingen	A	31,3	1970	Pr
Viadukt Eptingen	A/G	71,0	1970	Ex
Pont sur la Lutrive, Belmont-sur-Lausanne	A/B	131,5	1971–73	Pr
Schwarzwaldbrücke Basel	A/B	119,0	1971–73	Pr/Ex
Viaduc d'accès à la jonction d'Aigle	A/G	55,0	1972–74	Pr
Pont sur la Lutrive Bretelle, Belmont-sur-Lausanne	A/B	74,0	1973–74	Ex
Brücke Boli, Arth	A	42,0	1973–76	Pr
Brücke Linden, Arth	A	42,0	1973–76	Pr
Brücke Mettlen, Arth	A	38,0	1973–76	Pr
Saaneviadukt Wileroltigen	A	60,0	1974–76	Ex
Viadukt Weyermannshaus, Bern	A	38,0	1974–77	Pr
Lättenbrücke Glattfelden	A	65,0	1975–77	Pr/Ex
Viaduc du Lac de la Gruyère, Pont-en-Ogoz	A	62,6	1975–79	Pr/Ex
Grenzbrücke, Basel	A	35,4	1976–79	Ex
Lehnenviadukt Beckenried	A	55,1	1976–80	Pr/Ex
Allmendbrücke Kerzers	A	36,0	1977	Pr
Viaduc d'Yverdon	A	32,2	1978–82	Pr
Pont sur la Veveyse Fégire, Saint-Légier-La Chiésatz	A/B	106,8	1979–81	Pr/Ex
Sitterviadukt St. Gallen	A	80,0	1980–87	Pr
Autobahnanschluss Kerzers	A	27,4	1980	Pr
Rheinbrücke Hemishofen	A	75,0	1980	Pr
Viadukt von Galmiz	A	29,8	1981	Pr
Napoleonsbrücke Brig	A/G	83,0	1981–83	Pr
Seezviadukt Walenstadt	A	46,0	1982–87	Pr
Limmatbrücke A20, Dietikon	A	58,0	1983–84	Pr
Rheinbrücke Diepoldsau	B/F	97,0	1983–85	Ex
Neugut-Viadukte der Zürcher S-Bahn, Dübendorf, Wallisellen	A	44,0	1985–87	Pr
Weidenholzviadukt der Zürcher S-Bahn, Wallisellen	A	37,0	1985–86	Pr
Pont du Daillard, Ballaigues	A	50,4	1986–88	Pr
Pont sur le Rhône à St. Maurice	F/G	31,0	1986–88	Ex
Viaduc d'Orbe	A	47,4	1986–89	Pr
Aaretalbrücken Schinznach-Bad	A/B	90,0	1988–92	Pr/Ex
Hundwilertobelbrücke, Waldstatt, Hundwil	C	143,0	1989–91	Ex
Wettsteinbrücke Basel	C/G	66,0	1992–95	Pr/Ex
Viadukt Löwenberg, Murten	A	40,2	1995	Pr
Limmatbrücke Baden-Obersiggenthal	C	115,8	2000–02	Pr
Pont de la Poya, Fribourg	F	168,0	1989–2014	Pr

PROJEKTBETEILIGTE
PROJECT PARTICIPANTS

CASPAR SCHÄRER

*1973, Architekt ETH/SIA und Journalist; schreibt über Architektur, Städtebau und verwandte Disziplinen, seit 2008 Redaktor der Architekturzeitschrift *werk, bauen + wohnen,* verschiedene Publikationen und Buchbeiträge im In- und Ausland; Lehrtätigkeit seit 2010, unter anderem an der Hochschule Luzern (HSLU); seit 2013 Leiter des Seminars Architekturkritik an der ETH Zürich.

Born in 1973, the architect (ETH/SIA) and journalist Caspar Schärer writes about architecture, urban planning, and related disciplines. He has been Editor of the architecture magazine *werk, bauen + wohnen* since 2008 and publishes widely both in Switzerland and abroad. His teaching career began in 2010 at Lucerne University of Applied Sciences and Arts, among others, and he has headed the Architecture Criticism seminar at the ETH Zurich since 2013.

RALPH FEINER

*1961, lebt in Malans. Der Architekturfotograf ist der Chronist der zeitgenössischen Architektur Graubündens. Er erhielt 2013 den Kulturpreis der Stadt Chur.

Born in 1961, a resident of Malans, the architectural photographer Ralph Feiner chronicles the development of contemporary architecture in the Canton of Graubünden. Winner of the City of Chur's Culture Prize 2013.

DAVID BILLINGTON

*1927, Professor Dr. Dr. h.c. mult. an der Princeton University for Environmental and Civil Engineering. Billington verfasste mehrere wertvolle Bücher auf Grund sehr umfangreicher Forschungsarbeit, u. a. *Robert Maillart: Builder, Designer Artist; The Tower and the Bridge* (dt. *Der Turm und die Brücke,* Ernst & Sohn, Berlin 2014), *The Art of structural Design, a Swiss Legacy* .

Born in 1927, Professor of Environmental and Civil Engineering at Princeton University. Author of several books based on his own extensive research, including *Robert Maillart: Builder, Designer, Artist; The Tower and the Bridge,* and *The Art of Structural Design, A Swiss Legacy.*

LUZI BÄRTSCH

*1939, Dipl. Elektroing. ETH Zürich; Bündner Regierungsrat im Baudepartement von 1987–1998. VR-Präsident der Rätia Energie. Luzi Bärtsch führte das Baudepartement des Kantons Graubünden bei zwei ausserordentlich grossen und schwierigen Strassenprojekten: bei der Umfahrung von Flims und bei der Umfahrung von Klosters mit der Sunnibergbrücke.

Born in 1939, Electrical engineer (ETH), Chairman of the Board of Directors of Rätia Energie. Member of the governing council of the Canton of Graubünden from 1987 to 1998; as head of the Department of Buildings oversaw two exceptionally large and complex road-building projects in the Canton of Graubünden: the Flims bypass and the Klosters bypass for which the Sunniberg Bridge was built.

ISO CAMARTIN

*1944, Prof. Dr. phil. für Romanistik an der ETH und der Universität Zürich; Essayist und Literaturkritiker. In seinen zahlreichen Aufsätzen und Büchern hat er sich immer wieder mit der Geschichte und der Kultur seines Heimatkantons Graubünden auseinandergesetzt, wobei ihn die Passstrassen in der Berglandschaft besonders faszinierten.

Born in 1944, Professor of Romance Languages and Literature at the ETH and University of Zurich. As essayist and literary critic, author of numerous works concerned with the history and culture of his native Graubünden and his special fascination with its mountain passes.

MORITZ LEUENBERGER

*1946, Dr. iur.; Moritz Leuenberger führte in Zürich eine Anwaltspraxis und wurde 1979 in den Nationalrat gewählt. 1991–1995 war er Regierungsrat des Kantons Zürich. 1995 erfolgte seine Wahl in den Bundesrat. 2001 und 2006 war er Bundespräsident.

Born in 1946, Dr. iur., lawyer and politician, Partner in a law firm in Zurich; in 1979 elected to the Swiss National Council; member of the governing council of the Canton of Zurich from 1991 to 1995, when he was elected to the Swiss Federal Council; served as Swiss President in 2001 and 2006.

WERNER OECHSLIN
*1944, Prof. Dr. an der ETH Zürich; Studium der Kunstgeschichte, Archäologie, Philosophie und Mathematik in Zürich und Rom; Habilitation 1980 an der FU Berlin. Es folgten Professuren in Bonn, Genf, Zürich, Harvard und Montréal. 1987–2006 Vorsteher des Instituts für Geschichte und Theorie der Architektur (gta) der ETH Zürich. Gründer und Stifter der «Stiftung Bibliothek Werner Oechslin» in Einsiedeln.

Born in 1944, Professor of Art History and Architecture at the ETH Zurich, studied Art History, Archaeology, Philosophy and Mathematics in Zurich and Rome; habilitated at the Free University of Berlin in 1980; professorships in Bonn, Geneva, Zurich, Harvard and Montreal; from 1987 to 2006 headed the ETH Institute for the History and Theory of Architecture (gta); founder of the Stiftung Bibliothek Werner Oechslin in Einsiedeln.

JOSEPH SCHWARTZ
*1954, Prof. Dr. an der ETH Zürich. Joseph Schwartz ist ordentlicher Professor für Tragwerksentwurf am Departement Architektur der ETH Zürich. Er ist Mitinhaber eines Ingenieurbüros in Zug. Bekannt sind seine ausgezeichneten Hochbauten, die er in enger Zusammenarbeit mit Architekten realisiert hat.

Born in 1954, Professor of Structural Design at the ETH Zurich. Co-owner of a civil engineering firm in Zug known for its award-winning high-rise buildings realized in close collaboration with architects.

CHRISTIAN FRAEFEL
*1979, 1996–2000 Ausbildung zum Bauzeichner beim Ingenieurbüro A. Bärtsch in Chur. Seit 2001 Zeichner/Konstrukteur bei der Firma Bänziger Partner AG in Chur.

Born in 1979, trained as an architectural draftsman at the engineering firm A. Bärtsch in Chur from 1996–2000. Draftsman and designer at Bänziger Partner AG in Chur since 2001.

MARTIN DEURING
*1962, Dr. Dipl. Bauing. an der ETH Zürich, Studium der Ingenieurwissenschaften an der HTL Luzern und der ETH Zürich; Forschungsarbeiten an der EMPA Dübendorf. Mitinhaber der Unternehmungen des Ingenieurverbundes *dreiK* und damit engagiert in der interdisziplinären Erarbeitung von Hoch- und Brückenbauten sowie der Gesamtleitung von Brückenbauprojekten.

Born in 1962, studied Engineering Sciences at the HTL Lucerne and the ETH Zurich, followed by research work at the EMPA Dübendorf. Doctorate in civil engineering from the ETH Zurich. As partner in the dreiK network, involved in the interdisciplinary development and general management of major building and bridge projects.

EPILOG
EPILOGUE

CHRISTIAN MENN

Die Aufgabe des Brückeningenieurs ist faszinierend, aber auch anspruchs- und verantwortungsvoll. Sie ist eng mit dem überragenden Begriff des Gleichgewichts verbunden. Früher erarbeiteten die Brückeningenieure ihren Brückenentwurf fast immer selbst. Wegen der ausufernden Vorschriften und Normen konzentrieren sie sich heute oft nur noch auf umfangreiche Berechnungen; an der Konzeptentwicklung beteiligen sich hingegen jede Art von Architekten, Designern und Künstlern, was gelegentlich zu skurrilen Tragwerken führt.

Neben der Tragfähigkeit und der konstruktiven Effizienz spielt auch die Gestaltung eine wichtige Rolle: Am Pont du Gard in Südfrankreich fasziniert zum Beispiel die harmonische Balance von Bogenspannweiten und Brückenhöhe – eine wegen der veränderlichen Bogenlehrgerüste nicht kostenfreie Art der Verfeinerung, die bei vielen Brückeningenieuren in Vergessenheit geraten ist.

Bis in die Mitte des 20. Jahrhunderts spielte der Brückenbau in seiner Position zwischen Technik und Kunst eine bedeutende Rolle. Heute werden nur noch ganz grosse Brücken bewundert, allerdings auch wenn sie technisch-konzeptionell nicht überzeugen – was nicht selten vorkommt.

Was ist also zu tun, damit Brücken wieder als Bereicherung und nicht als Belastung ihres Umfelds wahrgenommen werden können?

AUSBILDUNG

Es ist bedenklich, dass die *structural art* als ein wichtiger Bereich der Baukultur an unseren Hochschulen – wenn überhaupt – kaum Beachtung findet. Wenigstens eine fundierende Lehrveranstaltung sollte für interessierte Studenten in den Lehrplan eingebaut werden. Dabei sollten sich die Dozenten durch Studien, Publikationen, Leistungen und Erfahrungen ausweisen können. Technisch-wissenschaftliche Arbeit, ein Hochschultitel oder gar selbstempfundene Kompetenz genügen hier auf keinen Fall.

The bridge builder's task is a fascinating one, but one that is also challenging and charged with responsibility. It is closely tied to the overarching notion of poise. Bridge builders used to draw their bridge designs themselves for the most part. These days, however, an overabundance of regulations and standards obliges them to concentrate on the math and the specifications, while architects, designers, and artists of all kinds have a hand in the conceptual work – which from time to time gives rise to some bizarre constructions.

Alongside load-bearing capacity and structural efficiency, design also plays an important role. What fascinates us about the Pont du Gard in southern France, for example, is the harmonious balance struck between the arch spans and bridge height – a refinement that did not come free of charge, since it entailed varying the falsework used to build the arches, and that has since been forgotten by many modern bridge builders.

Bridge building played a key role as an intermediary between art and engineering right up to the mid-twentieth century. These days, however, only the really big bridges draw admiration – even those whose underlying concept is not entirely convincing, which is by no means seldom the case.

So what can be done so that bridges are once again perceived as an enrichment of their environs, rather than a burden or even a blemish?

TRAINING

The fact that *structural art*, which after all is an important aspect of building culture, receives so little attention, if any at all, in our institutions of higher education is cause for concern. The curriculum should include at least one course on the fundamentals for those interested. Lecturers who teach such a course should have credentials in the form of studies, publications, reference projects, and experience. Theoretical work alone, an academic qualification, or competence that rests primarily on self-belief are not enough.

WETTBEWERBE

Projektwettbewerbe im Brückenbau sind unbedingt erforderlich. Normale, offene Wettbewerbe sind allerdings teuer. Der Aufwand aller Beteiligten übertrifft nachweisbar in vielen Fällen die Kosten des Bauwerks.

Das Ziel eines Wettbewerbs sind überzeugende Ideen und nicht ein paar Kilogramm bedrucktes Papier. Zur Kosteneinsparung muss deshalb ein Wettbewerb in einem zweistufigen Verfahren durchgeführt werden. In der ersten Stufe sollten aufgrund einfacher Skizzen drei bis fünf Vorschläge zur Weiterbearbeitung ausgewählt und erst in der zweiten Stufe die konstruktiven Details dargestellt und die technischen Nachweise erbracht werden.

Dieses Vorgehen erfordert ein klares Wettbewerbsprogramm und eine kompetente Jury. Brückeningenieure als Jurymitglieder müssen so viele Kenntnisse und Erfahrungen mitbringen, dass sie Machbarkeit und Kosten eines Projekts schnell abschätzen können. Leider ist das nicht immer der Fall und emotional beeinflusste Kriterien können dann eine viel zu grosse Rolle spielen, besonders wenn sie im Beurteilungsgremium gut vertreten werden. Der Wettbewerb wird dann zur Lotterie.

VERANTWORTUNG

Das Organigramm eines Brückenbaus weist im Wesentlichen folgende Funktionsträger auf: auf Seiten der Bauherrschaft den Projektingenieur mit seinem Prüfingenieur sowie weiteren Experten, dann den Projektverfasser und schliesslich den Bauleiter als Überwacher der Arbeiten sowie das Bauunternehmen und dessen Subunternehmer. Wie bei allen anspruchsvollen Arbeiten sind auch im Brückenbau Fehler unvermeidlich. Gefährlich sind vor allem grobe Fehler.

Brückenbau ist Teamwork, nicht das Werk eines Einzelnen. In einem Team müssen zunächst auf anspruchsvoller sozialer Basis allfällige zwischenmenschliche Probleme gelöst werden. Dies ist eine wichtige Grundlage jeder subsidiären Zusammenarbeit. Die Lösung der technischen Probleme ist mit mehr Arbeit verbunden, andererseits aber eher einfacher.

Die besten Garanten für das Gelingen des Werkes sind allerdings immer noch Interesse und Freude an der Bauausführung und gegenseitiger Respekt aller Beteiligten.

COMPETITIONS

Competitions for specific bridge projects are essential, yet the open competitions that are the norm these days are expensive: The total costs for those concerned have in many cases proven to exceed the costs of the finished structure.

The goal of any competition must be to find a persuasive idea – not to generate paperwork. To save costs, therefore, competitions should be conducted in two stages: A first stage in which entrants submit simple sketches and a second stage in which three to five of these sketches are fleshed out with details of the design and supporting documents for the engineering.

This method calls for a clearly formulated competition program as well as a competent jury. Bridge builders as jury members must have the know-how and experience needed to be able to estimate swiftly the feasibility and costs of a given project. This is not always the case, unfortunately, and subjective criteria can play much too great a role, especially if they are rather too well represented in any one specific jury. What began as a competition then becomes a lottery.

RESPONSIBILITY

The organization chart of a bridge-building project must identify the following functionaries: the client's own project engineer supported by an inspection engineer and other experts, then the author of the project, and finally the construction manager, as the one responsible for overseeing the works, and the contractor with subcontractors. As with all demanding projects, so in bridge building, mistakes are bound to be made. Of these, it is the really crass ones that are dangerous.

Bridge building is teamwork, never the work of an individual. The first job of a team must therefore be to resolve any interpersonal conflicts that there might be in a fair and socially acceptable way. This is essential to all collaboration based on subsidiarity. Solving the technical problems entails rather more work, but tends to be easier on the whole.

The best guarantees for the success of a project are still the interest and enjoyment of those executing it and mutual respect among all those involved.

DANK
ACKNOWLEDGEMENTS

DIE PUBLIKATION WURDE UNTERSTÜTZT VON / THIS PUBLICATION WAS SUPPORTED BY
HANS VONTOBEL · GEMEINDE KLOSTERS · STIFTUNG JACQUES BISCHOFBERGER · IMPLENIA AG · SBV BAUMEISTERVERBAND · KANTON AARGAU, DEPARTEMENT BAU, VERKEHR UND UMWELT · GRAUBÜNDNER KANTONALBANK · MAGEBA · STADT CHUR · KULTURFÖRDERUNG KANTON GRAUBÜNDEN

Die Publikation eines Buches, das sich mit einer technischen Materie sowohl an Laien wie auch an Fachleute richtet, gelingt nur dank der guten Zusammenarbeit vieler verschiedener kompetenter Hände und Köpfe. Als Herausgeber und Autor möchte ich an dieser Stelle allen, die diese Aufgabe übernommen haben, meinen wohl verdienten Dank aussprechen:

Zunächst dem Verlag Scheidegger & Spiess, namentlich Thomas Kramer und Cornelia Mechler, die bereit waren, die Produktion des aufwändigen Buches zu übernehmen; dann dem Mitherausgeber Caspar Schärer, Architekt und Publizist, der mit seiner grossen Erfahrung einen hochgeschätzten Beitrag leistete; weiter dem bekannten Architekturfotografen Ralph Feiner, der nicht zögerte, neben seinem fotografischen oft auch sein bergsteigerisches Können einzusetzen, um die Kühnheit einiger Brücken überzeugend ins Bild zu rücken; dem Ingenieur Dr. Werner Brändli, Partner des Ingenieurbüros Bänziger in Zürich, und seinem Zeichnerkonstrukteur Christian Fraefel für die Ausarbeitung neuer Katasterpläne sowie dem Ingenieur Dr. Martin Deuring für seine Beratung; den Buchgestaltern Susanna Entress und Urs Stuber für das sorgfältige Layout des Buches und den Übersetzern Prof. Paul Gauvreau für die technischen und Bronwen Saunders für die allgemeinen Texte.

Bedanken möchte ich mich auch bei Altbundesrat Moritz Leuenberger, der mir gestattete, einen Abschnitt aus seiner Rede anlässlich der Eröffnung der Sunnibergbrücke bei Klosters als Prolog zu übernehmen.

Des Weiteren danke ich den externen Mitwirkenden für ihre wertvollen Beiträge: Prof. Dr. Dr. h. c. David Billington, Professor für Structural Art an der Princeton University – meinem guten Freund und Kollegen seit 1972 –; Altregierungsrat und Baudirektor des Kantons Graubünden Luzi Bärtsch, der meinen Entwurf für die Sunnibergbrücke zur Ausführung bestimmte; Dr. Joseph Schwartz, Inhaber eines Ingenieurbüros und Professor am Departement Architektur der ETH Zürich; Prof. Dr. Werner Oechslin, emeritierter Direktor des Instituts für Geschichte und Theorie der Architektur (gta) der ETH Zürich. Nicht zuletzt danke ich meinem lieben Freund Professor Dr. Iso Camartin für seinen brillant geschriebenen Essay, mit dem er den Bogen zwischen Brückenbau und Literatur schliesst.

Christian Menn

The publication of a book whose subject matter is technical, but which is aimed at both expert and lay readers alike would have been impossible without the smooth collaboration of many different heads and hands. As author and editor, I would like to extend my sincerest thanks to all those who by embracing this challenge have done so much to deserve them:

The publisher, Scheidegger & Spiess, and specifically Thomas Kramer and Cornelia Mechler, who agreed to take on the production of this ambitious book; my co-editor, Caspar Schärer, whose contribution as an architect and publicist of considerable experience has proved invaluable; the well-known architectural photographer Ralph Feiner, who in his determination to convey the sheer audacity of some of the bridges shown here never once hesitated to apply both his photographic and his mountaineering skills; the engineer Dr. Werner Brändli of the Zurich-based engineering firm Bänziger Partner and his draftsman Christian Fraefel, who prepared the new cadastral maps; the engineer Dr. Martin Deuring for his sound advice; the graphic designers Susanna Entress and Urs Stuber for their meticulous layout; and the translators Prof. Paul Gauvreau for the technical and Bronwen Saunders for the general texts.

I would also like to thank former Federal Councillor Moritz Leuenberger for allowing me to use an excerpt from his speech at the opening of the Sunniberg Bridge near Klosters as a prologue.

Special thanks are also due to the authors of the essays: Prof. David Billington, Professor of Structural Art at Princeton University, a good friend and colleague since 1972; Luzi Bärtsch, a former member of the governing council and head of the Department of Buildings of the Canton of Graubünden, who selected my design for the Sunniberg Bridge; Dr. Joseph Schwartz, proprietor of an engineering firm and Professor in the Department of Architecture at the ETH Zurich; Prof. Werner Oechslin, Director Emeritus of the Institute for the History and Theory of Architecture (gta) at the ETH Zurich; and last but not least my dear friend, Prof. Iso Camartin, whose brilliant essay itself builds a bridge between civil engineering and literature.

Christian Menn

Bildnachweise / Credits

Alle Fotografien stammen von Ralph Feiner
ausser die im Folgenden aufgeführten:
All photographs by Ralph Feiner, except the following:
Christian Menn: 74 oben und unten/top and bottom,
130, 182 oben/top, 230, 266, 267, 270, 311, 312, 313, 315
Pia Zanetti: 10
Werner Friedli: 96
Bernard F. Gardel: 182 unten/bottom
Martin Deuring: 206
Tiefbauamt Graubünden: 84/85, 97
Abu Dhabi Department of Transportation: 281, 282/283,
284, 286/287, 288/289
ARGE Bänziger/Brändli, Martin Deuring,
Walt+Galmarini: 291, 292 unten/bottom, 294
Kraftwerke Oberhasli: 292 oben/top
Nevada Department of Transportation: 297
Anna Lenz: 298, 300/301, 320/321
Raumgleiter GmbH, Zürich: 303, 304, 306/307, 308/309
Orlando Monsch: 318 (aus/from: Gesellschaft
für Ingenieurbaukunst, Thomas Vogel
und/and Peter Marti (Hg./eds.),
Christian Menn – Brückenbauer, Birkhäuser, Basel 1997)
Ingenieurbüro Bänziger und Martin Deuring: 319

In einigen Fällen konnten die Urheber- und Abdruckrechte trotz umfangreicher Recherche nicht ermittelt werden. Berechtigte Ansprüche werden bei entsprechendem Nachweis im Rahmen der üblichen Honorarvereinbarungen abgegolten.

Despite best efforts, we have not been able to identify the holders of copyright and printing rights for all the illustrations. Copyright holders not mentioned in the credits are asked to substantiate their claims, and recompense will be made according to standard practice.

Impressum / Imprint

Konzept / Concept
Christian Menn, Caspar Schärer

Gestaltung / Graphic design
Susanna Entress, Urs Stuber

Satz / Typesetting
Daniela Bieri-Mäder

Übersetzung ins Englische / Translation into English
Paul Gauvreau, Bronwen Saunders

Übersetzung ins Deutsche / Translation into German
Harriet Fricke

Lektorat deutsch / Editing German
Caspar Schärer

Lektorat englisch / Editing English
Bronwen Saunders

Korrektorat deutsch / Proofreading German
Kirsten Thietz

Korrektorat englisch / Proofreading English
Benjamin Liebelt

Lithografie, Druck und Bindung / Lithography, printing and binding
DZA Druckerei zu Altenburg GmbH, Altenburg, Thüringen

© 2015 Christian Menn
und / and Verlag Scheidegger & Spiess AG, Zürich
© für die Texte bei den Autoren /
for the texts: the authors
© für die Fotografien: siehe Bildnachweis /
for the photographs: see image credit

Verlag Scheidegger & Spiess AG
Niederdorfstrasse 54
CH 8001 Zürich

www.scheidegger-spiess.ch

Alle Rechte vorbehalten; kein Teil dieses Werks darf in irgendeiner Form ohne vorherige schriftliche Genehmigung des Verlags reproduziert oder unter Verwendung elektronischer Systeme verarbeitet, vervielfältigt oder verbreitet werden.

All rights reserved; no part of this publication may be reproduced, stored in a retrieval system or transmitted in any form or by any means, electronic, mechanical, photocopying, recording or otherwise, without the prior written consent of the publisher.

ISBN 978-3-85881-455-5

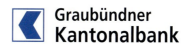

mageba ist eine weltweit aktive Herstellerin von Brückenlagern, Fahrbahnübergängen und weiteren Produkten und Dienstleistungen Hoch- und Infrastrukturbaus.

Dr. Deuring
 +Oehninger AG

Dipl. Bauingenieure ETH SIA USIC

Departement Bau, Vekehr
und Umwelt des Kantons Aargau

Gemeinde Klosters-Serneus

Stiftung Jacques Bischofberger